D1528905

Praise for *Lella Secor*

"Her beautiful and sensitive letters . . . gave me a feeling of the times in which she lived as no history book ever could. Her struggle for peace and equal rights for women makes us sisters."
Ethel Taylor, National Coordinator
Women Strike For Peace

". . . the struggles they describe—of a working woman trying to make it in New York—are disturbingly up-to-date. . . . deeply fascinating—"
Kirkus Reviews

"Lella Secor's career in the First World War as a pacifist agitator was meteoric. . . . I found her letters home from the front extremely readable: interesting as social history and . . . expressing a personality at once ingenuous and shrewd, impressionable and realistic, tender in idealistic hope and bold in practical action. . . ."
Dwight Macdonald

"Lella Secor's letters are a revelation and an inspiration . . . .a fascinating reminder to us of the spunk and the determination and the problems of those who came before."
Marjorie Lipsyte
New Directions for Women

"This collection of political and personal letters is one of the most exciting and important new contributions to peace history and women's literature."
Blanche Weisen Cook,
John Jay College, CUNY

"Women writing about women and women writing about themselves are two of the best things about contemporary literature. Secor's letters, vivid and appealing, are a rich and lively contribution."
Catharine R. Stimpson
Editor, *Signs*

"Adds a new name to feminist annals . . .a valuable resource in the history of peace and women's emancipation."
Madeleine B. Stern, author of
We The Women

"Reading this book was a great joy, bringing recollections of my work sixty years ago with Lella Secor. In publishing these letters you are making a great contribution to the cause of peace and international understanding."
Rebecca Shelley

Praise for The *American Women's Diary Series*

"The American Women's Diary Series is performing a double resurrection: it is not only unearthing forgotten manuscripts, it is also unearthing the hidden thoughts and feelings of women, frequently uttered nowhere but in these private "letters" to the self. To retrieve and restore the history of women, we must be able to read about their lives in their own words."

Laurie Stone, book reviewer,
The Village Voice

"The series is a way of personalizing history, making it less abstract. Works such as these show students that history is not limited to the study of the famous. These are lives that students can identify with and that give a true picture of daily life. I am sure that these books will be eagerly awaited and widely used.

Leonore Hoffman,
Project Coordinator,
"Teaching Women's Literature from a Regional Perspective"
Modern Language Association

"The American Women's Diary Series is a significant and exciting addition to the field of human studies, and I salute the publication of Secor's letters."

Eve Merriam, author of
Growing Up Female in America: Ten Lives

"Penny Franklin believes that an important part of history is 'knowing what one person felt at a certain time.' . . . She conceived a series of diaries and letters by American women. The first of these . . . is entitled Lella Secor: A Diary in Letters, 1915–1922. Lella Secor was a feminist, pacifist and journalist.

"Mrs. Franklin says she tries to keep the diaries geographically representative . . . . As general editor she works for a "unified editorial approach," avoiding the genteel deletions relatives are likely to make . . . . [The Series] reveals that women were not mute nonentities in American history after all."

Richard R. Lingeman
The New York Times Book Review

"An interesting, very impressive list."

Nancy F. Cott, author of
Root of Bitterness
The Bonds of Womanhood

"It is a wonderful series and I will spread news of it."

Tillie Olsen

LELLA SECOR

A Diary in Letters 1915–1922

American Women's Diary Series 1

PENELOPE FRANKLIN, *General Editor*

Lella Secor

LELLA SECOR

A Diary in Letters 1915–1922

Edited by
BARBARA MOENCH FLORENCE

Foreword by
ELEANOR FLEXNER

Burt Franklin & Company, Inc.
NEW YORK

Printed in the U.S.A.
Designer: Bernard Schleifer

The author gratefully acknowledges the courtesy of the following newspapers which have given permission to reprint articles:
The *Post-Journal,* Jamestown, New York, for "Miss Secor Was Disappointed," p. 279.
The *New York World* for "Since Ford's Peace Party Many Things Have Changed," p. 283.

Library of Congress Cataloging in Publication Data

Florence, Lella Secor.
Lella Secor : a diary of letters, 1915–1922.

(The American women's diary series)
Bibliography: p.
Includes index.
1. Florence, Lella Secor. 2. Feminists—United States—Biography. 3. Pacifists—United States—Biography. 4. Women journalists—United States—Biography. I. Florence, Barbara Moench. II. Series.
HQ1413.F58A34 301.41′2′0924 78-8374
ISBN 0-89102-071-3
ISBN 0-89102-114-0 pbk.

To Philip

About the American Women's Diary Series

The American Women's Diary Series is based on a simple, yet amazingly neglected, approach to the study of history—through the lives of individuals as recorded by themselves in the diary or journal.

Although professional historians regularly make use of diaries in their researches—and find in them one of their most useful sources of information about life in the past—relatively few of these journals have found their way into print. The majority of diaries that *have* been published are those of men, as are most of those preserved in libraries and archives. And yet, throughout this country's history women have kept diaries, and thousands of these records have been preserved.

The diary as a historical record has certain advantages over other first-person accounts. It is likely to contain details lost to the memory of the autobiographer. It is honest—sometimes in spite of itself—since it generally is not intended for an audience. And it communicates a sense of immediacy, of the process of everyday life, which is usually lost in a retrospective account.

We feel that the American Women's Diary Series fills a great need, both for feminists interested in women's past place in society and for students of American history searching for more than its standard version. We feel, too, the importance of making these works available to all women. For it is our belief that almost every woman can experience in their pages the shock (or the thrill) of recognition—the recognition that she has a feeling, an insight, or an experience in common with a woman who lived fifty or two hundred years ago.

The boundaries of the series have occasionally been stretched to include works—memoirs or collections of letters—that though not strictly diaries, have many of the qualities discussed above. All the works in the series have been chosen in an attempt to represent both the overall span of America's history and our national diversity of culture, race, region, and social class. They have also been selected and edited as works of literature, with attention to style, interest, and clarity. By applying uniform editorial standards to these varied documents, we hope to provide a useful basis for comparisons between the individual volumes.

Finally, we wish to emphasize that we have chosen to focus not on famous women, whose stories have been obscured by telling and retelling, but on the unknown women whose voices are yet fresh, and whose lives, upon examination, prove to be far from ordinary.

PENELOPE FRANKLIN
General Editor

Contents

Foreword

IT WILL perhaps come as a shock to readers of Lella Secor's *Diary in Letters,* especially those who are young, female, and consider themselves liberated, that an activist's life in 1915–18 in a city like New York was surprisingly similar to what it is in the 1970s. Then, as now, one could work around the clock on an occasional 36-hour shift—charged by the belief that one's efforts could make the difference between war and peace for a generation—raise money, demonstrate, organize delegations, and write home that everything was just fine despite the fact that the letter-writer was on the verge of a breakdown from exhaustion.

Lella Secor was just such a person. She would be totally at home on the staff of *Ms.* or N.O.W.—a young woman in her twenties, outraged at the cautious conservatism of the leadership of existing peace organizations, and convinced that a worldwide movement, sparked by Henry Ford's Peace Ship, would end the slaughter in Europe. She was pretty and piquant, blessed with a mop of golden red curls and total self-confidence—and not afraid to put herself and her idealism into words.

> I am experiencing again . . . that bounding, pulsing, thrilling, joy of life within me; that old feeling of confidence in my powers—as yet not fully tried or tested—and the sublime sort of certainty that I shall be able to fight my way, however difficult the obstacles. . . . What I am striving for more than anything else in the world [is] to be a great soul; to experience life so fully that I shall be able to understand the joys, the aspirations, the defeat, the struggle, the discouragements of those around me. For I have come to know that in just such a degree

as one lives, and experiences, in just that degree one can be of the greatest service to mankind.

Naive? Corny? We might think so—from *our* point of view. But it took not one but two world wars to shake us from the isolationism rooted in our less-than-300-year history, marred by only one fratricidal war and relatively untouched by the prejudice and distrust nourished by centuries of such warfare among the other nations of the world.

Lella Secor was born in Battle Creek, Michigan, and as a young woman moved to the West Coast. She became a journalist (which in those days spoke worlds for her ambition and self-confidence) and was sent by the Seattle *Post-Intelligencer,* an important paper then as now, to cover the Ford Peace Ship. Endowed by Henry Ford, the ship's mission was to carry several hundred delegates—men and women famous and unknown—to press the governments of warring European nations toward negotiating peace or, at the least, stating their war aims. The mission did not bring peace, but it did turn Lella Secor into a committed pacifist. When she returned to the United States she remained in New York to pursue two careers, that of a propagandist and organizer for the cause of peace and that of a journalist, for which New York seemed a stepping stone then as now.

New York in 1915 represented in many ways a much simpler world than ours. Celebrities were accessible. Journalism opened all doors. Lella Secor learned to know and wrote home about Henry Ford, Jane Addams, Charlotte Perkins Gilman, editors and publishers, and young hopefuls like herself—including the equally dynamic Rebecca Shelly. She must have thought of Wordsworth's line, quoted so often by young people in similar circumstances, "Bliss was it in that dawn to be alive." She must have paused occasionally, during those headlong days when everything seemed possible, to marvel that it was indeed she, Lella Secor, at the center of such historic events, in "bright, gay, wonderful old New York," where twenty-hour workdays were relieved by evenings at dinner and the theater with charming and attentive young men.

Lella's letters tell the story of the heartbreaking labors of the organizations she helped found, including the American Neutral Conference Committee and the Emergency Peace Federation. They tell of those and many others, of devoted men and women who made their marks in different ways later in life, of what it was like to live on two meals a day and little sleep, month after month.

Lella Secor and Rebecca Shelly, working together, tried everything to "keep the peace sentiment astir." They organized a delegation of American Neutral Conference Committee members which called on President Wilson, pressing him to live up to his campaign slogan ("He kept us out of war"). Wilson received them; they shook hands with the President of the United States, and then returned to New York with the situation much the same as it had been before. There was an "Open Letter to the President" from the English philosopher Bertrand Russell, smuggled into America and dramatically presented at a peace meeting, and a triumphant rally organized by Secor and Shelly, with both women sitting on the platform with distinguished speakers—an exhilarating experience for them.

With American involvement in the war looming closer, Lella and Rebecca pulled together two delegations, which traveled on special trains to demonstrate in Washington. And when the newly formed Emergency Peace Federation needed contributions, they put an advertisement in the New York *Times,* addressed to "Mothers, Daughters, and Wives," which they wrote themselves, and which yielded their cause some $35,000!

But in the end, America did go to war. Several months after the war declaration of April 1917, the two young activists chartered another special train, which they took into the Middle West, hoping to launch a new organization, the People's Council of America (somewhat on the order of a Russian soviet!), wherever they might be allowed to convene. But with America already hurtled into war, the erosion of individual liberties had begun. The Council members were barred from Minnesota and Wisconsin, and the governor of Illinois sent state police to break up their meeting in Chicago ("There will be no treason in the state of Illinois").

Lella Secor and her associates were not the only ones to suffer such harassment. So well established a reform figure as Jane Addams, who headed the Woman's Peace Party, was cast into disrepute—along with many others—because of the criticisms she voiced against American participation in the war. Even Henry Ford, patron of the Peace Ship mission, which had brought Lella Secor into the ranks of the pacifists, was pressured into withdrawing his patronage of the cause.

As time went on, many supporters on whom Lella Secor and Rebecca Shelly relied, whose names were needed to make organizations such as theirs "respectable," resigned from both leadership and membership. Jettisoning them, launching new organizations, finding new financial support, became progressively less rewarding—and less possible. For a considerable time Lella kept a job at *Every Week* magazine to pay her rent (food often came from supporters of the cause better off than she), while working at full speed after office hours at the task she considered her *real* job.

Coinciding with these pacifist activities was a whole world of struggle ending half a century of political campaigning on behalf of "Votes for Women." Lella Secor had come, most recently, from the state of Washington, which had emancipated its women in 1910. New York State—keystone of the nation—had defeated a woman-suffrage measure in 1915, but was headed for another vote in 1917. It was expected on all sides that this would be a showdown, and every available reform militant was corralled for suffrage work. The suffrage campaign had used many publicity techniques heretofore little known, such as leaflet distribution and parades. These tactics were later used to great advantage by the pacifist organizations.

Compared to the suffrage forces, pacifists were few in number. But such as they were, the many women among them profited from the general interest in women's activities. Women were news in those years, and the Secor-Shelly team tried to make the most of it. Considering their level of experience, they did very well indeed, and Madison Avenue today would clasp them to its flamboyant bosom.

Nevertheless, with women voting in the 1916 election in only six Western states and in Illinois (where they voted for president only), pacifists could not hope to win much political clout by appealing to them. Indeed, women never produced any recognizable "bloc" of votes; they made themselves felt more by contributing to the generally rising sophistication of the voting public than in any other way. The great achievement of women's emancipation is that today, women like Lella Secor and Rebecca Shelly could not only find their way into the political process—through the League of Women Voters, through the reshaping of the political parties (especially the Democratic Party), and through the labor movement—but that they would probably stay there, not be compelled to leave, physically and emotionally exhausted, as Lella Secor finally did.

And yet, who can say such efforts as theirs were wasted? Wendell Willkie's vision of "one world," the emergence and survival of the United Nations, had to wait on the preparatory process by which this country—self-sufficient and self-absorbed, its westward expansion finally halted by an ocean, and that not until 1900—slowly learned the necessary lessons. Learned them at Belleau Wood and Chateau Thierry; by defeating and then standing aside from Woodrow Wilson's cherished League of Nations, the "most essential" element in the peace settlement at the end of World War I. Learned them at the knee of Franklin D. Roosevelt, whose "fireside chats" took a whole country's imagination around a warring world where a generation of youth was scattered, from Guadalcanal to Anzio and Omaha Beach. Learned them at San Francisco at the founding of the United Nations, and in the countless crises through which that edifice has—so far—survived.

And may still learn them, through books like this one: accounts of earlier efforts to avoid war and heal the wounds of past wars, books that try to teach us what failed and what—in many ways that we forget or are unaware of—succeeded.

There was another aspect to Lella Secor's life, perhaps of equal interest to today's feminists: the years as a young married woman who had been rescued from the depths of physical exhaustion by one of her volunteer helpers, a young Englishman named Philip Sargant Florence. When her apparently indomitable physique finally gave way, he visited her in a sanatorium and their friendship ripened into marriage. They were, apparently, both ignorant of birth control (Lella devoted her later adult life to that cause), and she was forced to give up her ambition to become a journalist because domestic help within their means was simply not to be had, and she often had to care for her two baby boys and a household unaided.

Lella felt some bitterness over such a fate. Despite her feminism (in which she was staunchly supported by her husband), Lella does not appear to have seen the other side of her dilemma. She had not completely assimilated the teachings of Charlotte Perkins Gilman's classic book *Women and Economics,* although she did recognize the fact that better-paid jobs in war industries had taught domestic workers to expect higher wages generally.

And so, in the end, the young family moved to England, where Philip could support them comfortably on the salary of a Cambridge lecturer (ironically, in economics): where a servant class still existed that was satisfied to work for low wages and put its employers' interests before its own. We may criticize the couple's solution to their problem, but we must remember that Philip Florence's English upbringing had imposed a set of values different from those of his wife. Although Lella came from a working-class background, she assimilated some of Philip's very English, upper-class expectations. She learned to accept servants as a way of life, which gave her back her independence while not, in her own mind at least, causing the loss of any of her democratic ideals. In the end, we are left with the realization that few of today's militants and young mothers have solved the problems that confronted an earlier generation some sixty years ago.

Lella Secor's story, as she tells it in these letters, is autobiography, but it is history as well, as any good biographical work must be: part of our heritage, which reminds us of our roots and of the national experience that has contributed to making us what we are. We are reminded also, as with any account which is honest, that not all human problems are solvable. In the half century or more since Lella Secor's strivings, we have still not found a sure road to peace, or discovered how to reconcile our human obligations with our wishes for complete self-fulfillment and freedom. What is certain, however, is that each generation will have its share of Lella Secors, and that in each decade there will be some gains to show for their efforts.

ELEANOR FLEXNER
April 1978

Preface

THE LETTERS in this book were written during the years 1915–1922 by Lella Secor, a young New York journalist and peace activist, to her family in the West and Midwest. Her mother and sisters saved the letters and many years later they were returned to Lella, then living in England with her husband and two sons.

Lella Secor was my mother-in-law. I discovered these early letters on a visit to England in 1975, nearly ten years after her death. They had been carefully packed away, along with many documents relating to the pacifist movement of the World War I era with which she was passionately involved.

It seems to me that Lella's story, although rooted in the political struggles of another day, has much in common with the problems of today's women. Lella's commitment to her writing and her chosen cause, pacifism, was absolute. Yet her letters express poignantly her attempts to reconcile her independence with the enticements of domestic life. She strove to be a "great soul" in the service of man- (and woman-) kind, yet could also become absorbed in clothes, cooking, decorating her home, and later caring for her children.

In Lella's early letters I have made almost no cuts, deleting only passages which discuss hometown friends or family preoccupations. Later letters have been edited more heavily, eliminating repetitious accounts of her children's development and her household problems.

I have indicated deletions in the conventional manner. Spelling errors have been corrected, and punctuation has been changed occasionally when necessary for clarity.

I am greatly indebted to Penelope Franklin for her wise and tactful part in bringing this book to life. In addition, I would like to thank the following people for their help, interest, and encouragement: Philip Sargant Florence, Noel Florence, Tom Franklin, Mary Case Bird, Grace Collins, Barbara Neal, Sue Ratkiewicz, and January Adams.

BARBARA MOENCH FLORENCE

Introduction

LELLA FAYE SECOR was born in Battle Creek, Michigan, on February 13, 1887. Her mother, Loretta Reynolds Sowle Secor, was then almost forty-five years old, and had five children by her first husband, Joseph Sowle. These were a great deal older than Lella and her sister Ina, both born of a second marriage to William Secor. Lella, the youngest of the seven, was always known to her family as "the baby daughter."

Between Ina and Lella there had been another child, Ivy Golden, who had sickened and died. Loretta Secor believed that only because she was no longer nursing Ivy Golden had she conceived Lella. A bright and lively child whose red hair matched her enterprising nature, Lella soon learned to make the most of her fortuitous arrival on this earth.

Loretta Secor was a strong, devout, and resourceful woman but "a poor judge of men," who mothered her husbands as well as her children and managed alone when the husbands died or disappeared.[1] Lella's father, William Secor—an itinerant carpenter—drifted away from the family when Lella was very small.

The family's money ran low and in 1892 Loretta Secor went to Ventura, California, taking Lella, Ina, their half-brother Ellsworth and their half-sister Lena with her. She opened a restaurant called "The Enterprise," and Lena and Ellsworth spent their spare time plucking chickens for the kitchen. The restaurant was not a success, and several years later the family moved to Green Bay, Wisconsin, where Mrs. Secor worked as cook in a lumber camp, Lena in a doctor's office.

In 1898 Loretta Secor returned to Battle Creek and opened a boarding house. She did all the cooking herself, and Lella and Ina

OPENING

The new Eating House to be known as

The Enterprise!

Will be opened this noon on Santa Clara Street,

Opposite the Y. M. C. A. Rooms.

HOME COOKING!

A SPECIALTY. MEALS, 25 CENTS.

Meals and Lunches at All Hours

March 26, 1892. A share of patronage is solicited.

MRS. SECOR & MRS. TURRILL.

helped with the many other chores. This time the family's efforts were successful; the boarding house became very popular with visitors to Dr. John Harvey Kellogg's Battle Creek Sanitarium,[2] and was always full. Lella's special responsibility was the marketing, for she preferred this to looking after the guests. By the time she was in high school she had also taken a Saturday job in Woolworth's Five and Ten Cent Store, and later worked packing corn flakes at the Kellogg factory.

The family were staunch Baptists. As Lella later remembered, their whole social life revolved around the church and "even on Sunday there was a great deal of pleasant sociability and handshaking before and after the services."

> Sunday was a busy day, with morning service followed by Sunday school, Junior Baptist Young People's Union in the afternoon, and Senior B. Y. P. U. at 6, and then the evening service. Sometimes in the winter, when the snow lay deep on the ground and the temperature hovered around zero, my mother would pack lunch for the entire family, and we would spend the whole day at church. This always delighted me, for other families were certain to do the same, and Sunday lunch became a pleasant picnic.
>
> Fund-raising church suppers when the whole building was filled with the delicious smell of coffee and baked beans, church socials when the young folk managed furtive wooings, lectures, concerts, and entertainments, to say nothing of the gift-laden tree at Christmas-time, provided an endless succession of pleasant occasions, which served to link religion with everyday life. We learned how to organize societies, preside as officers, conduct our affairs according to Parliamentary rules, and become tolerably good public speakers.
>
> The choir played an important part, and always sang one or two anthems in addition to leading the congregation in hymns. . . . Boys and girls from childhood learn[ed] to sing part-songs.[3]

By 1906, when she finished high school, Lella had become interested in journalism, but her mother insisted that she be a teacher.

An interview was arranged: she was to apply for a position as mistress of a one-room country school. On her way to the interview, she met a friend who had not found a job and who wanted badly to teach. Lella gave the friend her letter of introduction. Then she went straight to the office of the Battle Creek *Journal* and talked them into hiring her, although she had never even used a typewriter. She eventually became the paper's society editor.

Within three years, living at home under Mother Secor's stern and watchful eye had proved too constricting for the young reporter. Lella's brother Ellsworth had gone West to homestead in the state of Washington and his stories of the area intrigued her. Deciding to stake out a claim for herself, she packed her belongings and traveled to the Coulee Wall country. There was no Grand Coulee Dam then, and the closest town, Coulee, consisted of a saloon, poolroom, grocery, and a few houses.

By this time Ellsworth had given up farming, married, and gone to live in Spokane, but Lella claimed land next to his and proceeded to live up to the federal laws. Of her 160 acres, she was required to cultivate twenty-five, so she borrowed four horses and plowed the land herself. With the help of a lovestruck cowboy,[4] she built a one-room shack and lived in it the fourteen months required to validate her title to the land. Rattlesnakes loved to sleep in the shade outside her door and she learned to scare them away by banging a shovel against the doorstep before running across the yard to the privy.

When the fourteen months were over, Lella decided to resume her career as a journalist. She ceded the land to Ellsworth and found a job with the *Inland Review* in Spokane, where she wrote features and ran a Sunday page, signing her articles "L. F. S." When she applied a short time later for a job on the Everett, Washington, *Herald,* the editor judged from these signed initials that she was a man, "and it took some tall talk to convince him that a woman could do the work."[5]

With her mother and sister Ina, Lella lived first in Everett and then in Bellevue, across Lake Washington from Seattle. For three years, Lella and Ina commuted by ferry to Seattle, where Ina taught school and Lella wrote for a hotel trade paper and the Seattle *Post-Intelligencer*.

In November 1915, this peaceful way of life abruptly ended when a telegram arrived from Lella's friend Rebecca Shelly in New York. Lella had met Rebecca in Ann Arbor, Michigan, where Rebecca—a Phi Beta Kappa student—had just received her degree from the University of Michigan. Lella had been deeply impressed by the young woman's enthusiasm, and an immediate bond was formed. The friendship had ripened when they met again in Everett, where Rebecca had taught school until she left, early in 1915, to go with Jane Addams to the International Congress of Women at The Hague. A dedicated pacifist, she had remained in New York upon her return, devoting herself to plans being advanced for ending the war in Europe.

Rebecca Shelly was soon to sail aboard Henry Ford's "peace ship," to help "get the boys out of the trenches by Christmas."[6] The *Oscar II* would carry a body of unofficial delegates to Europe, where they would join representatives of other neutral countries in a conference designed to establish continuous mediation of the conflicts in Europe, and hopefully to bring about a negotiated peace. Rebecca, who had influence among the expedition's leaders, offered to get Lella a position as one of the corps of reporters and journalists who would accompany the delegation.

Until that moment Lella had not given much thought to the war in Europe—nor to keeping America out of it—but the voyage of *Oscar II* was an exciting prospect. Henry Ford and other famous pacifists would be on board. The delegates would visit Norway, Denmark, Sweden, and Holland—meeting with local pacifist groups as they went along.

As Lella said later, she had always cherished a secret determination to go to Europe. She needed little time to make up her mind. Borrowing $76.00 for a coach ticket, she left Seattle the same night.

Notes

1. "Our mother had a great desire for education and attended a short time at Hillsdale [Michigan] College. I think of the ambition [she] had . . . keeping us well dressed, clean, and teaching us the reward of right living." Lena Sowle Case, "Some few items about our ancestors," a hand-written family memoir.

2. Dr. John Harvey Kellogg, brother of W. K. Kellogg the cereal manufacturer, was a surgeon whose special interests were nutrition and public health. His Kellogg Sanitarium, founded in 1876, advocated vegetarian dietary ideas; rich industrialists came there for the cure whenever they felt "the onset of managerial fatigue."

3. Lella Secor Florence, *Our Private Lives*, ed. P. Sargant Florence, *America and Britain*, vol. 3 (3 vols.), London, George G. Harrap & Co. Ltd. 1944: 53.

4. Bryant "Cowboy" Stafford was the brother of Mabel Stafford, Ellsworth's wife. Lella's family considered him "not good enough" for her, but he worshiped her and she appears to have treated him kindly.

5. From an interview in the Battle Creek *Enquirer and News*.

6. European fighting men; America was officially neutral.

I

The Ford Peace Ship

To Laura Kelley and Lida Hamm[1]

[On board *Oscar II*]
December 9, 1915

This is Thursday evening, and the first bugle has already sounded for dinner, but if I allow many more events to accumulate, I shall never be able to find a beginning for the wonderful story of this wonderful trip. Every day I try to rouse myself to an actual realization of the fact that I am here, and that I am I.

I had intended to keep an accurate daily account of all that transpired so that I should be able to mail it as a sort of diary from our first stop on the other side. But all of my good resolutions were swallowed up in the waves of seasickness which engulfed me Saturday evening, and from whose grip I am only today beginning to enjoy comparative freedom. At this present moment the ship is rolling to such an extent that I am never quite sure that my finger is coming down on the letter aimed at, so that you will know the many blunders are resultant from the fact that the machine seldom stays long in the same spot, and that I am really too dizzy to follow it with alacrity.

Where shall I begin? Perhaps I had better abandon newspaper style of attacking the most important thing in the first paragraph, and write this account in sequence. I reached New York Saturday[2] evening—bright, gay, wonderful old New York. Rebecca was not at the train to meet me, so I rode to the McAlpin Hotel in a cab, and was escorted immediately to her room. What a joyful meeting we had! She is a trifle thinner than when we last saw her, and I think considerably prettier. She was having luncheon [dinner] in her room with Louise Matheney, who visited her in Everett and with whom she used to teach school in Wisconsin. She called a waiter, and another table was brought for me—juicy porterhouse and ice-cream. I was really too excited to eat, or to embrace the opportunity of ordering anything I chose from a very elaborate menu.

After dinner we went at once to the Biltmore [Hotel] where the headquarters of the Ford party were established. Here were scenes of history-making activities. An immense force of clerks, stenographers, secretaries, transportation men and others were in the throes of final preparations for this great expedition which had been organized in less than ten days.

In the midst of this confusion, it occurred to me to inquire about my passport. I confess I had been entirely ignorant as to the procedure necessary for securing this document, and had rather depended upon Rebecca to attend to the matter for me. I learned that I should have made application before leaving Seattle, and that my passport should then have been forwarded to New York from Washington D.C. A rule had been made that no one would be received aboard the ship without the passport, and it looked for a time as though my wild rush to New York City would finally be in vain. However, Madame Schwimmer,[3] who is certainly a most resourceful woman, discussed the matter with Rebecca, and it was arranged that I should make application in New York, and ask Washington to forward my document to Copenhagen. Accordingly, after a couple of hours sleep, we started out on our mission. It is necessary to have identification by some person who has known you for some time, and on account of the tremendous demand for passports, the bars had been put up, and the federal office was rather stringent. Rebecca herself had had a serious time with identification, and had finally been forced to enlist the services of S. S. McClure,[4] whom she had fortunately met at the conclusion of the Jane Addams expedition[5] in the spring.

We boarded one of those infernal institutions, the subway, and rode to the federal building where, much to our satisfaction, we found that Rebecca's identification would answer for me. However, it was necessary to have a photograph taken, and by the time I had accomplished all these details, and secured my application, it was 12:30 o'clock, and the ship was due to sail at two.[6] A wild rush back to the McAlpin, and a ride via the "tube"—another infernal institution—and by taxi, brought us to the dock.

Saturday morning

Two days have elapsed since I have had an opportunity to write another line. I am feeling quite myself again, though I am finding it difficult to spur my lagging mind to action.

So much has transpired during these days, that the time of sailing seems a far distant event on which it is difficult for me to concentrate my attention, especially in view of the fact that there are scores of typewriters clicking in the office on a story of much importance which "broke" loose last night, and which you no doubt already read about in papers by this time, for it was put on the wireless at midnight by the associated press services. A half dozen men are dictating, and the ship's band is playing a stirring air on deck—and my mental activities have been on a prolonged vacation. However, to make everything clear to you, I think I had better stick to the sequence of my story.

I wish you could have seen the thousands of people who had assembled on the dock to bid the ship God-speed, and have felt the thrill and enthusiasm of the occasion. Mr. Edison, Mr. Bryan, and other notables were on board, but these two did not accompany the ship.[7] One after another, prominent people were brought to the rail of the ship while cheer after cheer broke from the multitude below. The crowd was so great that we had difficulty getting to the gangplank, and equipped with my transportation, I succeeded in avoiding the necessity of showing my passport.[8] I could scarcely believe myself, when I stood with the hundred and sixty passengers now on their way to Europe, and I am sometimes even now inclined to doubt my sanity.

An orchestra on shore and the ship's band on board alternated with stirring patriotic airs, and finally, almost two hours late, the great vessel slipped her mooring, and while the band played the Hawaiian farewell song, the *Oscar II* glided away from the pier, while the throngs pressed close to the edge of the dock to offer last good-byes.

As soon as the start was made, everyone, including myself, rushed for the writing room, and the next two hours were spent in a frantic effort to pen a few lines to those who were left behind in America, in time to have the letters returned by the pilot boat which accompanied us for a short time. It was growing dark when the mail was thrown aboard the pilot boat, and she returned to New York. I shall never forget the thrill I felt when we steamed away alone into the great ocean! We had time for a few turns on deck before the bugle sounded for dinner, but aside from this, I saw or learned little that evening. However, even the equipment of our little stateroom, which Rebecca and I share together, was full of the keenest interest to me. After an elaborate dinner—and what scrumptious meals they do serve!—everyone was engaged in identifying his baggage and getting settled in his quarters. Much to my surprise, I learned that the trip would take from ten to fourteen days instead of five or six as I had originally supposed, so that there was every reason for establishing oneself as comfortably as possible.

I began to feel dizzy and somewhat ill even Saturday evening, but I rather felt that this was the natural result of my hard strenuous day, during which I had found no opportunity to eat. But Sunday I was truly ill, and never left my stateroom, though I made a desperate effort to dress for afternoon vespers conducted by Dr. Aked[9] of San Francisco, and the evening service when Dr. Jenkin Lloyd Jones, a venerable and noted minister of Chicago, preached. The sickness which I experienced was in no sense different from the sort of vomiting spells to which I have so long been subject, and I fully expected that it would last no more than a day. However, by the end of the fourth day when the horrible nausea and vomiting persisted, I was fully convinced that I was seasick. Not until Friday did I venture into the dining room or really relish a meal. Thus you see, I was obliged to miss much of interest, for there have been from four to six or eight meetings daily, addressed by many of the keen thinkers of the day. The intellectual feast has been supreme. I have enjoyed intimate talks with Mr. McClure, Mr. Ford, Ellis O. Jones, the humorist and noted single taxer, Mrs. Sewall, president of the International Council of Women, Judge Lindsey, Madame Schwimmer, and others.[10]

. . . There has been a fine spirit of comraderie among the ship's company. There are a few of course who have gotten in on one excuse or another and who lack any ideals—in fact I think I may say there are many "among those present" whose acquaintance I have no desire to cultivate. This is notably true of some of the journalists, a large number of whom never saw active service in the newspaper field and hastily attached themselves to some paper in order to make the trip.[11] But the peace delegates, in the main, are an excellent company of people.

While all are possessed of a desire for peace, there is much divergence of opinion, which has found expression in various group arguments as to ways and means of attaining and perpetuating a permanent peace. But there has been no evidence of outward break until last evening. No, I should amend that, for on Tuesday evening, Mr. McClure read an advance copy of the President's message not yet delivered to Congress, which you have no doubt read by this time, in which he advocates the expenditures of enormous sums for the enlargement of the navy, in compliance with a policy of preparedness.[12] Now we who are thorough pacifists—and I may as well announce here that the study of the subject which I have made since leaving Seattle, and the thought I have given to the subject, has convinced me beyond any doubt of the possibility and the advisability of international disarmament and future settlement of all disputes by means of mediation—strongly stand against the policy of "preparedness," which is admittedly one of the reasons for the present outbreak in Europe. But we find that we differ as to the accomplishment of this ideal. I, with Madame Schwimmer and the core of the Ford party, favor no further expenditures for "preparedness" in America, whatever the rest of the world may do at the present time. I can scarcely go into details as to this opinion, but I personally am thoroughly grounded in it.

When the president's message was read, there was sort of an electric shock, which threatened to develop into a real storm when Ellis Jones who is, I am afraid, rather impetuous and a little hot headed, jumped to his feet and delivered a scathing denunciation of the President. Mr. McClure and some others who are in accord with international disarmament, favor preparedness in the United States until such time as international disarmament can be accomplished. I take strong issue with him on this point, but I really must not stop now for prolonged discussion. Suffice it to say that a sharp interchange of ideas was only avoided by the suggestion of Mr. Ford that the message be given consideration for several days, and then discussed.

Last evening Mr. Lochner,[13] secretary of the peace expedition, delivered a peerless address on "World Federation," and at its conclusion a "platform," drawn up by a committee of resolutions, was placed before the ship's company, each of whom was invited to sign it or not as he chose. The platform contained three planks, two of which dealt with the loyalty of the ship to Mr. Ford and his project, and the peace project, and the third of which contained an unqualified declaration against any increase by the United States of her naval or military forces. It was rather railroaded through, and though I conscientiously signed it because I could do so, I did disapprove of the rather dictatorial method in which the policy of the entire ship had been outlined by a committee of five.[14]

A tempest ensued which could hardly have been contained in a teapot. Journalists representing the big dailies and the associated presses rushed wildly about, and there were angry passes between various persons who accused intrigue, etc. The excitement continued well into the morning, and there rapidly developed a division of the pilgrims into two groups: those who endorsed the policy without hesitation, and those who refused to sign the platform. It was the understanding that only those who felt they could endorse the platform would be included in the peace party to continue negotiations at The Hague. I realize that some declaration of principle was essential, but I do regret that the method employed should have been so tactless. Fortunately we learned this morning [that] the wireless last night was unable to pick up any vessel westbound, so apparently the story did not reach the press. But of course it will do so eventually, and will, I am afraid, give the papers another opportunity to ridicule an effort which is far more serious and earnest than anyone who is not with us could imagine.[15] Just what the outcome will be, we do not know. Perhaps a new platform will be drawn up to which all can subscribe; perhaps the original few will proceed on the mission alone.

If anyone thought this was going to be a leisurely, delightfully restful voyage, he was mistaken. To be sure it is delightful and restful and exhilarating, but every day is filled to overflowing and the nights are the briefest space possible. Yesterday, for instance, was a typical day. I was up at seven—in time to see the miracle of the early morning sun breaking through the dull gray clouds in golden radiance. I think I have not mentioned the fact that since the second night at sea, I have slept on deck, swathed in steamer rugs and blankets, and comfortably ensconced on one of the deck benches. I simply cannot endure the air of the inside cabin which Rebecca and I were so unfortunate as to draw, and as all first and second cabins are occupied by members of the Ford peace party, the rules of the ship have been very largely cast asunder. At eight I breakfasted, and at nine enjoyed the luxury of a hot salt water bath. At ten I attended a student's meeting, and participated in a discussion concerning disarmament. Then lunch with the students, and a further discussion of the subject with Mr. Ford. That is, we discussed it and he said "yes" or "no" as the case might be. He is one of the most unique and most delightful men I have ever met. He is simple, unassuming, witty, and a man of great ideals and the courage to stand by those ideals in the face of any obstacle. Just to meet him and catch a gleam from his philosophy of life is reward enough if nothing else should come of my trip, which is of course quite impossible.[16]

After lunch there was a short time for an exhilarating walk on deck, and a chat with the representative of the *Christian Science Monitor,* before a lecture by Mrs. Sewall on "Women and the International Movement." After this, dinner, and then the lecture by Mr. Lochner which I have already mentioned. We discussed this occurrence informally wherever we chanced to meet, and at half past twelve, someone conceived the idea of having a mock trial, the idea resulting from the statement from one of the students that Mr. McClure had convinced him since coming on board that preparedness was the proper thing. So Mr. McClure was indicted on a charge of "Corrupting the Morals of Youth," and a very clever trial ensued, in which there were many brilliant passes.

I have never been any place in my life where so much food is consumed. The eating process starts with breakfast in the morning, bouillon and wafers at ten with fruit interspersed at any hour one desires, luncheon at noon, tea and cakes at four, dinner at six followed by coffee in the lecture room, and sandwiches and drinks—beer, ginger ale, etc.—from then until midnight.

Mr. Ford has left nothing undone for the comfort of his guests. Every stateroom was adorned with a flowering plant and supplied with a basket of fruit. Journalists are permitted to use the typewriters, of which there are dozens, . . . constantly in demand. I am at this very moment supposed to be writing a report for my paper, instead of this lengthy epistle, which I must bring to a close. You will perhaps not realize that I have been working steadily for several hours. A few moments ago we stopped long enough to go on deck to have some moving pictures made. By the way, moving pictures were also taken of the ship as she left the pier at New York, so it may be possible that you will have a chance to see them. I was standing at the rail, and purposely waved my handkerchief as the camera turned my way, so that I could perhaps greet some of you even while I am in distant lands.

I would suggest that you get the *P-I* [Seattle *Post-Intelligencer*] for accurate news of the ship's voyage, or better still New York or Chicago papers, which will no doubt carry fuller reports. Wireless messages are sent out every day.

I suppose I should not close this epistle without mentioning the weather. Today a young gale is blowing so that it is almost more than one's life is worth to venture out on the deck. With the exception of one or two sunny days, we have had rough weather all the way, but I have grown to love the rolling gait of this old ship. There is something mighty and inspiring in watching her mount the crest of a great wave, and then slide smoothly down into the valley of water, between a burst of emerald water into pearl spray.

To Laura Kelley and Lida Hamm

Wed. [December] 15, 1915

Dear Ones At Home:

This morning we dropped anchor in this beautiful little harbor of Kirkwall, a fishing hamlet in the islands near Scotland. We do not know how long we are to be delayed here. I have written a massive account of this wonderful trip, but I'm not going to mail it here, because everything must pass through the hands of the censors, and it is difficult for us who live in such freedom, to understand just what the censors consider it proper for us to say, and what not. We are told, anyway, that the delay occasioned by the need of censorship will prevent mail from reaching N.Y. as quickly as if mailed from Christiania,[17] a neutral port. So prepare for volumes to follow—or perhaps precede this letter.

I have thought of you all every day, and the only shadow on this marvelous experience has been that you could not all be with me. . . .

Our passports were examined this morning, and I experienced no difficulty whatever. It gave me such strange sensations to see the British soldiers standing at attention in the halls. Three inspectors sat at a table in one of the dining rooms, with the British lieutenant who boarded our vessel when we first entered the war zone. He was a jovial, ruddy chap who recalled me as one of the members of the Press Club, I think, for we exchanged pleasant smiles. When he came aboard, the Press Club invited him to join us in an informal reception. I think we all hoped secretly that he would drop some bit of news which would make a good story. But we were disappointed, for he never said a word, but just laughed uproariously at all the entertainment we provided.

They say the mail is leaving now—so I must bring this to a hasty close—

Loads of love,
Lella

To Loretta Secor

In the harbor of Christiansand
[December] 18, 1915

Dear Mother and Loved Ones at Home,

. . . I had no trouble about my passport. I guess I told you that I had just a certified copy of my original application, but they let me through without a question. I had such a strange feeling as I saw the armed soldiers standing about in the halls, and realized that we were virtually prisoners on this ship. The harbor of Kirkwall is thickly strewn with mines, which look something like the weights on the fishing nets we see in the Sound, only they are of iron and much larger. Little black menacing boats are constantly in attendance, and when a boat is to enter, the mines are carefully towed out of the way while the vessel passes through, then drawn back again. After three o'clock in the afternoon, no vessel dares to move.

This little harbor where we are now reminds one of the pictures in fairy stories—rocky snow-covered hills topped with the purple-pink glow of an early afternoon sunset. The windows of the houses are of gold just now, and little gold fleeced clouds offer the last remembrance of the vanishing day.

I had fully expected to have some money to send in this letter, but though my voucher has been O.K.'d it has not been paid yet. . . .[18] If possible, before I close this letter, I shall try to get a check made out to you. . . . I do wish I had time to tell you all about my plans or rather my hopes in this great movement, and the opportunities—financially as well as otherwise—which I hope may open for me. However, everything is yet in a state of uncertainty, because we don't know what we shall be able to do at The Hague. I have met such wonderful people, especially in the last few days I have become better acquainted with many. Some are friends whom I shall be proud to have all my life, and who will no doubt be of great service to me from time to time.

Every day I thank God for this marvelous change, and pray that it may open up something fine for us all. You are constantly in my thoughts, and my only wish is that you might be with me. Henry

Ford is a prince among men. I have never met his equal, and it has been worth so much to me just to have the chance to know him.

I wrote you at Kirkwall, but I'm afraid perhaps the letter will be so much censored that it may never reach you. I know what a sacrifice you are making to let me have this chance, and I hope I shall be able to more than repay you. If I do not, then you, too, shall have contributed to this wonderful cause of peace, to which I have become devoted heart and soul.

At my first opportunity, I want to tell you a few of the many things I have learned; but in the meantime, I wish you would study the subject as much as possible. . . . I have really worked very hard to get more written, but I've been busy so much of the time with Press stuff, and have also been helping the management, with whom I have come to stand rather strong. I think I shall share in any good thing which may offer, though of course nothing may develop.

Love unending,
Lella

To Loretta Secor

[December 1915]

[First page missing.]

Perhaps I had better try to begin back at Christiansand, where I mailed my other letter. . . . I believe a ship is sailing tomorrow so I'll send this even though I am not able to say all I want to.

One of the reasons why my time has been so full is that I have been assisting in the publication of a "Who's Who" of the ship's company. I have not received any compensation so far, and don't know whether I shall, but I am glad of the chance to help, and it has also given me the opportunity to establish myself in rather intimate relations with the executive force of the expedition. I don't know anything more definite about my prospects than when I last wrote you, but occasionally I hear little things which lead me to believe that I may hope to become one of the salaried staff. In the meantime I am collecting a rich store of material which cannot fail to be valuable for months to come.

I think my previous letter will doubtless have given you a pretty clear idea of the entire ocean voyage, which occupied just two weeks. However, I did not tell you about the captain's dinner served the last night on shipboard. It is a custom on all vessels, and this one was especially elaborate, in keeping with all the events of this history-making trip. The tables were gaily decorated, and everyone appeared in full evening dress. I have never seen so many dress suits so often in my life. Almost every youngster over fifteen is properly equipped with a swallow-tail outfit. In the center of the table were great cakes made of almond meal, and surrounded with brightly colored "snappers" and favors of various sorts. Each was topped with an American eagle, and as Rebecca and I were almost the only ladies at our table, the eagles were gallantly presented to us for souvenirs.

After dinner I still had some work to do on the biographies, which I did not finish until 2 a.m. Then I took a few rounds on deck, which I shall never forget. We were nearing land, and the water was as smooth as glass. A full moon hung in the heavens, and spilled its silver rays in a broad road across the sea. Far in the distance we could see the twinkling lights of land. When we woke in the morning, we had already arrived at Christiania, that wonderful city of Norway.

But before I go on with Christiania, I must tell something of Christiansand, where we anchored first, but where we were not allowed to go ashore. I think I have never seen anything more beautiful. A great rocky promontory glistening purple-pink under the rays of the late afternoon sun, forms a natural fort which protects the city, tucked snugly away in the little cove of land behind the promontory. Everything was freshly snowcovered—the strange buildings, and the sturdy little church towers. And while we looked, the sun dropped into the ocean in brilliant triumph, and left the little city with its wonderful hills shrouded in that quiet mystery of a long, purple-glowed twilight. Then while we still stood at the rail entranced, the pale moon peeped up behind the hills, and wonder was enveloped in new wonder.

It was almost noon before we finally disembarked at Christiania, and were whisked to our hotels in taxicabs. I have never gotten on such familiar terms with taxis before, and I never hope to again.

Especially the young woman and I who have been working on the biographies have been whisked here and there—always a taxi at our command. Truly the wildest *Arabian Nights* Tale has no comparison with the wonder of this trip. Mr. Ford is quite the most wonderful man I have ever known. In fact there are no words to describe his sweet simplicity, or the unspoiled beauty of his idealistic nature.

As soon as we reached our hotel—I have a sumptuous room with Miss Hopkins,[19] a well known magazine writer of New York—I dropped on the bed for a nap, for I felt that I should not be able to go on with all the demands on my strength which the day would bring without a little rest. I slept half an hour, and got up like a new person.

Mr. Ford had planned an outing for us at Hollen Kollen, a winter resort of Christiania, and Sunday forms a day which will stand out in my memory forever as one of the happiest I have ever known. We were taken from our hotels in taxicabs to a sort of interurban station, and there boarded cars which took us through the outskirts of lovely Christiania. It is crisp winter weather here—hovering around zero—and everything is white with snow. I can't describe the lovely hills and vales through which we passed—hills dotted with snow-weighted pine trees. I had become acquainted on the boat with a Mr. Sorensen,[20] one of the most substantial and splendid young men whom it has been my pleasure to meet, and he rather assumed the privilege of looking after me at Hollen Kollen. This is a delightful playground way up in the hills, where hundreds of Norwegians were skiing and coasting. We scattered in small groups and enjoyed long tramps before the hour for luncheon, which was served in a quaint little inn. I have taken on so many impressions, that I can hardly separate my thoughts in coherent fashion, so if I ramble terribly, you will know that it simply reflects the state of my mind.

Mr. Sorensen and I chose a path which brought us to an adorable little kirk hidden among the pines at the top of a high hill. It was built of natural pine, and finished after the style of the ancient kirks. We went in and my escort, who speaks a little Norwegian, was able to translate some of the inscriptions about the walls and over the altar. There was only a sort of janitor in the building, and we sat down in one of the pews with its wonderful handcarvings. I have never spent a half hour of more wonderful exaltation. One could not fail to catch the spirit of worship and adoration which enwrapped the little church, and though we tried in vain to translate some of the passages from the little prayer books, one did not need words to help one worship. Afterward we stood alone on the steps of the kirk, too far from the crowds to hear even a sound. A pink-purple mist enshrouded the valley below us, and it was not difficult to imagine that we had stepped into a new and strange sphere far removed from the mundane things of life.

A brisk walk in the crisp air sharpened our appetites for luncheon which we ate at about three o'clock. Mr. Ford, who has been ill in bed ever since we reached Christiania, was able to be with us on that occasion, but has not been out since—a fact which has been a great disappointment to all of us. He is much better today, and has promised the people of Norway that he will not leave until he has a chance to see them face to face.[21] It was announced that we would leave for Stockholm by train tomorrow, but I doubt whether we will get away, for today Lloyd Bingham, the husband of the actress, Amelia Bingham, died in a hospital in Christiania. He was ill on the boat, and was taken to the hospital as soon as we reached this city. This, and Mr. Ford's illness, may delay us still later, which I really hope may be the case, for I have seen very little of Christiania yet.

But to return to Sunday. We had luncheon in a long room with a big brick fireplace at either end. I have never seen anything quite like those fireplaces. They are immense, with a partition down the center, and the wood is placed on end at either side. Above, and around the room, were great sledges and skis used by famous explorers and captains. On the mantels stood the most adorable steins of strange pottery. I longed for a pocket big enough to hold one.

After one of these strange Norwegian luncheons—cabbage fried with caraway seed—wouldn't you love it though Ina?—we started back to the [train], and thence to our hotels via taxis—always taxis.

There was an informal reception in the Grand Hotel, the headquarters of the party, where I am now working, so I hastily dressed for this occasion. Afterward a dinner had been planned, but while the reception was still in progress, Miss Lawton, of the New York *Sun,* and I were asked to assist Miss Leckie,[22] the publicity manager, and were whisked away in a taxi and dumped out before a strange dark building. We went in and found a sign on the elevator which we could not read but which evidently announced that the lift was not working. So we started to climb. We didn't know the name of the printing office which we were seeking, or on what floor it was to be found, so we resorted to the expedient of opening every door we camc to. The halls were dark and silent, and we experienced a distinct thrill when we finally opened a door into a dimly lighted studio whose walls were lined with nude figures of various sizes and shapes. In the midst of this orgy of limbs and bodies sat some sort of an abnormal individual who croaked at us in broken English when we addressed him. We fled and continued our process of opening doors, until finally we discovered a small office where Miss Leckie sat working at a desk. I confess we felt rather relieved. We went in and worked until nine o'clock, and then had dinner served in Miss Leckie's room at the Grand Hotel, thus missing the evening meeting, which was said to have been very interesting.

Monday, too weary to waken, I slept right through until ten o'clock, and then hurried to the printing office. I have also become rather well acquainted with Mr. Heubsch,[23] a prominent publisher of New York, with whom I was whisked back to the hotel—in a taxi—for luncheon, then back to the printer's office. Between times of editing copy and reading proof, we had many merry moments during which the Norwegian publisher, who has done our work for us here, tried to teach us a few phrases in his language. I have found them very convenient in making myself understood. Late in the afternoon, Mr. Heubsch conducted me on a brief tour of the shops. He speaks a little German, and between us we had no difficulty in making our wants known.

After dinner Monday night—we all eat our luncheons and dinners at the Grand, no matter where we are residenced—we went, in a taxi, to a great hall seating 5,000 people, where a mass meeting was held under the auspices of the Ministers' Peace Union. It was thrilling and inspiring, but the necessity of repeating everything in both Norwegian and English made it rather tiresome and too prolonged so that the impression, we feared, was not as good as we should have liked. Two of the newspapers are very friendly toward us; some of the others are skeptical as to the possibility of our accomplishing anything, but all unite in great admiration for Mr. Ford.

I slept rather late yesterday again, for Miss Hopkins and I talk things over at night, even after we get to bed which is almost never before twelve, and I feel compelled to keep myself in condition to meet the ever varying events. Then after lunch, I remained on duty, to secure the biographies of the 25 persons or more who arrived on board the *Frederick VIII.*[24] I dictated probably two dozen biographies during the afternoon, and then at about five o'clock, went out with Miss Lawton to call on the American consul and his wife, who were having open house for the Ford party. Much to our disappointment, however, we were delayed so in finding the place, that we felt it was too late to go in.

At eight o'clock I attended a banquet given by the Norwegian Students' Association, or the Order of the Golden Pig, a very dignified and quite the foremost educational order of Norway. It includes not only students now in college, but scientists, and doctors, etc., who have completed their courses. Our conception of students is vastly different from that of the old world, for to them, educated men never cease to be students.

This was quite the most unique banquet I ever attended. On the small tables were simple wine glasses and napkins. Then the men at each table brought plates and silver from a long central table, and served each course from this table themselves. Everyone over here drinks wine and it's rather awkward to be a teetotaler when so many toasts are to be pledged. At the banquet, Mr. Ford's secretary announced a gift of $10,000 toward the building of a home for the Order of the Golden Pig, and this was of course received with tremendous enthusiasm. $10,000 in Norway is a princely sum.

Afterward Dr. Aked gave one of the most brilliant addresses I have ever heard. It left me tingling from crown to toe, and the audience gave him such an ovation as I have seldom witnessed. Everyone clapped, then shouted, then stamped on the floor, then rose and waved napkins and shouted some more. Afterward when Dr. Aked, arm in arm with the brilliant young president of the organization, led the way from the banquet room, everyone rose again and the demonstration was repeated. I had just returned from this wonderful meeting last night when I penned the first lines of this letter.

It is after one o'clock now, and I have an invitation to take dinner with Rebecca and one or two others, at the home of one of the big men of Christiania. In the meantime, I must try to get a story written for the papers; try to get a conglomeration of notes into some shape for future use before I take on any more impressions; dress, and attend to a dozen details.

. . . I have hardly at any time, I think, told you anything about my personal feelings regarding the expedition, and they have been evolved by such a process of thought and reasoning, that it would be hard to say much on paper. I am heartily in sympathy with the plan for continuous mediation until some satisfactory plan can be devised for all the warring nations, and it does not seem at all unreasonable or impossible to me. Neither does international disarmament seem so, as I shall try to tell the people of Washington when I come home. I have been accused, as have all the earnest members of the Ford party, of being an idealist, and I am proud to plead guilty to the charge, for certainly every big movement must start from the ideal. But all this must wait until I see you.

Mr. Heubsch very kindly got this money order for you today. I expected to send $100, but I forgot the $20 that I borrowed from Louise Matheney in New York. . . . I do hope the money has come from Michigan by this time. The thought of your struggles while I am having so much without paying out one cent myself, has really made me wretchedly unhappy. I don't know whether the *P-I* or the [Everett] *Herald* will use any of my stuff, for by the time it reaches them the news will be horribly stale. But if either of them do, I wish you would please tell [them] to forward to you, at my request, any compensation which may be due me. I shall be happy if I can simply keep my notes and impressions straight until I can find time to use them.

I made out my voucher to the full sum of a first class ticket, and also put in a reasonable sum for meals each day. . . . The whole came to $203, and I have kept the $103 to see me through Europe and get me back to Seattle. . . . So I shall have to spend very cautiously indeed. I am rather sorry, for there are so many things which seem very cheap to me here. By the time this reaches you,

Christmas will have passed. It hardly seems possible to me that the time is so near. Mr. Ford has arranged a fine celebration for us at the beautiful hotel in Stockholm, and you may be sure there will be nothing cheap about it.[25] You never saw such a host in all your life, for there is no other like him.

Even if it costs a good deal, I'm going to try to send a cable to you today, so that you will have word from me by Christmas day. . . .

. . . I am so eager to hear from you all, and to know that everything is well with you. I have felt confident that you have kept in touch with us through the wireless messages which have been sent back, but I have had no way to get the slightest word from you. Give my love . . . to Lena and Lew and the babies[26] when you see them, but keep loads for your own two dear selves.

Lovingly,
Lella

To Loretta Secor

HOTEL WITTEBRUG
S-GRAVENHAGE
[The Hague]

January 10 [1916]

Dear Mother and All:

. . . Some of the students are returning on a boat sailing tomorrow and I shall ask one of them to mail this in New York so you will be sure to receive it. . . . I finished a lengthy typewritten epistle which, in the horrible rush of leaving Copenhagen, was mislaid so it did not get mailed. Sounds as though it was the letter's fault, doesn't it? I am hoping that it found its way into a bundle of paper and things which I mailed home and that it will eventually reach you. That letter described in detail our wonderful stay in Stockholm and Copenhagen. . . . I'm just going to try to hit the high spots.

The two most important events which have happened to me personally are these: My sincerity and earnestness and my unshakable belief in our mission has won for me the hearty approval of the "administration" and at the behest of my good friend Mr. Heubsch, the publisher from New York whom I think I mentioned before, I was made a regular delegate. You see our company is divided really into 4 parts: the delegates who constitute a voting membership, the press representatives who are so scurrilous and vicious that I have entirely severed all connection with them, the students, and the business force.[27]

The second big event was the chance Mr. H[eubsch] gave me to address a splendid audience of 2500 people in Stockholm. This was really a great honor, for only a few of our company have been asked to speak at the mass meetings, and we now number nearly 2500. I wish I had time to tell you in detail about this wonderful meeting. . . .[28]

Our reception in Stockholm was simply a triumph and our stay there will always linger in my mind as one of the brilliant events of my life. In Copenhagen we were likewise cordially received, but [Denmark] is in such mortal terror of being drawn into the war that we were not allowed to hold any public meetings. Instead there was a ceaseless round of receptions, banquets, teas and excursions, all of which those of us who are conscientious attended with religious regulation. You see, that was the only chance we had to meet the people and get our plan before them. I think it was about the hardest week's work I've done. To stand for hours at a reception and make oneself understood [above] the rumble of voices, especially with foreigners who understand very little English, is a task which requires endurance.

Before going through Germany to Holland, it was necessary for us to dispose of every bit of printed matter, etc.[29] We left Copenhagen about 9 o'clock Thursday morning, and after changing from train to boat and from train to train four or five times during the night, we arrived at The Hague at 11 a.m. Saturday. The German officials passed us through the lines without even examining our baggage—an almost unprecedented condition, and therefore a real triumph for our cause. The German Lieutenant in charge even made a speech in the crowded waiting room in which he wished us

Godspeed on our trip, and fervently hoped that we would succeed in establishing peace. His speech met with a wonderful ovation.

The trip through Germany had a strangely wonderful effect on me. I felt the sorrow, the woe, the anguish of a great nation. Every darkened window of the houses we passed seemed to shroud an almost phantom woe, and every lighted window seemed to stifle the wails of wives and mothers. Everywhere were soldiers, soldiers, soldiers,—human stoics in uniform who neither smiled or frowned, but simply looked. Oh, you've no idea how awful it is—this hate and distrust and envy—this horrible slaughter of prime manhood and all to no purpose. My soul is afire with the vision of the future when all this barbarism will yield to reason and faith and brotherhood and love.

The trip from Copenhagen was very wearing, for we could obtain no sleepers because so many were needed to carry the wounded soldiers. Everywhere, however, we met courteous treatment, from the guards who traveled on our train to those who took charge of us at the stations where we got off.

Several members of our party, who had to leave early for one reason or another, passed through a most rigid examination. They were stripped to the skin and every article of clothing was most painstakingly examined. You can see what an immense concession was made for us.

The Hague is a splendid city. I have seen practically nothing as yet, for yesterday I staid in bed a good part of the day, trying to prepare for the rather strenuous program of the week.

I have thought of you all so often, and longed so much to see you and have you here. Your letter, Mother, written Dec. 12, was forwarded to The Hague and reached me yesterday. I was so glad to hear from you.

Love in big quantities to you both,

Lella

To Loretta Secor

S. S. Rotterdam
January 26, 1916

Dear Mother and All,

I feel almost disheartened when I think of writing any more letters, for I feel normally sure that half of those I have sent you have never reached their destination. However, since we are half way across the Atlantic, and out of the toils of those poor, war-distracted countries, there is perhaps some hope that this may be delivered. . . .

We left Rotterdam, Holland, on Jan. 15,[30] and dropped anchor in The Downs off the coast of Dover, England, the next day. We were detained there a day, and then went on through the English Channel to Falmouth. Here we were held up three days while the English officers came aboard and examined passports and luggage. This was a much more thrilling experience than that we experienced at Kirkwall, but we had become so inured to the sight of officers and the process of being examined, that we missed many of the thrills, I fear.

The first day they were on board, all the men were examined, and we women had our turn the next day. I had gone into the magnificent blue room to get a book from the library, and when I was ready to go out, I found myself a virtual prisoner with other women of the ship's company. One by one we were hailed into a corner before the stern automaton of war. Our passports were examined and were scrutinized by many eyes. Each of us was asked whether she was carrying any letters for other members of the Ford party, and if so, to kindly produce them. It happened that my good friend Mr. Huebsch, whom I've mentioned in the letters which you have doubtless not received, had given me two letters to post in New York in order to avoid the delay of English censorship. I either had to deliver them to the authorities to be posted by them goodness knows when, after they had been duly read, or else I could open them myself, allow the officers to read them, and get them back again providing there was nothing objectionable in them. I chose the latter course, though some members of our party who had mail for folks left behind at The Hague, elected to give up the letters under protest, rather than open them. This seemed to me a false standard of honor as long as the letters had to be opened anyway and I felt that I could depend on Mr. H's approval.

So undoubtedly, all the mail which we sent with the students, who left several days in advance of us on the *S. S. Noordam,* is now in the hands of the English. I have little hope now that the stories I have sent back have ever reached their destination.

We could not quite understand the reason for the painstaking examination to which we were subjected when we were about to leave for America, but it became more apparent when, the night before we sailed from Falmouth, one of the English passengers on board, was taken off as a German spy. He claimed to be an American citizen, and was traveling under an American passport. But for some reason, suspicion was aroused, and when his trunk was searched, much German literature, picture films, etc., said to be designed for pro-German propaganda work in America, was found.

In consequence, a much more thorough search of everyone was made. In cases of suspicion, even the carpets in the staterooms were torn up, and mattresses were ripped open. At last, however, we were released, leaving our suspected friend to face the prisons of England, or the firing squad. He was taken off just as dinner was in progress, and the meal went merrily on while the orchestra played its liveliest tunes. How strange that we can yet be gay while tragedies are being enacted under our very noses!

As soon as we cleared the English Channel—and we were all more or less glad to be free from those floating-mine-infested waters—we began to encounter very high seas, which developed into a real storm. The *Rotterdam* careened about like an empty egg shell, and nearly everyone, even those seasoned sailors, was seasick. I began to feel the symptoms, and straightway set about to overcome them. I threw all the willpower I possessed into the fight, and won out triumphantly. I have been on deck every day, and although I confess to feeling "green" on some occasions, I never gave up for a moment, and had the keen and superior delight of smiling at the poor crumpled seasick sinners.

For three days we plowed through a magnificent storm. The

Rotterdam is a 24,170-ton streamer, and eleven stories high, so you can imagine the force of a storm which could shake such a vessel almost as a dog would shake a rat. The storm reached its climax when a huge wave broke over the sun deck, or very top of the vessel. For two nights the rolling and pitching of the boat was so violent that I hardly slept at all. A British freighter sent out an SOS call which we were about to answer when an Italian vessel nearer than we responded and took off the crew before the ship sank. You can hardly imagine what a strange sensation it gives one to see and feel the great vessel sink down—down—down into a valley of water, and then as surely rise again—up—up—up onto the crest of another great wave.

Most of all I think I have enjoyed my evening walks on the sun deck with Mr. Sorensen—to whom I have already introduced you, though perhaps the introduction has failed to land—when the storm would be raging so that I did not dare venture around the deck alone for fear of being blown overboard. The great, vigorous, seething sea, the wild untamed winds, and around all, great limitless space, gave me a new and inspiring awe of the mightiness of Nature. It is much calmer now, and I suppose we shall not encounter such a grand storm again.

Saturday morning

Today we are nearing New York, and this wonderful voyage will soon be over. I have just come in from a turn on the sun deck, and wished every step of the way that my little sister[31] could be walking beside me. It is the most marvelous day—in distinct contrast to the severe storm through which we have been traveling. The sun is radiantly bright, and the sea and the sky reflect each other in a glorious blue, while the wind is sharp enough to keep one moving.

I can't tell now just exactly when I'll reach home. So much depends on how we find matters when we reach New York. If Mr. Ford approves of some of the peace plans we have in mind, and will finance them, or rather us, I shall try to have a share in the work, for it will mean financial gain, beside giving me an opportunity to do some really big work. However, all this is purely visionary at this moment. I am hoping earnestly that some mail may await me in New York. I'll send a night letter as soon as I arrive, and will keep you informed as fast as things develop.

Loads and loads of love,

Lella

Notes

1. This letter was printed in the Battle Creek *Moon-Journal* of January 15, 1916, with the following preface:

"MISS L.F. SECOR WRITES OF THE FORD PEACE TRIP/Former B.C. Girl Tells in Lengthy Communication Many Very Interesting Details/LETTER IS A MASTERPIECE/*Tells Of The Discord Among The Peace Delegates That Originated Early In The Great Trip.*

"Happenings aboard the Ford Peace Ship the 'Oscar II,' from the time it sailed from New York City until it approached the Denmark shore, are told in detail by Miss Lella Fay[e] Secor, a native Battle Creek girl, in a letter to her two sisters, Mrs. W. C. Kelley and Mrs. Lida E. Hamm, both of whom reside at 158 Grove Street.

"Miss Secor has a wide circle of friends in this city, although she has not been a Battle Creek resident for several years. She is a graduate of the local high school with the class of 1906, after which she entered newspaper work, taking a position as society editor on the Battle Creek Journal. Her advancement in this line of endeavor was rapid and after serving an apprenticeship of two or three years on the Journal, she was offered a position at Everett, Wash., which she accepted. Since leaving this city, she has made rapid advancement in the newspaper field and has held many responsible positions . . .

"Interesting personal experiences as well as descriptive articles of various conferences held on the ship are told by Miss Secor in her communication to her local relatives. She also deals lightly with the unexcelled treatment afforded the delegates by Mr. Ford and other prominent members of the delegation, of the excellent food served aboard and personal interviews with some [one line missing]."

2. It would have been Friday evening because *Oscar II* sailed Saturday afternoon.
3. Mme. Rosika Schwimmer, Hungarian author and feminist, had been instrumental in convincing Ford of the need for mediation.
4. Editor of the New York *Evening Mail*.
5. Following the International Congress of Women at The Hague in April 1915, Jane Addams and others had traveled in Europe, gathering evidence that both neutrals and belligerents were ready to consider mediation.
6. "I . . . arrived breathless at a small official window just as it was closing. I put my head through to stop it, and I begged the young official to give me a passport, and if he couldn't do that, something that looked like one. I don't suppose I shall ever reach such heights of eloquence again. It fired the young man's imagination, and there and then he concocted a fake passport, adorned with my cock-eyed photographs, and embellished with more official seals than have ever graced a simple, honest passport." Lella Secor Florence, "The Ford Peace Ship and After," in *We Did Not Fight: 1914–18 Experiences of War-Resisters*, ed. Julian Bell, London, Cobden-Sanderson 1935: 99.
7. Thomas A. Edison and William Jennings Bryan, both committed pacifists.

8. "The official who inspected passports at the gangway of the ship was overcome by the crush, the excitement, and the proximity of so many great ones. . . . I waved my document and slipped up the gangway." Florence, "The Ford Peace Ship": 100.

9. Charles F. Aked, clergyman.

10. May Wright Sewall was also president of the Women's Peace Congress in Chicago; Ben Lindsey was a well-known judge from Denver, Colorado.

11. "[Of the] journalists on board . . . I don't suppose half a dozen . . . ever tried to discover just what the promoters of the expedition had in their minds, or to examine dispassionately the merits or flaws of their proposals. . . . To this day [1935], I feel ashamed of the unscrupulous behaviour of my colleagues. We were treated with extraordinary kindness. . . . This was repaid, on our part, by insolence and scandal-mongering. . . . Hardly a fair and decent story was sent out from the Ford Peace Ship." Florence, "The Ford Peace Ship": 100-101, 106.

12. Wilson's message went to Congress on Wednesday, December 8.

13. Louis P. Lochner, former secretary of the International Federation of Students, had been a prime mover of the expedition.

14. See Appendix A for a fuller discussion of this meeting.

15. American newspapers seized every opportunity to ridicule the undertaking. When Ford announced his peace plans, one headline had read, "Great War Ends Xmas Day, Ford to Stop It." *Oscar II* was called the "flivvership" and its passengers "a bunch of nuts."

16. Ford "preferred the young and unsophisticated members of the party, and nearly every morning he breakfasted with the student group with whom I early allied myself. . . . At that particular time he was engrossed in the Fordson Tractor which he was just bringing out. He talked in raptures throughout one breakfast about revolutionizing farming. . . . I tried to appear as interested as I could, but I hardly understood any of the mechanics he explained to me in great detail." Florence, "The Ford Peace Ship": 108.

17. Now Oslo.

18. Her expense voucher, issued by the Seattle *Post-Intelligencer*.

19. Mary Alden Hopkins, free-lance magazine writer.

20. Christian Sorensen, a young lawyer from Lincoln, Nebraska.

21. In fact, Ford slipped away the next morning to board a boat for America. "Officially it was given out that he had never intended to remain longer than to launch the undertaking and give it his blessing. Unofficially it was whispered that influential officials from the Ford plant who had accompanied him . . . had subtly poisoned his mind against the whole expedition as something quixotic and absurd." Florence, "The Ford Peace Ship": 108–10.

22. Katherine Leckie, journalist and peace worker.

23. Benjamin W. Heubsch, of B. W. Heubsch, Inc., later Viking Press.

24. A Norwegian ship carrying additional student delegates from America.

25. "We spent Christmas at the Grand Palace Hotel in Stockholm. The orchestra in the flower-scented Winter Garden played Sousa's 'Stars and Stripes' to please the Americans. I walked lightly in a lovely dream, but I seldom saw Madame Schwimmer and the other leaders of the expedition, and when I did, they seemed anxious and worried." Florence, "The Ford Peace Ship": 109.

26. Lella's sister Lena, her husband Lewellyn Case, and their two daughters lived in Seattle.

27. According to the list published on board, *Oscar II* carried 67 delegates, 36 students, 3 foreign participants, 28 journalists, 2 photographers, 23 members of the business staff, and 7 "miscellaneous," but other accounts differ. At any rate, the American contingent was swelled along the way by great numbers of delegates from host countries.

28. "I had memorized in Swedish a graceful compliment to the Swedish people which I delivered with an appalling accent. But the audience loved it, and their loud cheers and friendly, smiling faces put me at my ease. . . . I said among other things that women weren't going to be willing to bear children if death or mutilation on the battlefield was the only future society could offer them. There was a good deal of ragging [in the Swedish news-

papers] over this. 'School-girl speaks for American mothers!' . . . [But] I know that . . . I was nevertheless voicing the thoughts of thousands of mothers all over the world." Florence, "The Ford Peace Ship": 110–11.

29. "We [had to] even remove labels from bottles or jars of face cream—every possible source of suspicion that we were carrying messages. . . . I gathered all the precious papers and documents relating to the Expedition which I had collected along the way and posted them off to America." Florence, "The Ford Peace Ship": 111.

30. All of the Ford party were returning home, except those who would remain as delegates to the Neutral Conference for Continuous Mediation in Stockholm.

31. Ina was in fact two and half years older than Lella.

II

New York: Journalism

To Loretta and Ina Secor

Wednesday, February 2, 1916

Dear Mother and Sister:

I know you will be surprised to learn that I am still in New York, though by the time this reaches you I may be on my way to Washington. I have gone over the situation again and again in an effort to decide just what will be best for us all, because of course in whatever degree I prosper and advance, in the same degree you will be affected. This is the dual situation. There are several movements in the peace work now under foot, which will develop within the next week or so, or more likely within a few days. It is quite likely, if Mr. Ford approves certain plans we have, that I will be given a more or less prominent part. It is needless for me to say that however much I am devoted to the peace cause, I am not for one moment forgetting my home obligations, and will not consider any work which will not make it possible for me to fully meet my share of the home expenses.

Rebecca is today awaiting a wire which may call us to Detroit to interview Mr. Ford. If this does not develop soon, Rebecca will go to Detroit at all events, and in the meantime, I am turning my attention to some unusual opportunities in New York which I felt I could not afford to miss.

INTERNATIONAL THEATER
CHARLIE CHA
The WORLD'S GREATEST WHEEZE:
HENRY FORD
IN HIS
HOSCAR THE DEUCE
FAMOUS FOUR REEL FLIVVER FARCE
"NOBODY HOME"
STAGED BEFORE THE CROWNED HEADS of EUROPE!
Passed Up By The Board of Censorship
A GREAT CONTRIBUTION TO THE GAIETY of NATIONS.
HURD

Through the acquaintances made on the Ford trip, I have been given letters of introduction to some of the prominent publishers and literary people of New York. Mr. Heubsch, the publisher whom I've mentioned several times, has given me letters to Miss Reed, editor of *McCall's,* and Miss Levieu of the *Metropolitan Magazine* staff. Others have presented cards to newspaper men, sociological workers etc., while Miss Leckie, the publicity manager of the expedition, with whom I stand solid, is one of the best known editors in America and has promised me access to numerous sources. So you see, something very good may open in New York—an experience which would be a valuable education to me, and which I feel I could hardly afford to miss. I can live very cheaply in New York, so that at a fair salary I should be able to send considerable home—more than I could get in Seattle under present conditions. It would hardly happen once in a lifetime that a girl—unknown as I—could come to New York and have access to so many valuable people. It may be a little harder for you for a week or so more, but I know that I should always regret not having taken advantage of such rare opportunities as are offered me here.

My chief adviser has been Mr. Heubsch, the publisher, a man of about forty, with whom I have a most substantial and delightful friendship. He is an intimate friend and adviser of Mrs. Joseph Fels, widow of the famous single tax exponent, and had a prominent part in the Ford expedition. Between him and the attorney, Mr. Sorensen of Nebraska, . . . my stay in Europe was made very agreeable. [Mr. Heubsch] is thoroughly all right, and fully to be trusted. He remained in Europe, but expected to return on the next boat, and quite insisted that I remain in New York until he comes, quite certain that he would be able to influence something good for me. He insists that if there is any need, he will finance me until I get work, and knowing him as I do, I would not hesitate to accept money from him.

Of course all that I have told you is simply more or less visionary, and it may finally transpire that I shall simply come back to Washington and await the first opening which I feel reasonably certain will develop from my trip to Europe.

I am so sorry that all the long letters in which I described our wonderful trip so minutely never reached you. . . .[1] I can only say that from Christiania, Norway; Stockholm, Sweden; Copenhagen, Denmark; through Germany to Holland and The Hague, including also trips to Amsterdam and Rotterdam, the trip was wonderful beyond words. And in spite of all the difficulties, the ridicule, the lies and the slander, it was a splendid success. The neutral conference, which will seek to suggest terms of peace and arrange the beginning of international disarmament, has been started, and that was exactly what the expedition started out to do.[2] Much more was accomplished besides, but I shall have to leave details to some future time. I am hurrying through this so I can go to call on the *McCall* lady yet this afternoon.

The two important events which happened to me in Europe were [first] my appointment as a voting delegate, which was really the work of Mr. Heubsch, and was the logical result of my enthusiasm and earnestness. Of course you don't understand that the company consisted of delegates chosen because of some special fitness (more or less imaginary in many cases), the press of which I was a member, the students, and the business staff. Of course the delegates were the core of the expedition, and I was happy to be given a definite place among them. My [second and] greatest triumph came when I was invited to speak at one of the great mass meetings in Stockholm. I shall never forget that night, or that wonderful audience of 2500 seated in the Circus, a great circular building. Judge Lindsey and Mr. Weatherly, the Nebraska minister, were the other speakers, and we reached the high water mark of enthusiasm. I bought a picture of the hall, taken during my speech, and sent that, together with papers containing cartoons of me and reports of the address, home, but I dare say the whole bundle is in the possession of some English or German censor. It *was* a great honor to be chosen among the dozen or more speakers who addressed the great throngs as we moved from place to place, and I appreciated the prestige of being counted an international speaker.

How I wish I could go on and on, telling you of this wonderful trip and all that it has meant to me. I suppose from the tenor of my letters, you will already have known that I have become a radical pacifist.

Rebecca and I last night left the McAlpin and are staying with her friend Louise Matheney out in the [Columbia] University district. My address while here will be 106 Morningside Drive, New York. I should have added Apartment 75. I was so relieved to get your telegram.

Loads of love including
Lena and the rest,
Lella

To Loretta Secor

My address—106 Morningside Drive
Apartment 24, New York
[February] 1916

Dear Ones,

Just a line this morning before I go to the city. . . . My plans are still somewhat indefinite. That is, we are still waiting for word from Detroit to know what we shall do. In the meantime, I have been busy from morning till night calling on magazine editors and making acquaintances which cannot fail to be of distinct advantage to me. I shall be in New York at least until next Wednesday, for I have a position in view which will give me a wonderful experience, and which ought to pay a very good salary. It is in connection with the Bureau of Investigations of the N. Y. *Tribune*. The bureau is the only one of its kind in existence and was itself started only last May. One of its principal functions is to expose fakers of all sorts, and especially false advertisers. For some purpose, which I have not yet learned, they want to gather certain statistics concerning New York. They expect to divide the city into districts and gather information regarding nationalities, incomes, foods, methods of living etc. This is the immediate work Mr. Le Vigne, the head of the bureau, has in mind for me, and I someway feel rather sure that I shall land it. . . .

In the meantime, also, I have an engagement with one of the *Metropolitan* editors for next Monday (today is Saturday). Also there is a tentative opening on *McCall's*. It is more or less a mechanical job—someone to take charge of the head of a department which will handle the thousands of letters asking various questions—but it would give me a chance to study magazine methods first hand.

The other position, however, would bring me into intimate touch with all classes of people, and ought to be prolific of much valuable material for magazines, etc. . . .

New York is a wonderful city and I am glad of even this brief experience here, but I should hate to be sentenced for life. I have not seen one single home, such as we understand the term to mean, and I guess there are practically no homes in the whole city. Everyone lives in apartments—great square buildings ten or twenty stories high. Conditions here are as different from those in Seattle as Europe is different from America. New Yorkers think the world revolves around New York, yet almost all of them hate their unnatural lives, especially those who have lived in other places. Everyone has to live out a considerable distance, for rents near town[3] are prohibitive. We are a half hour from town, via that infernal institution, the subway. Do they have those in Chicago, Ina? I never rode in one until I came to New York. You descend into the bowels of the earth and are whisked through space. Always everyone hurries.

We were delighted to learn for a certainty this morning that Mr. Ford and Mr. Bryan will sail about Feb. 13 to join the other delegates at the neutral conference, and that the conference will be formally started with the members already present on February 7.[4] So you see, ridicule, or any amount of evil influence, has not been able to turn the big idea from its course. I don't know just how much you know about the peace expedition. I don't know what the Western newspapers used, or how much of the information you have is correct. If you'll tell me, I'll try to give you the exact "straight" of the whole matter. . . .

My love to all the dear ones, but a triple share to my Mommie and Little Sis.

Lovingly,
Lella

To Loretta Secor

[February] 1916

[Fragment]

A big mass meeting is being planned which will take place in about a week, and I have the chance to do the press work for it. There will not be a great deal of money in it—perhaps fifty dollars—but it will add materially to my fund of experience, and the money as well will be worth waiting for, I think. Mr. Ford will come then, and we are all expecting that something definite will result. If he has any plans for fighting preparedness in America,[5] there is a very good chance that I will have a good position. Of course, this is just speculation but well worth a little investment of time and patience, for if I did secure a definite position as organizer, lecturer, secretary, press agent, or such, there would be a good salary attached. So you see, as I tried to tell you before, the delay of these few weeks may seem hard to you, and it may appear that I am just thoughtless of you and seeking my own advantage only, whereas I have acted wholly in the belief that the possibilities of the future, if not the probabilities, were well worth taking a chance with. I do hope you will understand the motives which have prompted me.

I have been in New York two weeks today, and wonderful weeks they have been! I spent day after day just doing nothing but going from one magazine to another and talking with editors. Three weeks ago, the *Designer* took on a new woman to handle the social department, which I am sure I could have had, had I been here then, for I seemed to have made a fairly good impression on the editor. But perhaps it is better that I did not get it. At all events, I shall feel that if nothing opens up for me here, it is for the best.

While I have worked constantly since I came, my stay has by no means been devoid of interest and pleasure. The first night after we arrived from Europe, all the members of the Ford party who were still in New York had dinner together at the Dutch Oven, a queer little bohemian sort of place where artists and literary people hang out. We had such a merry time, but it was rather sad too, for many of us parted that night, knowing that we should not meet again. You know, after you have traveled and dined and slept with folks for eight weeks, you know them better than you know friends in the ordinary way after two years of acquaintance.

Then Louise Matheney, Rebecca's friend at whose apartment house we are staying, gave us several fine treats. We heard Caruso and Amato[6] in *La Bohème* at the Metropolitan Grand Operahouse, and the Symphony Orchestra with Emmy Destin as soloist at the famous Carnegie Hall; and saw Ethel Barrymore in *Our Mrs. McChesney*. Miss Blake, principal of one of the New York schools, and a member of the Ford party, entertained Rebecca and me and her nephew, Mr. Robinson,[7] at dinner one evening, and last evening, after we had had a meeting of the Ford group to work on plans for the mass meeting, Mr. Mandel, one of the young men who was interested in me on the trip but who didn't have much chance because I found two or three others more interesting, took Rebecca and me to one of the Broadway cabarets, where we had a little supper, and watched the dancers and entertainers until midnight when we formally christened the affair a birthday party.[8] Mr. Mandel is a fine young fellow and thoroughly trustworthy. He wants to show me the sights and lights of New York, but I shall not have time, for if we have the meeting on February 21, we shall have to work night and day next week.

Tomorrow night, three of the Columbia College men who are friends of Louise, have invited the three of us to dinner and theater, and I rather think that will conclude my festivities here.

To Loretta Secor

New York
February 29 [1916]

Dear Mother and All:

When I left the house this morning, I fully expected to return at noon and get several letters off before dinner. It is now eleven o'clock p.m., and I have just gotten around to start this message. Life in New York is certainly strenuous even in its simplest forms, and one never can reckon on any given time being enough to accomplish a task in.

First I must tell you of my success in my work, for I know of course that you will be glad with me.[9] I turned in my stuff this afternoon, and the [managing] editor seemed very much pleased, although she is one of those stoical sort of women who let you know very little of what she really thinks. But the associate editor, a charming, eccentric sort of little woman to whom I have taken rather a fancy,[10] followed me out of the office to tell me that she wanted to warmly congratulate me, for I had made a great hit with the editor [-in-chief]. I was immediately given another assignment, so that means I shall be in New York another week, at least, and of course as long as the work keeps coming my way, I shall feel that I had better stay and do it. I shall receive $30 for this one page feature, and $50 for any double pages which I may do. Each feature is likely to take about a week in preparation, though some might be done in much less time, and I would thus have considerable leisure for other work. I figure that I ought to earn $40 or $50 a week. Of course this estimate may be too high for a beginner, but I think I can do it. It's a hard trick, you know, but I can do her.

My idea now is to remain here at work as long as there are features to be done, until I am thoroughly acquainted with the magazine and its methods. Then I see no reason why I could not continue much the same sort of work in Seattle. I have somewhat hesitated about coming home so long as there was any prospect here, because I don't know whether I still have a job there. . . . A combination of *Hotel News, Every Week,* and a few other magazines might make a profitable combination if I could manage to swing them all.

Ina, I wish you would send me the contents of my file. . . . Also if I am to be here long, I shall need some of my clothes. I was going to suggest that you send my nightgowns, but on second thought, I think I had better buy cheap crepe ones which are easy for me to launder. But I would like those two light blue dresses. They will at least make a change. I so often regretted that I didn't have them with me on the trip, for I could have used them to such advantage. I haven't bought a thing for myself since I left Seattle except some shoes, but I am on the ragged edge of nothing and shall soon have to invest in a waist. I am still wearing Mabel's hat decorated with the quills from the drake's tail. Everybody on the trip admired that hat. I don't know whether I ever mentioned that Lou Rogers, a very clever little cartoonist and artist, said it was the most artistic hat she had seen. Mr. Huebsch was remarking one day that it was becoming, and so, with some glee, I told him—he spends a great deal of money on his own wardrobe—how I had needed a hat, and had run up to the garret, and found this; and how I had gone out and taken some feathers out of the drake's tail to decorate it with. I suppose he had never heard of anything quite like it, for his eyes bulged with genuine surprise. He was gracious enough to say that he had admired me before, but that his admiration had taken a great leap. That, of course, was one of those futile phrases which men hand about with such alacrity. Rebecca insists that I am bitterly skeptic so far as men are concerned. Heaven knows, I should hate to be that.

Your letter of February 24 was here when I got home, Mother, and I was so happy to have it. I do look forward with such impatient interest to the hour when I come home at night and sometimes discover messages from loved ones. It must be lovely in Bellevue now. I can just see how everything looks, and I wish with all my heart that I could have a whiff of that wonderful air, and the good brown earth, and all the green shoots coming up out of the ground. New York is still in winter's grasp, although it was sunny today, and less bitter than yesterday. But there are still great patches of ice in the streets, and dirty piles of snow in the fence corners.

I guess I have not written you a real letter since Saturday, so I'll try to remember all I have been doing in the interim. Sunday morning, I had an interview with Amato, the famous baritone whom I heard when I first came to New York. He was simply splendid, and I fell quite in love with him. In the afternoon, I attended services in the Fifth Avenue Presbyterian church, listening to the famous Dr. Jowett. . . . At six o'clock, I went to the home of Mr. and Mrs. [Thomas] Seltzer, where Rebecca and I had supper, and spent a very happy evening. Mr. Seltzer was a member of the expedition. He is a queer little Jew—very brainy and rather likeable in spite of, or perhaps because of, his many eccentricities. He is an author, and also has translated many books into the English language. He has a perfecly splendid library, and an altogether intellectual and charming little wife, both of which rather surprised me.

We left at about ten o'clock, and then went to call on Mrs. Lochner, wife of the secretary of the expedition, who is in New York expecting to sail soon for Europe, and Mr. Kliefoth, Mr. Lochner's assistant.[11] We staid some time talking over the peace situation, and got home rather late. Yesterday, after a rather hard day, I went with Rebecca and Mr. Mandel to call on Mr. Golden in his bachelor apartments. Mr. Golden is employed in the social service department of the New York Ford establishment, and is a decidedly interesting man of about 35 or 40. We went over this blessed peace situation with him, and incidentally talked of many other things, and I got material for a splendid story. Afterward, Mr. Mandel took Rebecca and me to a German café, to hear Rigo and his famous Hungarian orchestra. . . . He is of Gypsy origin, married a princess, was kept in a dungeon, and had many thrilling experiences. Mr. Mandel introduced us to the swarthy gentleman.

I forgot to mention Saturday. In intervals when I was awaiting appointments for interviews, I went with Rebecca to call on Mrs. Villard,[12] publisher of the New York [*Evening*] *Post,* a very wealthy, delightful and radical old lady, of whom, I think, I made a friend who may be of value at some future time. I mentioned that I had tried to secure connections with her newspaper, and she seemed much interested, taking my name and address. In order to call on her, I rejected an invitation to have tea with Mary Alden Hopkins, the magazine writer who was a member of our party. But Rebecca and I had dinner with John E. Jones, of Washington D.C. and afterward attended a concert at the Waldorf-Astoria. . . .

. . . Mr. Mandel has really been very pleasant to me and has already spent considerable money in showing me the sights. (It makes me shudder the way men throw money around.) He is quite anxious to continue the process, but I really can't indulge in so much social gaiety and still do my work. This noon I had lunch with Louise Eberle, the adorable associate editor and fiction buyer for *Today's Magazine.* She is so eager to have me stay in New York that she has even invited me to share her room with her to cut expenses, but I didn't feel that I could do that. We have discovered a strong mutual interest in each other. She is clever, and just bulging with ideas which she turns over to me in great quantities.

Everyone is, and has been wonderfully kind to me, and I do love all the dear people I have met.

Mother, I do so much need some corset covers. Do you think you could find time to make me some very plain ones? I will send back that *point de Paris* one which just fits. It has all gone to pieces, as have most all of mine. If you have any old material around the house, use that, but if not, tell me how much to get and I'll send some from here. I think, as a matter of fact, that crepe would be the most profitable, because I can wash them myself. I have done all my laundry work since I came back from Europe, but I find it difficult to get things ironed. There is a place over at the university near here, where you can iron for five cents an hour, and I am going to introduce myself. . . .

Now I must stop, for it is twelve o'clock and I am not sure that my neighbors like to hear my typewriter click. Last night I worked until three o'clock. That is the beautiful part about this magazine work I am doing. It gives me so much freedom, and if I want to work late at night—which you remember is always my liveliest time—and sleep late the next morning, I am at perfect liberty to do so.

Please tell me every little thing that happens in Bellevue, for I do so like to get the mental picture of all that you are doing. What gay times you must be having with your ponies. How I wish I might take a canter with you. Please write, all of you soon,

Lovingly, and lots of it,

Lella

To Loretta Secor

106 Morningside Drive,
New York
March 4, 1916

Dear Mother and All:

How little possible it seems that time is creeping on into March, and I am still in New York. It sometimes seems to me that I have been living in a constant dream ever since Rebecca's telegram came to me in Bellevue.

I have had not a letter for two days, and now I must patiently wait until Monday. . . . How I should love to see you all! Someway Saturday night and Sunday bring the heart-tugs for home, even when the rest of the week finds me too busy to remember all that is so dear back there.

I am getting along with my work surprisingly well. I expected to get my check for the first feature [in *Every Week*] today, but the office closed at one, and there was so much to be done that I said it could wait. Besides, the editor is considering the possibility of using it for a double page instead of a single, in which case it will mean $50 instead of $30. I'm just praying that she will. I have about half the material collected for my second "spread," as we call them technically, and have begun to collect facts for a third.

The third is to deal with laws which are on the statute books of various states and are not enforced, and in this connection I had a very pleasant little outing this afternoon. Louise Matheney had introduced me to a Mr. Sage, a New York attorney and a rather agreeable person. We had had dinner together [in the dining room] several times, and he and Dr. Curtis had taken Louise and me to dinner and theater one evening. He seemed quite willing to promote the acquaintance, but I have really had little time, and have not often eaten in the apartment dining room because it is too expensive. It occurred to me, however, that he might be able to suggest sources of material, and I told Louise to mention that I would like to ask him some questions about an article when I had the opportunity.

She saw him at dinner last night, and he immediately suggested that I come to his office at the earliest convenience. Then, having cogitated the matter for some time, apparently, he suggested that Louise and I take lunch with him and then go on a little sight seeing excursion, today.

His office is in the beautiful new Woolworth Building which is, I think, fifty-four stories high. From his window we had a wonderful view of the city—the great throbbing center of the universe, with its broken skyline of towering buildings which house so many thousands of human interests and activities. The throngs of pigmy people in the streets below reminded one of nothing so much as swarms of black ants hurrying here and there, apparently without rhyme or reason.

The Woolworth building is a marvelous work of art, and recalled to my mind quite vividly some of the great buildings of the old world. The halls are of variegated marble in pearl white and brown, and the domed ceilings are of exquisite mosaic design. Mr. Sage took us into the lovely Rathskeller, a story below the surface of the earth, where we had a princely lunch to the tune of nearly five dollars, and an exceptionally fine orchestra.

Afterward we went to Trinity Church which has stood there close to two centuries. The historic chimes, which called George Washington and Alexander Hamilton and many other notables to worship, peal out today with the same soft notes of a century ago, but their melody is swallowed up in the greedy roar of heedless Broadway.[13] Surrounding Trinity is an ancient graveyard whose stones are fast crumbling to earth, and whose inscriptions have, in many cases, been entirely obliterated by the relentless hand of Time.

Only a little distance from Trinity stands St. Paul's Cathedral which likewise has supplied spiritual food to many men and women whose names are now blazoned on the pages of history.[14] Surrounding this, too, are ancient graves—silent, age-long sepulchres which have not yielded to the onslaught of commercialism. These peaceful spots, couched in the center of surrounding skyscrapers, present a curious incongruity. We went into both churches, and someway all the spirit of the past seemed to be collected within those silent, reverent walls.

From St. Paul's we walked down Wall Street, which is a narrow canyon of a street flanked by busy marts of business on either side. Here is J. P. Morgan's bank, and the stock exchange where fortunes are won and lost in a day, and the offices of the Standard Oil, and all the great competing concerns. We topped off the excursion with a jaunt down to the Battery and a visit to the Aquarium. Wall Street and that busy part of New York known as Park Row, where most of the newspaper offices are located, I had traversed many times during the course of my work, but it was interesting to have things pointed out and identified. I was surprised to find that I had seen more of New York than Louise, who is attending school here, and has been here since last September. In search of material, I have wandered all over the East Side—where, in places, strange antiquated horse cars still prevail—through most of the business district of greater New York, and yesterday, my work called me to Brooklyn. It was the first time I had crossed the famous Brooklyn Bridge. I can hardly believe that I am actually seeing these things which have so long been only sort of story-book lore to me. Louise confided to me that she had never been in anyone's office before, and she was, in fact, quite amusingly ignorant. I could hardly believe that a girl lived who had been so rigorously sheltered.

Rebecca has gone to Washington, D.C., and I miss the nightly talks which we always managed to have, although we often saw very little of each other during the day.[15] I am not sure whether she will return to New York, or go on to her home in Chesaning [Michigan].

I have just been interrupted by two events, one of which was so pleasant as to overbalance the other. I have had a mouse in my chiffonier drawer, and a letter from Lew with a dear little letter from Esther[16] enclosed. The letters, and not the mouse, of course, constituted the pleasure.

Tomorrow afternoon I am to address the Y.W.C.A., and I must stop now so as to gather a few thoughts together, and also investigate my dubious wardrobe.[17]

Heaps and heaps of love,
Lella Faye

P.S. to Laura Kelley and Lida Hamm

This above, is a carbon copy of a letter I wrote home. I wanted to tell you all the same facts, and it saved just half my time to write both letters at once. I do hope you are not impatient with me for my vacillating plans. It has seemed quite impossible for me to avoid this uncertainty, for I have not known from day to day how this thing or that was going to develop. I feel a keen disappointment in not seeing you. . . . As you can all well imagine, I have my hands full with letters, especially since I seem always to have so much to say.

Love again,
Your baby sister

To Loretta Secor

New York
March 11, 1916

Dear Mother and All:

Just a few lines this morning before I settle down to work. . . .

I am about to finish my second feature. It has hung around longer than necessary, for I have had a dozen errands to do this week which have taken so much of my time. Miss Eberle has convinced me that I can get a much better room than the one I have, for the same money, and put me in touch with a Mrs. Googins, with whom I am quite sure I shall be settled after next Wednesday. I did not meet the lady herself, but both Miss Eberle, and the woman who showed me the room, say she is a delightful person. She has this five room apartment with bath, and lives alone, so that I shall have many home privileges which are impossible in a great apartment house like this where girls just live alone, each occupying one room.

This room I have now opens into a court—a sort of narrow canyon formed by high brick apartment houses on three sides. The sun never reaches my room, for it is on the second floor, and there are ten or twelve stories above me on every hand, to shut off the warm rays. My new room will be on the fourth floor, with a big window overlooking the street. It is much larger, and so neat and dainty. It is a regular $6 room, but Miss Eberle said so many pleasant things about me, that Mrs. Googins phoned her later and said she was convinced she wanted me, and would let me have it for four dollars. This includes bath, kitchen privileges, and the use of her parlor. So I think I shall be quite cozy. I had another streak of good fortune when Miss Eberle asked me if I could use her typewriter and desk indefinitely, as she has no place to put it, having changed her quarters. There is plenty of room in my new room, so that expense is saved me. It is quite essential that I have a typewriter at home, for I do most of my writing—in fact all of it—there. . . .

I had a number of other rooms which I wanted to look at to make sure that I should be satisfied, so I spent my entire morning yesterday at our old occupation of hunting houses. My conclusion was a unanimous decision for Mrs. Googins. So I expect I shall move next Wednesday, and then settle down to real business. Miss Eberle has turned over to me a load of material which she has accumulated from time to time, and which she hasn't time to use, so that I fully expect to sell some real articles before long.

Yesterday afternoon I spoke before an enthusiastic group of women in the fashionable apartment of some woman, and there met . . . Dr. Martin, pastor of one of the fine churches here, who was the other speaker. He invited me to take dinner at his home, where I met a delightful group of young people, especially interesting being his daughter, a young woman who is just beginning to blossom out into a fine thinker. Dr. Martin asked me to address his congregation Sunday evening, and his family urged me to take supper with them before the service, which I promised to do.

I had a letter from Lida yesterday, in which she sent me a clipping from the *P-I* which I was very glad to read; she also sent a copy of the *Journal* containing my letter.[18] I was simply dumbfounded when I found the space they had given to it, and I read it with fear and trembling lest I should have said things in a perfectly private letter which would not do for publication. Had I known that it was to be published, I would have sent a much more carefully written letter, but I just pounded it out, using the first expression that came into my mind. It behooves one to always do one's best on all occasions, doesn't it?

Now I must get to work. It is ten o'clock, and I have not yet had breakfast. I usually breakfast in the middle of the morning, and dine about five o'clock, which is less expensive than three meals, and seems to be quite satisfactory. My board has really cost me very little lately, for so many people have invited me to take a meal here or there. All such contributions gratefully received.

STILL NOT A LINE FROM INA!

Much love to all,

Lella

To Loretta Secor

1 Convent Avenue
March 15, 1916

Dear Mother and All:

Your long and very welcome letter came this morning before I was out of bed, and I had the pleasure of reading it before I got up. You know it always was a luxury for me to read in bed.

I am moving today, and O, what a horrible day it is to step outside. Yesterday it was much milder, and began to rain. It is colder today with flurries of hail and "hard" rain, and the sidewalks are a glare of ice. I have not been down town yet, and it is noon now, but it has taken me all the morning to pack and move, for I have had to make two trips. I finished a maline hat this morning. It is just a plain black hat with a band of greenish gold and velvet ribbon across the front. The whole thing cost me 98 cents. And now it's too cold to wear it. Ain't it awful?[19]

I wrote a note to Ina yesterday and sent some money—also a bulletin of the church where I spoke Sunday evening. I have made quite a hit with the Martins. They had me there to supper again Sunday night, then to young people's meeting where I spoke briefly, and again at the church service. Dr. Martin gave a short sermon on "Preparing for What?"—being a talk against the present madness which has seized America—and I spoke for nearly an hour to a fine audience of about 800 people. Scores of people came up to speak to me afterward, thus giving me a chance to meet some delightful folks. . . . Also, a fine young man asked me to address the Y.M.C.A. which I promised to do. I have come in contact with so many splendid people through these little talks I have been giving.

I was quite delighted to find my check [from *Every Week*] for $50 instead of $30 as I had anticipated. When I went to the office yesterday, Miss Lewis, the editor, said that Mr. Barton, the chief mogul, had given explicit directions that the next time I came in he was to meet me.[20] So she ushered him in and he was tremendously cordial; said he was delighted with my work, that I had fallen into their way of doing things right from the beginning without "previous condition of servitude" etc. Then he said he hoped I was going to stay in New York, and I said that depended on whether or not someone provided my bread and butter. Then he said they would certainly be Elijah's manna to me if I'd stay, etc. So it looks as though I stand pretty solid, if I can just keep up the pace.

I had a letter from Lida the other day in which she said again how much she wished you could visit them, Mother. So I am writing them that we are going to see someway that you can do it. Altogether I think it will be a splendid change for you, and it will be more fair to all of us, now that we are so widely scattered, to have you in the middle, rather than so terribly far away. I shall feel much better when I know you are in Michigan, where I could get to you within 48 hours if need be. In fact, it would not be at all surprising if I could run down this summer to see you. I think now that I shall settle down to the probability that I shall remain in New York several months, and while I am here, I think it would be delightful for you to be with the girls in Michigan. Then, when I get ready to go back, we could make the trip together. . . .

I think you had better to plan to leave next month, for then it will be delightful to travel. I would suggest that Ina advertise in the paper that you want a companion to Chicago, and offer to pay part fare. You could undoubtedly find some nice, competent woman who would look after you and see that your trip was made pleasant, though I think you are quite competent to attend to this latter yourself, for you so soon make friends with the people you meet on the way. But I would not want you to start out alone. . . . I will ask some of the B[attle] C[reek] folks to meet you in Chicago. In the meantime, I really think you ought to spend a little time with Lena. You know how hurt she always feels when you do not come, and it wouldn't be right to start off on a long visit without giving her some time first. . . . I do wish I were to be home to help you get ready. I feel all thrilly and excited just to write about it. . . . One of the gifts I am planning to send is something especially for traveling, and I had intended it for Ina. But now, I'm going to change my mind, and send it to you, and I've decided that your birthday present is going to be something else that you need to travel with.

I think I am going to like my new quarters so much. There is such an atmosphere of home about the place. My landlady is a Christian Scientist, and that was one of the reasons why I was so anxious to live with her. Scientists are sure to be lovely people. Louise Eberle, the girl I like best of those I met on the Ford trip, and the one who has done so much for me in order to make it possible for me to stay, just because she liked me, is also a Scientist. . . .

Mr. Kliefoth, one of the fine young men of our party, spent last evening with me. He is sailing for Europe today, and I want to get down to the boat, so I shall have to hurry.

I'm going to try to get some clothes just as soon as I can, Mother, for I certainly am shabby, and rather hesitate to accept the invitation of any of my friends, all of whom patronize rather scrumptious places.

Loads and loads of love to all, and much for yourself and little sis.

Lella

To Laura Kelley and Lida Hamm

1 Convent Ave.
Apartment 45
New York
March 20, 1916

Dear Sisters and All:

I am making a wild dash to get some more letters written tonight, for I have agreed to do some extra work this week . . . for *Today's Magazine,* and I don't expect to have a single minute to myself for the rest of the week. I am going to read hundreds of answers to a prize contest conducted by that magazine, and decide who shall be awarded the prizes.

New York is just teeming with opportunities, and I am so happy to have the chance to take advantage of them. Everyone seems to think that I have been unusually lucky in finding such profitable things to do right away, for they tell me that most people who come to New York expecting to do literary work are thankful if they can barely earn enough to keep the wolf away from the door. If it wasn't that I realize that it's my faith in God, pure and simple, that gets me things, I'd feel quite "cheasty."[21]

I have changed my address, and am much more pleasantly situated. I have a room with Mrs. Googins, a widow lady who has a five room apartment, and no other guest but myself. She lets me have the run of the apartment, which makes me feel much more at home than to be shut up in one tiny room as I was at the other apartment. She gives me the use of the living room in which to entertain my friends, and I really need it, for I have suddenly discovered myself quite "poplar." Mr. Huebsch, the publisher whom I have mentioned before, has returned from Europe, and we have already had some very pleasant times together. He came up shortly after six last evening, and at eight we went out to a fashionable restaurant for dinner. We lingered to listen to music until nearly midnight, so that I did not have time to write the scores of letters I had expected to do yesterday. Then I have an invitation from Mr. Mandel, another of the Ford party, for dinner and theater this week. Mr. Mandel is a Hungarian, a graduate of the New York University, and speaks five or six languages. Mr. Huebsch is a German Jew, so you see I lack nothing in interesting variety. My latest conquest is an attorney, Mr. Sage. . . . So little Faye is going to gobble in all the good times she can while they're on the wing. . . .

There are a few others whom I want to tell you about sometime, but I think I have prattled on about myself quite long enough in this letter.

I was so happy to get both of your letters. You have no idea how welcome are messages from loved ones. Even though I am very busy, and have many interests here, I often realize how far I am from home and loved ones.

I don't remember what I wrote in my last letter, but I do remember that I raved on at some length. [22] I think I must have given you a wrong impression if I made you think that either Ina or I had stagnated. The years have brought us rich experiences, but we have not been able to develop fully and freely and naturally while we were held under a sort of system of suppression. But all that does not matter. I don't regret any sacrifice I have made in my effort to make Mother happy. The only thing I regret is that so much of the time our efforts have met with no result. Mother and Ina have both quite reached the limit, I guess, and an immediate change is essential for both of them.[23]

I have written to Mother that you girls were anxious to have her come for a visit, and that she had better plan to come during April, while the weather will be pleasant for traveling. I know that Mother will enjoy the change immensely, and I know, too, that you will all enjoy Mother, for she will be quite happy and contented probably at least for a time. I sometimes think we'll just have to accept the situation as it is, and not try to struggle against it any more; that is, when Mother gets too unhappy for endurance, why we'll just have to try to make a change for her which will relieve us all. I will try to keep Mother in what money she will need for clothes and incidentals, so that the burden will not be too great on you. I have suggested that Ina advertise for someone to travel with Mother. . . . She really is not able to travel alone, and I would not listen to the idea of her taking even a day's trip without someone to look after her. I would suggest that you extend the invitation again, urging her to come in April. I have already told her to plan to make the trip then. Ina is very near a nervous breakdown, and an immediate change seems essential.

In the meantime, I urged her to visit Lena, whom she hasn't visited since I came away. Mother has not been nearly as shut in this winter as she thinks she has. The jitney bus has always been available, but the truth is that going out is such an effort for her that she just dreads to undertake it, and then in her own mind she thinks it is the fault of someone else, when in reality it is simply the result of advancing years.

I myself, however, am going to try to take the matter a little less seriously. That is, I'm going to indulge Mother as much as I can without actually impeding my own progress, for after all, I suppose we will have her only a few years more. Let me know just as soon as you can what you think of my plan, so that I can get things in motion. I thought it might be possible that I could run down to Battle Creek sometime this summer to see her, and at all events, I should feel much better about her to know that she was near enough so that I could get to her in a few hours if need be.

Why Lida, Brooklyn Bridge and all these wonders are not in the least impossible for you. In fact, I have often planned what fun I would have showing you and the rest of the folks this big town. I have thought so especially about you, because, since you haven't any family to look after, you are just a bit more free than some of the others to get about.[24] And then, for such a long time I have been just crazy to see you. We would have some grand old larks together. I wish you wouldn't think it impossible for you to take advantage of some of the Eastern excursions this summer. You see, some member of my family ought really to censor my friends and acquaintances—for I'm only thirty years old, or thereabouts. I started out to say for I'm the baby, but a sudden realization of my advancing years descended upon me.

I have kept pretty closely at my work since I last wrote to you, and I haven't scouted around quite as much as usual. One day last week I went over to Jersey City, New Jersey, to see some folks off to Europe. Mr. Kliefoth, one of the fine young men on the trip who came back to America to attend to some business matters, and who has been delightful to me during his brief stay in New York, went back, accompanied by the wife of the general secretary, her mother and baby. They had four hours to wait so Miss Watson and Mr. Schultz, also former members of the Ford crowd, and myself had luncheon with them on ship board. It was one of those typical Swedish feasts with a dozen different kinds of fish. We all felt as though we were going right back again.

A week ago Sunday I spoke in the Mount Washington Presbyterian Church. I had a fine audience of about 800 people, and they seemed to like my spiel, for they kept me at church until nearly eleven o'clock, answering questions, etc.

I met a Mrs. Clarence Secor and two charming daughters at one of the meetings. She came to the church Sunday night on purpose to hear me speak again, and seems quite interested. She is a charming woman, and wants to entertain me at her home, but frankly I dread to submit to the questions her husband would probably ask me. No rattling of skeletons please, if the bones can be kept quiet!

Now I must close this epistle, and get at a dozen others. I have some little trinkets I brought from Europe which I shall send you just as soon as I have time to mail them. . . .

Loads of love from your baby sister,
Lella Faye

To Loretta Secor

March 20, 1916

Dear Mother and All:

This is Monday morning, and I must get a letter off to you before I start to work. I intended to write so many yesterday, and never scratched a single line all day long. In the morning I went to Mount Morris Baptist Church on Fifth Avenue. It is only about eight or ten blocks away from this apartment, so I presume I shall often go there. I am sending you a bulletin so that you can see what a live church it is. I came home and had dinner with my landlady. She has agreed to let me have an occasional meal, which will sort of help to balance my restaurant fare.

I am using Miss Eberle's machine, which is an old style Remington like the one I used on the ranch, and I am not quite accustomed to it yet. It sort of bucks and kicks once in a while. I just finished dinner when Louise Matheney came up. I presume you met her in Everett. She is a short, rather dark girl, not at all pretty, but a very nice little thing. She spent the afternoon with me so that I had just time to dress before Mr. Huebsch came. He arrived at about 6:30, and at eight we went out to a fashionable restaurant for dinner. It's astounding the amount of money men spend on food here in New York. It seems almost wicked to me. We lingered to hear the music until nearly midnight, so it was too late to begin to write when I got home.

I have just about finished up two more features, so I shall be able to send some money, I think, in my next letter. Also, I want to get that package off to you this week, for I'm going to include in it your birthday present, Mother.

Your long letter arrived about 10 o'clock Saturday night, Mother, so I had the pleasure of reading it the first thing Sunday morning. We have wonderful mail service here. Mail is delivered almost every hour until ten o'clock at night.

I had a very interesting letter from my attorney friend Mr. Sage, who said he would be delighted to call, if I would permit him to do so, and also suggested that there were "a great number of places which you would enjoy visiting, and there is no reason why we should not take excursions of exploration into these fields of historic, bohemian, and artistic interest according as your choice lies." So I am looking forward to some pleasant times with him. Louise, who introduced us, is much interested in the progress of what she insists is a "case." I discovered yesterday that he is a Baptist, and quite a prominent worker in one of the churches here.

I was just interrupted by a note from my friend Mr. Mandel, who has invited me to dinner and the theater. They ain't nothing like being "poplar," is there?

I am going to get some clothes, Mother, just as soon as I feel that I possibly can. When my men friends suggest, as Mr. Huebsch did last night, that I get some pretty new things, I think it is quite time that I did something to my wardrobe. He is so delightfully frank that I can't help liking him.

I wish, Ina, that you would send me the clothes I asked for, just as soon as possible. I know they are not suitable to wear out, but they will be something I can put on when I come home from the office, or street. Now I haven't a thing but the few duds I have to wear almost every day, and I do so like to have something different to get into for the evening. Will you also include my plume, or what there is left of it?

Mr. Barton came into the office Saturday, when I was there, and told me to consider myself a member of the staff. I really feel that I have something very good there. I don't believe I ever earned $50 any easier than the 50 I received for that first feature. Just as soon as any of my stuff comes out, I'll send you the magazine, so you can see the sort of work I am doing. In the meantime, I am rounding up any number of ideas for other stuff, and I shall begin this week to develop some of them. I am going to try to do a little personality sketch of Mr. Huebsch for the *American*. He has done some original things in his publishing house, such as introducing Hauptmann,[25] the wonderful German author, and his works to America, and establishing a definite system for training men and women as professional book sellers. Then I have ideas, and partial material for an article which I think *Everybody's* will buy, and another which may sell to *Collier's*. Of course, none of them will give me an order, because they don't know my work, so there is little I can do but just plug ahead, and trust that they'll like the stuff when I get it done. There is the big advantage here, though, that I can talk over ideas with the editors, and find out just how they would like to have the matter worked up.

But now I must hurry along, for I mean to cram this week with work. Mother, I think that when you come to Michigan, you had better bring my trunk on your ticket, as excess baggage. Then it can be shipped on from Michigan at much less cost. As long as I'm going to be here even a few months, I might as well have the use of what few things I have. I think most of the stuff now in my trunk would have to be packed in a box. Ina, you'll do that for me, won't you? Then put in my trunk my bathrobe, my fine underwear, nightgowns, etc. I have accumulated so much printed matter and junk that I can't possibly get everything in my suitcase now, and I think my trunk will be almost essential. Also, I suppose I might as well mention now the books I'd like to have. I'd like that little Good Cheer book . . . and that lavender book in which I was pasting poems; also that little book of quotations with the blue cover, and the quotations written in; that green volume of poems, Whittier, I think; Emerson's essay on Friendship and others—that soft brown leather book; Ralph Trine's *What All the World's Aseeking;*[26] and any others you think I ought to have. I hope, though, that you will send the dresses right away, and not wait for the trunk.

Heaps of love to all, and especially to Mommy and Little Sis.

Lella

Ina, have you had any new clothes yet, and if not, what are you planning to get? I don't want to spend any more for mine than you do for yourself.

To Loretta Secor

Sunday Afternoon,
March 26, 1916

Dear Mother and All:

This has been such a lazy, restful day, except that the noise and hubbub on the street is much like we used to experience on Rucker Avenue in Everett, except that it is multiplied many times in volume. In spite of it, however, I have dozed nearly all day, for I have a heavy week's work ahead of me, and want to be prepared to meet it. I haven't been out of the house today. I got up late, had a hot bath, then made a cup of cocoa and some toast for myself, and went back to bed. Now I am hurrying along to try to make up for these hours of leisure, for I am going to have dinner with Mr. Mandel this evening, and then go with him to some settlement house, where he is going to give a stereopticon lecture on the trip. I suppose that I shall have to say something too. Thursday evening I had dinner with him—this time in a gay French restaurant where everyone laughed so much, and seemed so engrossed in having a good time, that I wondered how they ever got anything eaten. Afterward we went to see *The Fear Market*, a much talked of play running at one of the theaters here. Both of us, however, were a little disappointed in it.

After the theater we went to a café for more refreshments, and then home "at a late hour."

Spring seems to have arrived with all her baggage, quite unexpectedly today. It has been so snowy and cold and disagreeable until this morning, when we woke up to discover that it was too warm to close the windows. The sun has been shining all day, and it has seemed so good, although I confess this lovely day has reminded me rather forcibly of a certain little brown bungalow on Lake Washington. . . .

Don't worry about my eating, Mother. I have really kept in fine physical condition, although I think it is more because I have had a good deal of sleep. Sleep seems to supply every deficiency for me. However, I have been eating I think all I need. I have not always had just what I would choose, but I have tried to select wholesome and nourishing dishes. Besides, you see I'm invited out . . . two or three times a week, and that helps some. Some of these invitations to lunch have come from various girls, however, so that I am not much better off, for I shall have to return the compliment sooner or later. When I know I'm going to have a big feed at night, I cut down on rations during the rest of the day. For instance, I had such a late breakfast this morning that I have not had anything else since, and still do not feel painfully hungry.

I was so glad to learn something about your Christmas. Indeed, it seems to me that you had quite a scrumptious Christmas. I have seen so much misery and destitution since I came to New York and while I was in Europe, that I have come to look upon our own circumstances as princely. During the bitter cold of this winter, when I have seen poor, aged, white haired women selling a few papers on the street corners, or braving the cold blasts with a little tray of candies and gum, or carrying great loads of packing boxes and scraps of wood on their backs, or picking bits of coal out of some one else's ash can, or even hitched like horses to pull the canal boats in Holland, I have looked upon them with a sob in my heart, and a prayer of gratitude has gone up from my soul to know that my Mother was warm and fed and sheltered. Christmas of 1915 will always stand out in a unique place in my memories. And one of the unique features was that I received not a single gift—gifts as we have been accustomed to think of gifts—except flowers. Instead I had the gift of Life itself—Life rich in new experiences and new visions and new dreams and new ambitions.

I suppose I shall never be able to repay all I owe Rebecca for having made this trip a possibility for me. I am experiencing again, as I did when I first went to Spokane, except in a much greater measure, that bounding, pulsing, thrilling joy of life within me; that old feeling of confidence in my powers—as yet not fully tried or tested—and the sublime sort of certainty that I shall be able to fight my way, however difficult the obstacles. Mr. Sorensen in his last letter was kind enough to predict that "some day you will be famous and great in the eyes of the world." And someway—in a cool, matter-of-fact way, without thought of self-praise or self-esteem—I have sometimes felt that this might be true. And the reason why I think it might be true is because of my unwavering belief in the God-given powers which lie within us all, and which most of us have only begun to try out. There was a good deal of satisfaction, too, in his added statement that today, "you are a great soul in the eyes" etc. etc.[27] For after all, that is what I am striving for more than anything else in the world—to be a great soul; to experience life so fully that I shall be able to understand the joys, the aspirations, the defeat, the struggle, the discouragements of those around me. For I have come to know that in just such degree as one lives, and experiences, in just that degree one can be of the greatest service to mankind.

But I had no idea of delivering a sermon. Besides, the hour has come when I must be gone. I have promised to meet Mr. Mandel downtown, because he had another engagement this afternoon which made it impossible for him to come after me. So I shall have to finish this when I get home tonight.

Monday night

This is the close of another perfect spring day, but along with it has come a sort of spring lassitude which makes it hard for me to work. I expected to finish this and get it off this morning, but I had an appointment with a woman at nine-thirty, and did not have time before I had to leave. I have undertaken this week to do some work also for a Press Service Bureau here. They are conducting a publicity campaign for the Society [for] Ethical Culture, and invited me to do some feature stories. So you see, opportunity seems to follow close on the heels of opportunity. I feel so happy and so profoundly grateful for God's goodness to me. I had surely expected a check today so that I could send some more money home, but the mailman has not brought it. However, it will doubtless arrive sometime this week, within a day or so.

I had such a pleasant evening last night. It was a new experience to me to visit a settlement house, and one in which I was much interested. The audience consisted largely of young people of the middle classes—largely Jewish and foreigners. Mr. Mandel gave a very interesting lecture with slides, and then insisted that I say something as well. He gave me such an extravagant introduction that I was ashamed to face the audience. I felt almost that some apology was due, so I said that I was afraid it would be difficult for me to live up to such a flattering introduction. Much to my surprise, a number of young men in the audience called out "not at all, not at all," and gave me such an ovation that I was terribly fussed. I met one of the young women workers—a charming girl—who invited me to visit some of the larger settlements with her. I have intended to offer my services in some sort of social work while I am here, for the experience would be so gratifying.

Before the meeting, we had dinner in a gay little Hungarian restaurant. I had really intended to urge Mr. Mandel to select some little inexpensive place, for I felt rather alarmed at the amount of money he was spending on me. Dinner is always two or three dollars, and sometimes more, and I wasn't sure whether he could well afford it. But before I had a good chance to make my suggestions, he bluntly asked me if I would not please call on him in case I should get out of funds, and said that he hadn't any special use for money, and could always let me have some whenever I wanted it. Of course I shall not have occasion to borrow any, but I love the frank delightful way in which he offered it. He is a civil engineer in the employ of the city, and owns and edits as well a weekly newspaper in his own tongue.[28] So I guess he has plenty of cash, and I will not offer any objection to his spending a little of it on me. He is making rather extensive plans for showing me the interesting sights and entertaining places, including the theaters. My only worry is that I may start something which I can't finish.

I shall love to have the apron you made, Mother. It will seem so good sometimes to get into a real domestic garment. Mrs. Googins is just as dear to me as she can be, and I have the use of the kitchen whenever I want it. Sometime, I want to cook a little supper for Mr. Huebsch, and another perhaps for Mr. Mandel. Then I thought perhaps I could return some of the compliments which Louise, Dr. Curtis, and Mr. Sage have bestowed upon me, by inviting the three of them to a little supper with me. I didn't have time to answer Mr. Sage's cordial note until Saturday, so I have not yet heard from him, but I told him he could call some evening this week so I suppose I will have the pleasure of entertaining him.

You spoke about Ina and Mr. Chapin rehearsing for a play. . . . I am so happy to know that Ina is enjoying so much social and outdoor life. Go to it, little Kid! We have been grownups too long. Let's have a little fun now, while the pickin's good. How I should love to run in and join you at some of your frolics.

And now I must stop, for I've such loads of things to do. Your letters never come too often, or are too long to suit me, Mother.

Heaps of love to all,
Lella

To Loretta Secor

1 Convent Ave.
N.Y.C.
Easter Sunday
April 2, 1916

Dear Mother,

This has been rather a lonely Easter Sunday, and one during which my thoughts have often sped Westward. I had hoped to have Easter dinner with Mrs. Googins, but she had been cleaning house, and was too tired to get it. So I ate dinner alone in a crowded restaurant, and without much relish, for my thoughts led me across a continent to a little brown house on the hill, where I knew there was a feast of fresh eggs and all the fixings going on. I pictured you all sitting around the table together, gay and merry, and I wondered if any of you noticed that Lella Faye was not there.

I went to church in the morning, and heard John Haynes Holmes, a Unitarian minister whom I very much admire, preach a powerful sermon on the immortality of the soul. I am enclosing the bulletin and also a picture of St. Paul's Chapel, one of those old churches which I told you about in a previous letter. One day during Holy Week, I had to wait for a man to return to his office, and in the interim I dropped into St. Paul's to listen to the Easter music. New York churches of every denomination seem so much more practical than most of our churches in the West. The downtown churches are never closed, and you are free to go in for rest or meditation whenever you choose.

Easter morning was ushered in here with a cold wind and intermittent showers. The sun never has appeared all day, and the gloom without has perhaps served to add to the depression of folks away from home.

I indulged in a new hat to the tune of $1.15. It is a tri-corn shape of nice neutral color, something the shade of my coat, and I trimmed it with shirring of narrow corded ribbon of a very bright blue. I guess I forgot to tell you that Louise Matheney changed her mind about that blue dress, and I had to give it back. I have been trying to fix over my brown dress. Something got spilled on it on board ship coming home, and the cleaners couldn't take it out. However, it didn't seem to go through, so I've ripped the dress apart and turned it wrong side out, but I haven't yet got it finished, for I have so little time and am so slow and awkward. . . .

I have had very little time for social pleasures lately. I have been compelled to reject a number of invitations, including two from Mr. Sage, because I couldn't afford the time. However, I do not intend to cut all my social life off, for I realize that one must have a limited amount of diversion in order to keep in trim. The two weeks I spent trying to finish up those two features have put me back financially, but I don't think that will happen again. I have three assignments of articles to do for *Every Week* now, and also an offer from Mr. Jones of a position at $25 a week, which will not take all my time. If it does not require too much time, I shall accept it, for it will be comfortable to feel that a weekly salary is coming in at all events, and then my work for *Every Week* and the other magazines will be extra. . . .

Heaps of love,
Lella Faye

To Loretta Secor

Saturday evening,
April 8, 1916

Dear Mother:

I have just finished the "family" washing, and now I'm trying to get off a lot of letters, first of which shall be to my dearest. . . .

. . . The week has been a crowded one. I have spent much time trying to collect final material for two features. I never saw anything the way they have hung on. I surely expected to finish this week, but I shall not be able to now before Monday. In addition to this work, I have tried to do a little in the peace cause.

Monday morning, I went with a friend I met at Welcome Settlement House, to visit Clark Settlement House on the East Side. It is one of the big settlement houses in New York, and is wonderfully equipped. There the children of the poor, for the sum of one penny a day, have the advantages of a most modern, up-to-date kindergarten. For similarly small fees, young people of all ages may take advantage of classes in cooking, gymnasium, studies, etc., and may have the uplifting influences of a splendid atmosphere. It made a tremendous impression on me. It seems so wonderful that children can be lifted out of such sordid surroundings, and have a chance to get something like a fair start. They were intelligent, charming children—mostly Jews and Italians—and I could have loved any one of them. We spent the entire morning watching the various classes, . . . I think the teachers and helpers must get very good salaries. There is even an air of luxury about the place—especially in the rooms of the resident teachers.

[This was] my first great glimpse of the ''East Side.'' I thought I had seen something of the slums but I found Clark Settlement neighborhood vastly different from anything I had yet seen. The streets are narrow and filthy, and lining the curb as thickly as they can be placed are street merchants' carts, on which every conceivable kind of ware is displayed for sale. One may purchase atrocious pictures and other ''art'' works of one merchant, and onions or cheese from his neighbor. At noon, as we passed through, it was almost impossible to make one's way through the crowds. One wonders how so many people ever survive in so small a space.

At noon, Miss McCallister, who had given her morning to me, invited me and two others to have lunch with her in a cunning little Italian restaurant. Tuesday night, Tracy Mygatt and Miss [Fannie] Witherspoon came to my house for a conference concerning the Anti-Enlistment League in which we are interested.[29] Wednesday night, I went with Miss Splitstone, one of the editors of *Today's,* to a business women's banquet, which puts me still further in debt to her. I don't know when I'm ever going to return all these compliments.

Thursday night I went to the great mass meeting at Carnegie Hall. I sat on the platform, and it seemed like old times in Europe. I think if they had announced that I was to be the next speaker, that I should probably have gotten to my feet without being the least bit surprised. This meeting was the first of a series which are to be held in all the states where Wilson campaigned. The speakers are men who are opposed to preparedness as advocated by the president. Carnegie Hall seats about 4500 people, and it was full. There was tremendous enthusiasm. The mention of Mr. Ford's name brought a volley of applause. Dr. Curtis, one of the young men to whom Louise introduced me and who asked to go with us, walked home with me after the meeting, and kept me standing in the hall discussing certain points, on which we disagree, until one o'clock in the morning.

Last night I went to a little farewell dinner for Emily Balch,[30] professor of economics and sociology in Wellesley College, who sailed for Europe today. She was one of the American delegates chosen for the neutral conference, and we are all so glad to know that she is going. I had such a time over that dinner. It was during the afternoon that I lost my purse with my keys in it. I came home about 5:30 with just barely time to get into my clothes and get back to the Cosmopolitan Club where the dinner was held. When I got to the apartment, I found that Mrs. Googins was not at home, and by no means or process could I gain entrance to the apartment. I had on that little light silk waist I bought in Seattle, which was very soiled, my black skirt, and my old hat. I debated which would be better taste: to telephone eleventh-hour regrets or to go as I was, and I chose the latter. I philosophically dismissed the thought of clothes, and had a delightful evening. I met Charlotte Perkins Gilman, the author, whose stuff you have doubtless read.[31] She is a charming woman.

Today we were welcomed by a lively young snowstorm which developed into almost a blizzard before the day ended. It has been horribly nasty to be out. Mr. Mandel has invited me to take a little jaunt to Staten Island, with dinner at a cunning bohemian place, tomorrow, and I certainly hope the weather is more agreeable. For Monday, I accepted a dinner invitation extended by Mary Alden Hopkins, the magazine writer whom I met on the Ford trip. It is astounding how many things there are to be done, and the worst part of it is that they're all things I want to do.

But I think this is enough about myself. I think you must be laboring under the same delusions regarding mail as I did at first, and still do sometimes now unless I actually figure up dates. Ten days is the very minimum in which you could get word to me and receive a reply. It would be more likely to be twelve days, counting time for mail delivery after it reaches the city. . . . I can't quite understand why there was a whole week when you did not hear from me, for I can never remember a week when I have not written at least once or more. . . .

You certainly have been dissipating, Mother. It's either a feast or a famine, isn't it? I'm so glad you've had a chance to get out and see new faces and new places. One needs to have a change. . . .

Well dear, I think I have raved on long enough. In fact, I'm getting so sleepy I can hardly hold my eyes open. . . .

Heaps and heaps of love,
Lella Faye

Notes

1. Many of the letters did arrive, but others were lost or held back by censors.

2. "The pilgrims' return was accepted generally as the collapse of Ford's project, although actually it marked the beginning of real work, the task of continuing mediation. The conference which developed from the cruise was to labor for a solid year, seeking to halt the war." Allan Nevins and Frank Ernest Hill, *Ford: Expansion and Challenge 1915–1933*, New York, Charles Scribner's Sons, 1957: 26.

3. Midtown Manhattan. Morningside Heights, Lella's home, was an outlying district.

4. In the end, neither Ford nor Bryan attended the conference.

5. Ford was taking large newspaper advertisements at this time, opposing preparedness.

6. Enrico Caruso, world-famous tenor, and Pasquale Amato, leading baritone at La Scala, who had come to New York in 1908.

7. Freddie Robinson, who was to become a close friend.

8. Lella had her twenty-ninth birthday on February 13, 1916.

9. Lella had had an article accepted by *Every Week*, a Sunday news magazine, and the managing editor had given her an assignment to write captions for an upcoming picture story.

10. This was Anne Herendeen, who became Lella's lifelong friend.

11. Lochner himself had stayed on in Stockholm as a delegate.

12. Mrs. Villard's son, Oswald Garrison Villard, was publisher of the *Post* and had helped organize the Ford Peace Ship expedition. Fanny Villard was a pacifist and daughter of William Lloyd Garrison, famous abolitionist.

13. The original Trinity Church was built in 1776. Hamilton is buried in its churchyard but Washington never worshiped there. The present edifice dates from 1846.

14. St. Paul's *Chapel* is New York's only surviving pre-Revolutionary church and was the site of a special service after Washington's presidential inauguration.

15. "Rebecca Shelly's . . . steadfast faith was the admiration of everyone who knew her. . . . I spent hours in my free time debating Rebecca's schemes, helping her with letters, typing out appeals, and such like." Lella Secor Florence, "The Ford Peace Ship and After," in *We Did Not Fight: 1914–18 Experiences of War-Resisters*, ed. Julian Bell, London, Cobden-Sanderson: 116.

16. Lella's niece, younger daughter of Lew and Lena Case.

17. Lella was beginning to be invited to speak to small groups about the Ford Peace Ship.

18. The Battle Creek *Moon-Journal*, which had printed Lella's letter of December 9, 1915, on the front page.

19. Edward Streeter's *Dere Mabel* was a popular book of the time; the phrase "Ain't it awful?" appears frequently throughout.

20. Bruce Barton was editor-in-chief of *Every Week*.

21. Apparently a colloquialism for "chesty," i.e., puffed up, proud.

22. This letter has not survived.

23. Ina felt increasingly trapped and imposed upon by Lella's "desertion" and the additional responsibilities it had forced on her.

24. Lida was a widow and childless.

25. Gerhart Hauptmann, German playwright and 1912 Nobel prizewinner.

26. Ralph Waldo Trine was a popular author of books of spiritual uplift.

27. Lella leaves her mother to guess at the rest of Mr. Sorensen's words, which may have been "in the eyes of those who know you," or even "in the eyes of God."

28. *Amerikai M. Nepszava*.

29. Tracy Mygatt and Fannie Witherspoon founded the War Resisters League.

30. Emily Greene Balch, one of the alternate delegates to the Neutral Conference for Continuous Mediation in Stockholm; later (1946) a co-winner of the Nobel Prize for Peace.

31. Charlotte Perkins Gilman was a leading feminist theorist, pacifist, and reformer. In her book *The Man-Made World*, widely read at this time, she asserted that men were genetically inferior to women, and were the cause of most of the world's evils, including war.

III

New York: Activism

To Loretta Secor

Monday
May 15, 1916

Dear Mother and All:

I feel as though I must stop and write a few lines before I go out this morning. . . . Unless I keep at my correspondence every day, it piles up until I don't know where I'm at. . . .

I am devoting every spare moment these days to the fight against preparedness, and if I neglect you, you will know it is because I am giving my minutes to a good cause.[1] Last Saturday the Navy League—backed of course by the munitions makers and the political preparedness crowd—had a tremendous parade in New York. There were over 400,000 people in line, and it lasted from nine in the morning until ten o'clock at night. They have, of course, all the money they need, and there were bands and banners galore. Anne Herendeen, Mrs. [Margaret] Lane of the Woman's Peace Party, and a few other young women decided that the day ought not to pass without some protest on the part of those who see the thing as it is and are not deceived or scared by the munitions crowd. So we planned a little stunt which worked beautifully, and we were able to reach thousands of people with our ideas.

Needless to say, the experience was a brand new one for me,

REAL PATRIOTS ATTENTION!

KEEP COOL!

"Preparedness"—What for?

DEFENCE ? or DOMINION ?

Our present "preparedness" program surpasses in expenditure any military program ever adopted by any nation — not excepting Germany.

Can we hope to control this monstrous machine when once we have set it in motion?

Let's not start something that will finish us.

Are we "preparing" ONLY to defend ourselves?

"Strictly speaking, if national defence applies solely to the prevention of an armed landing on our Atlantic or Pacific coasts, no navy at all is necessary." — FRANKLIN D. ROOSEVELT, Assistant Secretary of the Navy, October 5, 1915.

"The coast fortifications of the United States are impregnable." — Gen. E. M. WEAVER, Chief of the Sea Coast Artillery Corps, March 15th, 1916.

"Nobody seriously supposes that the United States needs fear an invasion of its own territory." — President WILSON, January 28, 1916.

Watch your step!

Are we, in reality, "preparing" to crush others?

"A nation has a right to improve its position by every legitimate means, including world conquest." — *The Seven Seas*, Official Organ of the Navy League.

"World-empire is the only logical and natural aim for a nation that really desires to remain a nation." — *The Seven Seas*.

"We must play a great part in the world and .... perform those deeds of blood, of valor, which above everything else bring national renown. By war alone can we acquire those virile qualities necessary to win in the stern strife of actual life."
— THEODORE ROOSEVELT.

The hope of the world is that the present war will end militarism.

America armed to the teeth is MILITARISM VICTORIOUS.

We, the undersigned, hereby petition the Members of Congress from New York State to vote against unusual increase in Army and Navy appropriation during this Session

THE REAL PATRIOTS, 70 Fifth Avenue, N. Y.

and one which I shall never forget. The plan was to have a crowd of girls all dress in white and with identical hats, so as to stand out from the mob, and circulate among the crowds distributing literature which would set forth the other side of the question. We wanted to carry sandwich boards—a sign which covers the person both front and back, the like of which I don't remember having seen out West—but we found that almost anything we might wish to do would infringe upon the law, and we had every reason to believe that the strictest censorship would be exercised over all those not with the preparedness crowd. It was I, fortunately, who finally struck upon a happy idea. I suggested that we paint the legend on the back of our middy blouses. Thus it would become part of our clothes, and policemen would be unable to do anything about it. Out of this suggestion evolved the final plan of using large black letters which were pasted on, and looked really quite startling. When we walked in front of anyone, he had to read this sign: "Real Patriots Keep Cool." We all wore white skirts and middies—I borrowed mine from Louise—and little ten-cent open-work sea-shore hats. Sort of hyphenated hats it would appear from this description.

I had to finish some work at home before going down Saturday morning, so that by the time I reached Fifth Avenue, the parade was well started. I have never had anything affect me more deeply. In spite of my best efforts, I could not keep back the tears, and for blocks down Fifth Avenue I wept over the pitiful spectacle. I could not look at those long lines of fine looking men, marching so gaily along, and with so little realization of what it all means, without a fresh outburst of tears. How little they realized that they were endorsing a system which means that great armies of splendid manhood shall go forth and slay other great armies. And why? Because stupid diplomats were too avaricious, too selfish, too ambitious to sanely handle the affairs entrusted to their care. All the lunatics turned loose from all the hospitals in the world could not have made so sorry a mess of things as have the diplomats of Europe. And yet we, blind and stupid as we are, are rushing into the same horrible cataclysm.

In a flash I was back in Europe, on the streets of Holland, watching the steady tramp, tramp, tramp of young men and boys being trained in the gentle art of murder. But their faces bore none of the lightness and frivolity which could be seen on the faces of those marchers Saturday. By the time I reached the peace headquarters, I was so wrought up that I could hardly control myself long enough to speak to anyone. Only those who have been to Europe during this brutal war, and have seen the horrible results of militarism, can realize or understand completely what it means. Anne Herendeen and I decided to go out together, but first we went for lunch, though I was scarcely able to eat anything.

Then, with white bags slung over our shoulders and filled with pamphlets, we started out. New York women, who have fought for suffrage and free speech and social betterment and every other thing, are accustomed to such stunts. But I confess that my heart was beating like a trip hammer. We started down Fifth Avenue, and almost the first person we met was Mr. Huebsch, with whom I have been carrying on a polite little quarrel over certain differences of opinion. He disapproved of our plan, and did not want me to go in on it. At first I pretended not to see him and was going to pass by, for I was in such a state anyway that I hardly felt fit to undertake anything more. Then I thought that very cowardly, and turned to overtake him and show him how I looked and what I was doing. As I turned, he turned also to come back to me. We exchanged just a few words, and then I went on. This morning I have a note from him telling me how charming I looked, etc., just by way of amelioration. But I am not so easily satisfied.

We began to hand out our pamphlets, and were astonished at the eagerness with which people took them and read them. We had 50,000 copies, and within a few hours they were all handed out. We met with courtesy on every hand, and only those violently pro-English or pro-German had anything to say against our program. On the other hand, when people read the signs on our back, they would often come up by the dozens, asking for our pamphlets, so that many times it was difficult to hand them out fast enough. There were many comments such as, "That's the dope!" "I sympathize with this idea!" "I'm interested in this; give me all the different kinds you have!" etc. By evening my spirits had risen. I began to feel that after all the preparedness parade did not represent such prodigious strength as it appeared to represent. As someone suggested, most of the preparedness people were marching, and the crowds on the street were either against preparedness or mildly indifferent.

Hundreds of those who marched did so not because they sympathize with the effort to line the munitions makers' pockets with more money, but because they were practically compelled to do so by their employers. A number of them came to our headquarters after their part was over, and signed a petition to Congress asking that no great preparedness program be entered into.

The "war against war"—as we peace people like to call ourselves—contingent has opened an exhibit on Fifth Avenue which is attracting much attention. At six o'clock, the woman who had it in charge, and who had already worked eight hours, announced that the place was to be closed. I felt that this was a big mistake, since the parade was still to be in progress for several hours. So Anne and Mr. and Mrs. Seltzer and a few others, with myself, offered to remain and keep the place open. Anne and her husband took me to a fine restaurant near by for dinner, and then we began our work of the evening.

Little groups gathered here and there for discussion, and the first thing I knew, I was the center of a large crowd which had gathered to listen to my debate with a man who favored preparedness. We thrashed the thing out, and the crowd agreed that I had won. It's thrilling work, and I love it, especially since I feel confident that whenever folks are started thinking on the right lines, they will see the thing for themselves as it really is. This idea that vast armaments is going to preserve peace is the biggest fallacy that was ever perpetrated on a reasonable people. But I must stop preaching on this subject. I am sending copies of our literature which we handed out. Oh how I wish that I might be financed so that I could simply devote my whole time to this work. I CAN grip the attention and interest of an audience. Everyone who has heard me speaks of it, and I feel it myself. So I think it seems like sort of a waste of talent which might be used to good advantage in this needed field. Over 11,000 people visited the exhibits on that one day. . . .

I have been having little spells of homesickness lately, which of course I must put out of the way. I cannot afford to waste any time mooning. But New York is such a deadly place to live in that I can't help sometimes longing for the green fields of home. There seems to be something about this place which saps my vitality. I am perfectly well—I'm sure I weigh more than I have for some time—but I seem to have no energy. I think it is because I do not get enough fresh air, so I am going to try to go into the country somewhere every Sunday as soon as the weather is better. This morning it is raining and cold, so cold that I am uncomfortable, even in my hug-me-tight.[2] . . .

Don't stay home from prayer meeting to write to me, Mother. Of course I do miss your letters when they are long in coming, but I don't want you to deny yourself any pleasure in order to write.

. . . I don't believe I'll bother about piecing down that blue dress, for I only wear it around the house, and skirts are so short now anyway. . . .

Now I must stop, for the morning is slipping away, and I still have loads to do. . . .

Lovingly,
Lella

To Loretta Secor

Every Week CORPORATION
95 MADISON AVENUE
NEW YORK

[June 1916]

Dear Mother and All:

Just a line or two this morning before I start for town. I have so many things on the way and so many irons in the fire that these days I hardly have time to breathe. For all of which I am very thankful. . . .

If I do not come West on the lecture tour I spoke of, I shall change my abode, I think. I find that I need more social relaxation, especially at meal time. When Rebecca is not here, the only companionship I have is Mrs. Googins, who, although she is very nice, is still very tiresome, and not particularly congenial to me. Besides I can get only an occasional meal here, and the rest of the time I am eating alone around at restaurants. The possibility of living at a settlement house was presented to me only yesterday, but it made a great appeal. One can get room and board for $26 a month, I am told, which is of course very cheap. There are about twenty girls in a house, and one has the opportunity of meeting such fine people. I shall look into the matter at once, and try to get a place as soon as I possibly can after I find out whether I am going West.

The American Neutral Conference Committee, which Rebecca is working on, is progressing slowly but very satisfactorily. I am not able to take a very active part at present, because I cannot give my time. However, Rebecca expects that funds will be available in a short time, in which case, I shall give more of my energies. At present I act as a sort of safety valve and advisor for Rebecca. In addition, I attended the initial meeting, and have had interviews with several people of more or less note. Yesterday we called on Rabbi Wise, who is one of the most delightful men I have ever met. I am afraid I am cultivating a growing admiration for Jews. I have had several delightful times lately with my friend Mr. Huebsch. . . .

I have been made a member of the organization committee which will launch this big neutral conference idea. The other members are Hamilton Holt, editor of *The Independent,* Dr. Lynch, who manages Andrew Carnegie's $12,000,000 peace fund, Dr. [James J.] Walsh, author and lecturer, Dean Kirchwey of Columbia University and now acting warden and prison reformer at Sing Sing, Bishop Greer, and possibly the millionaire Jacob Schiff. It is rather laughable when you think of two kids like Rebecca and me pushing these notables into action. At the first meeting the other day, Charlotte Perkins Gilman took my hand and said: "It seems funny to see you kittens running things."

"Do you think it is FUNNY?" I asked her. Then she got quite serious and said no, she did not. That she was glad to see the power of youth exerting itself. We are more and more convinced as we see the inertia and conservatism of older people, that this movement which so largely affects the future years which are ours to live, is essentially the movement of the young people. . . .

Now I must stop and hurry to town. Give my love to everybody. I just don't have time to write. Haven't written to B.C. in weeks and weeks.

Lovingly,
Lella

TERMINAL HOTEL
EUROPEAN
IN THE
Union Station, St. Louis.

Dear Mother and All June 18 1916.

I'm not sure where I am, but I think it is somewhere near Toledo, Ohio. I am on my way home from St. Louis after the most strenuous 4 or 5 days I have ever experienced. I slept but three or four hours a night while I was in St. Louis and was pretty well exhausted by the time I left Chicago at 1:45 today. I didn't have a moment in which to eat until after I got on the train which is taking me to New York. So immediately I had luncheon and then a long sound nap. Now I feel much refreshed and am anxious to tell you all about this wonderful trip.

Of course you know that Rebecca has been working on the neutral conference idea, and I have been helping her all I could

To Loretta Secor

TERMINAL HOTEL
UNION STATION, ST. LOUIS

June 18, 1916

Dear Mother and All—

I'm not sure where I am, but I think it is somewhere near Toledo, Ohio. I am on my way home from St. Louis after the most strenuous 4 or 5 days I have ever experienced. I slept but three or four hours a night while I was in St. Louis and was pretty well exhausted by the time I left Chicago at 1:45 today. I didn't have a moment in which to eat until after I got on the train which is taking me to New York. So immediately I had luncheon and then a long sound nap. Now I feel much refreshed and am anxious to tell you all about this wonderful trip.[3]

Of course you know that Rebecca has been working on the neutral conference idea, and I have been helping her all I could.[4] Launching a movement of that sort is such a slow, laborious process. People in the mass always are afraid to stand for an idea itself, but they are not afraid if men of prominence have given their support. So it has been our job to enlist the support of men whose names were known. After several weeks' effort, we succeeded in organizing [an executive] committee composed of ourselves, Jane Addams (advisory),[5] Doctor Kirchwey, Rabbi Wise,[6] Dr. Lynch, Hamilton Holt, and Paul Kellogg, editor *The Survey*. Our plan was to organize a Committee of 100 prominent men all over the United States, through whom we could work. As soon as we had action, Rebecca had been assured of financial support.

[Monday] night, we decided that in some way or other, we must startle folks into action, and we felt that the best way would be to send someone to St. Louis to lobby for the neutral conference.[7] [Tuesday] morning Rebecca went out into the country to the palatial home of Mrs. Villard, a daughter of [William] Lloyd Garrison, and a thorough pacifist. Rebecca laid before her our plan and returned to the city in the afternoon at 5 o'clock with money to finance the venture.

Immediately we began to set wheels in motion and, in the face of seemingly impossible odds, we had printed over a thousand copies of the neutral conference plank, which we had already wired to Secretary Baker[8] and President Wilson, and a letter urging its adoption in the Democratic platform. The letters were delivered to us at 2 o'clock in the morning and shortly after, I boarded the train for St. Louis.

Every day I am learning more and more to subordinate the unimportant to the vital things. I had put on my brown dress in the morning, and to start on my journey I wore just what I happened to have on. I didn't even have time to comb my hair.

On the way to St. Louis, I devoted myself to a study of the question at hand. I got there at about 7:30 on Thursday morning, and by seven at night, with the aid of a stenographer and office boy, I had sent out a thousand letters to the Democratic delegates. It was a stupendous task, and I did not stop even to eat all day long.

This accomplished, I planned to devote the remainder of the convention period toward securing members for the Committee of 100. Thursday night I was thrown into something of a panic by the announcement that the convention business was to be rushed to a close and the delegates would depart a day sooner than anticipated. I worked until 2:30 Friday morning and then took a taxi to my hotel, and piled in, too weary for words. In spite of this, I woke at 5:30, too burdened with the responsibilities I carried to sleep longer. I got up and started to dress, tormented with an increasing fear lest the unexpected turn of affairs should leave me high and dry, and I should be obliged to return without fulfilling my mission. I hope I shall never again experience such a case of nerves. My pains increased until it seemed as though I should actually die. At last in sheer desperation, I stripped off my clothes, filled the tub with cold water, and plunged in. The shock had a salutary effect, and I began to plan my day with more assurance.

Mr. Villard, son of the woman who financed me, and editor of the N.Y. *Post,* had invited me to breakfast with him. He also introduced me to three young men, one of whom—Mr. Davis, a former member of his staff—was detailed to assist me. I regained my poise and started out on one of the most remarkable days I have ever lived. At the outset, I succeeded in enlisting the sympathy and cooperation of several judges, senators, and persons of note, which made further effort less difficult. At length Mr. Davis had a brilliant idea. We went to the convention hall, and I had no difficulty in getting in on his press ticket, which admitted me to the floor where the delegate bodies were sitting. By working quietly, I succeeded in visiting various delegations and making appointments with a number for the following day. Then *I* had a brilliant idea. In the afternoon there was to be a meeting of the national committeemen and it occurred to me that I might get an audience before them and present the matter *en masse*. So I began to pull one wire after another and finally secured an introduction to McCoombs, the chairman, who very graciously promised me five minutes. I was elated, but someway I almost feared it was too good to be true. As soon as the meeting was called, it adjourned until 7:30, but I was on hand again at that hour. But I was destined to be disappointed and also to learn that a politician's promise amounts to nothing, and that the only way to get anything is by having a colossal amount of nerve. I sat through a most stupid meeting which broke up finally at 12:30 in such confusion and disorder that it was impossible for me to get my hearing. It was a great disappointment but a fine lesson.

Monday a.m.

I was present at the Convention during the suffrage debate. A plank recommending suffrage to the states was included in the majority report, while the minority report was against it. It was the first time in history that suffrage was debated at a national political convention, and the enthusiasm was unbounded. All but four states voted for the majority report, which was a great victory, although I consider that a mere recommendation to the states of suffrage by the Democratic party amounts to very little.

I wish I could tell you about every wonderful experience I had while in St. Louis. I doubt, however, whether you can even read this, for it is so hard to write on the train. But it was a liberal education. I had a letter from Jane Addams to Mr. Bryan, which I presented. In addition I met many senators, governors and people of note all over the United States. I left St. Louis Saturday night, arriving in Chicago Sunday morning. Mrs. Lloyd[9] and Miss Holbrook, both Ford folks, came down from Mrs. Lloyd's lovely home at Winnetka to meet me, and after a brief conference with them, I rushed off to the home of Miss Addams. I staid with her until I had just time to catch the train for N.Y. I feel much disappointed that I missed seeing the girls at B.C., although a stop of one day might have been more of an aggravation than none at all. Rebecca had telephoned Mrs. Lloyd from N.Y. saying that a meeting of big men was to be held in N.Y. this afternoon, and that it was imperative that I be present. So I of course had to abandon my B.C. plans and rush past. I shall have just time to reach the meeting at the Astor Hotel by rushing directly from the train. I certainly hope something may come of all these efforts.

My own plans for the next month or so are somewhat unsettled. I have some work started for *McCall's, Every Week* and *Today's* which I expect to finish as soon as I get back. If the neutral conference funds develop I may come West to work for a time. Otherwise I shall stay on in New York with my magazine work.

I feel as if I had lived a year in the last few days. Until last night I did not sleep more than 3 or 4 hours a night after I left N.Y., so I was pretty well tired out. I had a good night's rest last night, however, and feel much rested. I am eager to get my mail, for I had none forwarded because of the uncertainty of my plans.

Now I must get at the report I am to make this p.m.

Much love to all,
Lella

To Loretta Secor

Every Week
95 MADISON AVENUE
NEW YORK

Saturday night,
July 1916

Dear Mother and All:

It is exactly a week since I have written to you, and it has been such a full week that I hardly know where it is gone. I am too tired to think consecutively tonight. It is eight o'clock and after and I am still at the office, although we have a half holiday on Saturdays. I found my new office[10] in such a chaos, that I felt it would pay me to stay down one afternoon when the others would be all gone, and I could work without interruption for a time.

I'll try to tell you what I've been doing since last I wrote. I wrote from Croton.[11] I did so enjoy being in the country, although I didn't particularly enjoy that particular vacation. The crowd was not congenial to me, and it was a great disappointment to me that I should have found so many there when I had hoped to be alone. In consequence, I didn't get nearly as much done as I had hoped.

I came back to town Tuesday afternoon, and found some important telegrams awaiting me from Rebecca who was in Chicago. They needed immediate replies, as there had been a change in Jacob Schiff's luncheon, and she was bringing on some Chicago people to attend. So I had to get busy at once by telephone and telegraph. I worked at a public phone booth in the Western Union office until one a.m. but it was too late to head off either Rebecca or the Chicago people. However, we went ahead and had a very successful luncheon at the Astor Hotel anyway, as the guests of Dr. Lynch. I sat between Prof. Irving Fisher of Yale and Hamilton Holt, and enjoyed myself much, although it was rather a strain.

Rebecca and I, together with Mr. Huebsch and Mrs. Baker,[12] stand for radical action, and we have to fight the old pacifists every step of the way. However, we succeeded in getting through some measures we wanted, and the work of the American Neutral Conference Committee now looks very hopeful. I am facing quite a problem in this connection just now, but I shall not be called upon to settle it until a little later. As soon as funds for the peace work are available, I can have a position at $50 a week at least. Of course that is the work which my heart is really in, and I AM needed tremendously. Rebecca and I work splendidly as a team, and there are so few who stand for radical, and constructive, work.

On the other hand, I have this very good editorial position at $30 a week, and of course good prospects of working up, though it will be more or less slow. The peace job might last for months, and it might last only a short time, but in considering that, I have to consider the great possibilities of national and international work which would be quite likely to open up for me. I am quite certain that I have most of the qualifications which are needed by workers in great movements, and I do have great dreams of the possible part I may have in the great reconstruction work after the war. Of course all this is more or less visionary. . . .

I am enjoying my work here immensely, except that it is rather difficult for me to be confined in an office from nine until five, when I have been free for so long. However, the discipline is good for me, I guess, especially as it isn't discipline at all, hardly. Members of the editorial staff come and go as they like, and no one pays any attention to them. If we want to spend two or three hours at lunch, or stay home for half a day, we can, but of course the work is too heavy most of the time to permit of much dallying.

On Friday, the School Peace League, which is connected with the National Educational Association, gave a luncheon, and I was invited. I always accept all gratuitous invitations. It was certainly a feed! It began with cantaloupe and bouillon, capered along with lobster, chicken, salad, green peas, etc., and ended with fancy ice cream and confections. This was also at the Astor. I am beginning to feel entirely at home. I can hardly make it seem possible that hardly a year ago I was not absolutely sure what one was supposed to do when one went into a hotel. I am still wearing my old black dress, but as I have said before, I do expect to get some clothes before long. If ever I get my work done for *McCall's* and *Today's,* I shall perhaps use some of that money.

. . . Today, we had luncheon with Miss [Caroline] Cumming, a delightful little English girl who has just arrived in America. She is very active in the Union for Democratic Control, an organization which has had a phenomenal growth throughout England. She has come over with the express purpose of telling America that there is a strong desire throughout England for an end of the war, which has not seeped through the censors.

. . . I actually haven't had a moment of leisure with Mr. Huebsch in weeks. He has been frightfully busy, and so have I, and whenever we have had time to see each other at all, there have been so many peace subjects to discuss. . . .

. . . I felt very sorry to learn of the death of Mrs. Mills.[13] Sometimes I feel too burdened with all the sorrow there is in the world, to live. The dreadful world tragedy which is enveloping us now has depressed me more and more, until, during the recent Mexican crisis,[14] I had to stop reading the papers; I was unable to throw off the horror. I am certainly happy that the crisis is past. It has been a wonderful demonstration of what the American people themselves can do toward influencing the president if they try. The result has given us new heart in our neutral conference fight.

. . . I used to think I lived strenuously, but it was a quiet little existence beside this life. I have at least learned the value of time. I almost never squander a minute.

I am glad you are not in New York now. The hot weather has begun—though very mildly everyone says—and now at nine o'clock every breath of air from the open window is like a whiff from a desert. Even a nightgown seemed too much to have over one last night. Oh I am SO glad that Lena and Lew are living out there where there is plenty of God's country in which to rear the children. I am sick at heart every time I go into the streets here and see the thousands of children at play. I have never been able to get used to it. We are having a terrible plague of infantile paralysis. Hundreds of babies are dying every day.

Ina, I was able to send a little more money this week, because Mrs. Lloyd sent me a little check the other day to help out on the work I have done in the peace cause. She didn't want me to take a position so that I would not be free to give my time to the movement. . . .

Lovingly,
Lella

To Loretta Secor

July 24, 1916

Dear Mother,

This is Saturday night, and I am still at the office. I am going to take enough time to dash off this hasty letter to you, although I've had no letter from you in days. In fact I have heard from practically no one in weeks. Of course, I can hardly blame people, for I haven't written a line to anyone since I came back from St. Louis except to you. But just the same I miss hearing from folks terribly. I wish everyone would not hold me so rigidly to the rule, "I'll write when you do." They wouldn't if they knew how much a girl alone in a big city appreciates hearing from the people she knows.

. . . The time has simply sped by in a maze of work, which has been shot through with a few pleasures—as many as I could afford to take. Emily Greene Balch has come back from Europe to consult with Mr. Ford,[15] and Rebecca, Mr. Huebsch and myself had a delightful dinner with her one evening. Afterward Mr. Huebsch took Rebecca and me to a Fifth Avenue candy shop where we ate terribly expensive ice cream. I quite often dine or lunch with him. In fact we are getting along rather well. He has gone to Chautauqua this week to give a series of lectures,[16] so I shall have to shift for myself for a time unless some of my other friends bob up serenely, which they do from time to time. But mostly I work—from nine in the morning until eleven or twelve at night. I'm really enjoying it immensely, though.

. . . Rebecca is now staying downtown at a hotel, although we usually manage to see each other daily. My room was really too cramped for a prolonged stay together. I'm still keeping an ear out for [a] good place to stay, but I have almost no time to look for any.

I have been invited to join the Civic Club, a new club composed of some of the brightest men and women of New York. The dues are fifteen dollars a year, but I think I shall try to get that much some how. It gives one so much better standing to be affiliated with some club. They have delightful quarters in one of the downtown hotels, and members get special rates in the dining room, and so forth. I feel quite delighted to have been included.

Now I must run along, for Rebecca has come, and we are going out for a bite of supper together. Then I'm coming back to work again. . . .[17]

Much love to all,
Lella

To Laura Kelley and Lida Hamm

AMERICAN NEUTRAL CONFERENCE COMMITTEE

70 Fifth Avenue
New York
September 4, 1916

Dear Ones All:

I can hardly believe that all these weeks have passed since I last wrote to you. I have not written a single letter since I returned from St. Louis, except to Mother and Ina, and I have neglected them frightfully. I am enclosing a carbon copy of the account of my summer's activities. I wanted to send it to some of the others whom I have neglected, and it takes so long to write, that I decided to duplicate that part of my letter. I have thought of you all a thousand times in these busy, strenuous weeks. I can't tell you how keen my disappointment at not getting to Battle Creek was. I had looked forward with such joyous anticipation, and then to be suddenly cut out of even having a glimpse of you—it was really a bitter pill. . . .

I have been with *Every Week* only such a short time, but they are going to give me one week [of vacation] with pay. How I wish I could afford to spend the time with you! I had it all planned out how I would leave New York Friday night and I would not have to be back until the next Monday morning. But it is quite out of the question, for Mother's expenses and everything else will be piling up now. I shall be so happy if I ever get my head above water. I think I shall try to spend my one week in trying to earn some extra money.

I'm not going to weary you with much more of a letter, for I have already been at my machine over five hours, and I guess you know how nerve-racking that is. I am terribly weary, and I know you will be by the time you wade through these volumes. . . .

I do hope you are all feeling in much better health. Loads of love from your baby sister,

Lella Faye

This brief summary of my activities during the past few months, will perhaps explain my criminal neglect of everyone I hold most dear. I think my last letters to everyone except Mother, date back in April, so I'll rush over those months which have intervened since that time, as briefly as possible.

Sometime in May, while I was still doing feature work on *Every Week* and while I was still casting about in New York for some opening which promised action in the peace work, Rebecca telegraphed me from Chicago, saying that she had been able to interest several wealthy men in a project she had for organizing an American Neutral Conference Committee for the purpose which appears now on the letterhead.[18] They had promised financial support if the project seemed practicable, and she urged me to have a conference with Hamilton Holt . . . who has always been active in peace endeavors. He is, however, one of those old peace workers whom Rebecca and I call "peace hacks" because of their stupidity and conservatism and fear. I had the conference, concluded that no action could be expected from him, and wired Rebecca to come on to New York and we would see what could be done about organizing such a committee.

It would require a volume if I went into detail concerning all the complications which arose from the time we returned from Europe until Rebecca's return to New York. Suffice it to say that we have little hope of financial assistance from Mr. Ford, . . . after he had said to go ahead and organize such a committee. In passing, I might add that Rebecca and I had many other schemes which elicited even more enthusiasm from us both—especially a tremendous international young people's movement, which we still expect to pull off—but an official conference of the neutral nations seemed to be the only plausible means of hastening the end of the war at all, and the only hope there seemed to be for the neutral conference lay in the United States' taking the initiative. All the neutrals of Europe are ready and are waiting only for action from America, the largest and most powerful neutral. So we decided to bend our energies toward the organization of a committee which should work for that one thing, and that only.

Some day I hope to write an account of all the agonies of soul through which Rebecca and I have passed in bringing these efforts to fruition. From the beginning we have been handicapped with youth and sex. I used to think that there was nothing so desirable in the world as to be young and to be a woman. But there have been moments when I have felt that both of these were a curse. Many nights we planned and worked and reasoned until well into the morning. At the outset we discovered that Americans have not moral courage to stand by an ideal or even an idea itself. If you approach them, they ignore the idea and ask instead, "Who is behind it?" We had decided to ignore Hamilton Holt, Dr. Lynch, and those old peace conservatives, and to launch our committee without them. Then we came to realize that without a few "big names" to start with, we could do nothing at all. We found no one who would stand on his own feet and say, "I'm with you because I believe in the idea and it's reasonable." Instead they would say, "I'll do it if so-and-so will."

Finally, little by little, we began to build up a strong committee. It was to consist of one hundred of the most representative citizens of America, and we have them. I tell you, we are proud of them too! They include governors, statesmen, university presidents, authors, lecturers, etc.

About the time when our initial efforts were rounding into shape, the convention of Democrats was called in St. Louis. Rebecca and I had felt that it would be of the greatest advantage to have someone at the convention to sound out the sentiment, and to do whatever was possible to further the interests of the committee. Late on the night when the convention assembled, we decided that someone must go. But we had no funds. Rebecca, however, is one of the most resourceful of persons, and once we decided that we should be represented in St. Louis, she cast about for the money. She spent the next day at the magnificent summer home of Mrs. Henry Villard—daughter of [William Lloyd] Garrison of anti-slavery fame. Her husband was one of the promoters of the Northern Pacific railway out West, and also supported the University of Washington at Seattle when the state was still a territory and the university was without funds. She is a Tolstoyan, and one of the most charming old women I have ever met. She immediately agreed to finance me to St. Louis. Rebecca returned at five o'clock. Between then and two o'clock in the morning, we had browbeaten a printer into setting up and running off for us a thousand letters to the Democratic delegates. At three o'clock I took a train to St. Louis.

It was another of those miracles which seem to happen to me over and over again. I feel almost that I have lived twenty years since last November. Certainly it has been the most strenuous and the most broadening nine months of my whole life. I really had a wonderful time in St. Louis, though I carried the weight of my responsibilities so heavily that I slept only seven or eight hours during the four days I was gone. I found when I arrived that I was too late for a personal hearing before the resolutions committee, which had already had its meeting. So I spent my first day with the aid of a stenographer, and a boy, in getting out the thousand letters. It was a tremendous task, which I didn't finish until nine o'clock at night. Then I sat down to my first meal that day.

I met many of the famous personages whose names appear in the papers every day. I had a letter of introduction from Jane Addams to William Jennings Bryan, and had a very pleasant little chat with him and with Mrs. Bryan. I interviewed Secretary of War Baker, Senator Stone of the Foreign Relations Committee, and dozens of others. I was privileged also to be on the floor of the house during the final session of the convention, when the historic suffrage debate took place. This was the first time in history when suffrage was debated as an issue from the floor of a political convention. Altogether, the convention seemed to me a little disappointing. It was so frightfully cut and dried—there was evidence everywhere that a group of political dressmakers had cut and basted the pattern. The most enthusiasm was called forth during Senator Reed's speech when he dwelt at length upon the peace policies of the president, and during the suffrage debate.

At the risk of seeming to dwell too long on this ancient history, I want to tell you a little more about that debate, because it seemed so clearly to me an evidence of the method by which national suffrage will probably be won. The majority report had a very spineless clause in which the party endorsed woman suffrage, but in the same breath recommended that the individual states handle the question. This, of course, meant precious little, since it left the question practically where it is today. But it was a slight step ahead of past platforms, which have merrily ignored the suffrage issue. The minority report carefully avoided any reference whatever to the suffrage question. For a time it actually seemed, in spite of the chivalrous oratory of several senators, that the minority report would be adopted. Then one long-headed politician explained that in the suffrage states out West there were ninety electoral votes.[19] "Can we," he cried, "afford to lose these votes?" And the convention, including conservative New York and the southern states as well, immediately decided that they could not. So the majority report was adopted. That noon I lunched with Hon. Dooley, Democratic delegate from Puerto Rico, who had the temerity to brag that the triumphant thing about the adoption of the majority report was that it was done on the merits of the suffrage cause, and not as a matter of expediency. He scorned to accept the obvious truth—that ninety electoral votes had done it. Wait until a few more states have suffrage, and we'll show 'em a thing or two!

But I haven't any notion now of going off on a suffrage tangent. But I can stop to say this. I never realized how frightfully humiliating it is to be classed with imbeciles and criminals, until I lived in a state where woman is [not] accredited with human intelligence. Coming from Washington to New York has taught me a number of things. Here women plead in vain for the decent conduct of children's homes and asylums—such frightful conditions have come to light lately—for laws which will protect the rights of the helpless. Politicians laugh them to scorn. Not so in Washington, where women have the power of the ballot behind them. If I were not so engrossed just now in stopping the war and working toward certain international ideals, I think I should be compelled to cast my lot with the suffrage cause.

But to return to the main track. I staid in St. Louis until Saturday night, ending my visit there with attendance at the Congressional Union dinner which was attended by many of the women most prominent in the woman suffrage cause.

I left St. Louis about midnight—the weariest person who ever climbed into an upper berth. I got into Chicago the next day about nine o'clock. I had expected to go on from there to Battle Creek, where I planned to stop off a day. I was looking forward with so much eager happiness to this brief visit, and was dreadfully disappointed when a long distance [call] from Rebecca in New York urged me to hasten back on the fastest train, in order to be present at an important meeting the next afternoon. Of course there was nothing for me to do except to listen to the call of duty. Mrs. Lloyd, wife of the millionaire socialist, a charming woman whom I met on the peace ship, came down from her country home to spend a few minutes with me in the depot. I had about an hour left until train-time, and I spent this with Jane Addams in her Chicago home. It was the first opportunity I had had of meeting her and getting personally acquainted, and I was delighted with my visit. She is so sweet and simple; in fact one might easily expect her to be an every day sort of mother to an every day sort of family.

I got into New York just in time to rush to the meeting, and was able to give the cause quite a push, I think, by a rousing report of my St. Louis activities. From that time on, the organization of the committee progressed more or less rapidly, although we might have been at least a month ahead of our present activities if we had not been held back at every turn by the other members of the executive committee. Rebecca and I represent the radical wing of a very conservative group, and everything which we have been able to accomplish so far has been through constant fighting. But right through, the experience, trying as it has been, has been tremendously worth while.

After the committee had gotten a fairly good start, Rebecca concluded that she would go back to Chicago and stir things from that

AMERICAN NEUTRAL CONFERENCE COMMITTEE

GENERAL OBJECT

To Support Our Government in Any Effort it May Make Towards a Just and Lasting Peace

SPECIFIC OBJECT

To Urge Our Government to Call or Co-operate in a Conference of Neutral Nations Which Shall Offer Joint Mediation to the Belligerents by Proposals Calculated to Form the Basis of a Permanent Peace

EXECUTIVE COMMITTEE

Bertha K. Baker
B. W. Huebsch
Dr. Frederick Lynch
Lella Faye Secor
Dr. James J. Walsh
Rabbi Stephen S. Wise

CHAIRMAN

Hamilton Holt

TREASURER

Central Trust Company of New York

SECRETARY

Rebecca Shelly
Telephone, Chelsea 5458

VICE-CHAIRMEN

Jane Addams
Gov. Arthur Capper
Prof. Irving Fisher
John Hays Hammond
Dr. John Harvey Kellogg
Dr. George W. Kirchwey

GENERAL COMMITTEE

Judge Charles F. Amidon
Prof. Emily Green Balch
Hon. Cassius M. Barnes
Bishop William M. Bell
Charles L. Bernheimer
Rev. Herbert S. Bigelow
Desha Breckinridge
President Melvin Brennon
Bishop Benjamin Brewster
President Samuel P. Brooks
Luther Burbank
Prof. Henry Smith Carhart
Rear-Admiral French E. Chadwick
Dr. Francis E. Clark
Hon. Philander P. Claxton
George W. Coleman
Dr. Frank Crane
John D. Crimmins
Henry Williamson Dooley
Gov. Edward F. Dunne
Dr. Samuel T. Dutton
President W. H. P. Faunce
Mrs. Joseph Fels
Gov. Woodridge N. Ferris
President William T. Foster
Prof. Kuno Francke
Herbert Friedman
President William Goodell Frost
Zona Gale
William R. George
Charlotte Perkins Gilman
Dr. Washington Gladden
Julius Goldzier
Dr. Sidney L. Gulick
Hon. J. Frank Hanly
Dr. Abram W. Harris
Morris Hillquit
Dr. John Haynes Holmes
Hon. Frederic C. Howe
Prof. William I. Hull
Dr. David Starr Jordan
Paul U. Kellogg
President Henry Churchill King
Hon. William K. King
Prof. Edward B. Krehbiel
Judge Ben B. Lindsey
Lola Maverick Lloyd
Prof. Jacques Loeb
Hon. John A. McCandless
Bishop William McDowell
Judge Julian W. Mack
Robert Emmet Manly
Dean Shailer Mathews
Dr. Mark Allison Matthews
Senator Samuel D. Montgomery
Angela Morgan
Henry C. Morris
John Nolen
Fremont Older
Senator Andy O'Brien
Hon. Thomas Mott Osborne
Mrs. Percy V. Pennybacker
Prof. Arthur Upham Pope
Hon. Nicholas F. Reed
Senator Helen Ring Robinson
Prof. Leo S. Rowe
Jacob H. Schiff
Prof. Vida Scudder
Dr. Charles M. Sheldon
President William F. Slocum
James Speyer
Prof. Frderick Starr
President Henry Suzzallo
Mrs. W. I. Thomas
Hon. C. C. Thompson
President H. R. Thompson
William Bess Thompson
Mrs. Henry Villard
Oswald Garrison Villard
Lillian Wald
Frank P. Walsh
Rev. Arthur Weatherly
President J. Campbell White
Mornay Williams
Hon. Amos P. Wilder
President Mary E. Woolley
Gov. Arthur Yager
Ella Flagg Young

Membership of The American Neutral Conference Committee, showing the "Committee of 100" prominent citizens.

end. That left me with the full responsibility here, and in addition to my daily work at *Every Week* it was almost more than I could manage. It was during her absence, too, that I was invited to become associate editor of the magazine, an offer which I felt I could not ignore. Rebecca and Mrs. Lloyd wired me frantically from Chicago not to accept, for they felt that my assistance in this peace effort was imperative, and both expected that the necessary funds would develop at once. However, acting on my own judgment, I accepted the position, because I knew how uncertain a "cause" always is, and to what extent one must sacrifice oneself. I could sacrifice my leisure and my energy, but I could not afford to give my earning capacity as well. My move was a wise one, for the conservative and slow policy of the executive committee has largely hampered the collection of funds.

And now I come to the most recent events, which, according to every newspaper law, should have been recorded first. At last we secured our one hundred "big names," and the time came when we wanted to go to Washington to interview the president. Rebecca and I saw in it tremendous possibilities, and the fact that it fell so far short of our original plans is a bitter recollection for us. Would that there could be found in America a group of ten people who are unafraid and daring! We wanted first to gather enough money—we have five or six multimillionaires on our committee—to finance the entire Committee of One Hundred. It would have been a notable gathering, such as Hamilton Holt is always puffing about. We figured that we could get probably seventy-five of the committee members to go to Washington, and with proper publicity methods we could launch the work of our committee in a big way. But we were so long delayed by the conservative wing that when we finally asked the president for a date, he named Wednesday, August 30, which was just a week away. Under the circumstances, the delegation was a tremendous success. The conservatives said that we wouldn't be able to get fifteen. On the second day we had sixteen telegraphic acceptances to our telegraphic invitations, three of them coming from the Pacific coast. Finally, nearly thirty people gathered in Washington.

Dr. [John H.] Kellogg came from Battle Creek, and every moment when we were not at some conference, we chatted together. I suppose he will never know what a comfort he was to me! It seemed so wonderful to find a clear-headed, brainy man, who was at the same time fearless and splendidly radical. We found ourselves standing exactly the same on most questions, a fact which developed a delightful bond of sympathy between us. Twice, by stepping into the breach at the proper moment, he made a motion which kept the committee off the rocks of inactivity and ultra-conservatism. It was I who had suggested his name for the committee, and I felt as proud as though this splendid man was the product of my own efforts.

We traveled all night, and got into Washington at about seven o'clock in the morning. It was my first visit to the national capital, and I experienced countless thrills as the White House came into view. Washington is such a quiet, drowsy little old town that it hardly seems capable of holding the momentous events which have taken place within its boundaries. We went at once to the New Willard Hotel and had breakfast, which Rebecca and I ate with Mrs. Villard, Emily Greene Balch of Wellesley, and Caroline Cumming of London, England. She has been here for a few weeks in the interests of the Union for Democratic Control, organized in England since the outbreak of the war. We have established a delightful friendship which I know will be very profitable. She returned to London Saturday. After breakfast, the entire delegation had a brief consultation during which we outlined our plan of attack, and at noon we started out in a body for the White House. The Capitol buildings are not so large or portentous as I had expected. There is an air of quiet nonchalance about the entire place which belies the activities which go on. We waited a few minutes in the hall, and then we were ushered into an inner room. I had someway formed the mental picture of our group sitting about in dignified fashion, waiting the appearance of the president. Fancy my surprise, then, as I stepped inside the door, saw a hand extended in front of me, and looked into the face of the president.

He is rather interesting to look at. His iron gray hair seems to call attention to the fact that he is no longer a young man, a fact one would be quite likely to overlook otherwise. His eyes—small but brilliant—look very steadily through eye-glasses which are NOT tortoise shell (thank God for that). His jaw is, of course, the most prominent feature. It seems to be built on an iron frame, though it is padded quite generously with flesh. He wore a white flannel suit, and stood at alert attention quite as though he had not been up a greater part of the night trying to figure a way out of the strike.[20]

Dr. Irving Fisher of Yale, Dr. Mary Woolley of Mount Holyoke, and Dr. David Starr Jordan of California, presented our case.[21] Mr. Holt, who is a massive, good-natured easy-going sort of chap, introduced the speakers.[22] Obviously he was more than ever impressed with the magnificence of the chief executive. I rather expected to see him twist his hat like a school boy when he presents his first apple to his sweetheart. I felt that the thing was not brilliantly handled. After the three had spoken, the president spoke. He was less frightened than anyone else. Obviously, his personality, coupled with his assurance, placed him on an enviable elevation. He assured us most suavely, that he was going to open his heart to us, and that, therefore, we must regard his words in absolute confidence. I rather fancy that I shall be one of the few who are true to that trust, but at all events, I shall refrain from repeating what he said.[23]

During the moments when he was speaking, I thought him a truly wonderful man. My first thought was that we had been a very stupid lot of people not to reason the matter out in a similar fashion. Then he gently dismissed us, and we all slipped out, after shaking hands all the way round again. I was not the only one who was impressed for the moment by what he had said. Others, whose clear thinking habits I profoundly respect, were fooled in the same way. But as soon as we got into the open air, we began to analyze his remarks. Before we had left the White House grounds, I had concluded that they could be shot full of holes.

We had a big luncheon at the New Willard Hotel immediately after the interview with the president. Again we ran up against a conservative element which practically wanted to tie up further action lest we should "offend" the president. But Rebecca and I fought a good fight, aided by my beloved Dr. Kellogg and Mr. Huebsch, who is classified in the same pigeon hole in my affections. We are to have a meeting of the executive staff tomorrow evening, when we expect to tell them quite openly that their policy of inaction must come to an end. We expect a merry fight.

We caught an afternoon train back to New York, arriving at about ten o'clock in the evening. It was truly a wonderful day, and I felt that the mere opportunity of meeting all those fine people, and of visiting the president, compensated for all our efforts.

On the way back, Mrs. Villard asked me to arrange a little dinner party for the following evening at her country place, to honor any who might be remaining over. So I invited Dr. and Mrs. Batton—he is connected with the International Church Peace Union, and has spent the last two years traveling in the belligerent countries of Europe, Prof. [Arthur] Pope, a fine young radical from the University of California—he has the chair of philosophy—Mr. Huebsch, and Laiput Rai, an East Indian who has achieved considerable fame through his efforts to liberate his country from the thumb screws of England. Mr. Huebsch recently published his book *Young India* which is a wonderfully clear exposition of the present-day conditions in India. He has himself been sentenced to death for sedition; needless to say he escaped. He has had a most thrilling and interesting career.

Mrs. Villard sent her car in for us, and we had a most wonderful ride out to Dobbs Ferry, where the Villard mansion stands in the midst of a hundred acres of lawn and parks overlooking the Hudson. I think I have never been in a more magnificent home. The reception room is in gold and white, and the magnificent concert grand piano is of white inlaid with gold. In the drawing room there was another baby grand piano—I don't know how many more were scattered about the house. It has been many a day since I have tasted such food. We had a wonderful feast served in royal style on plates inlaid with gold vines. But I am becoming so accustomed to elegance that I am afraid I am losing my youthful thrills over it. And I am sorry for this.

This brings me, I think, up to this Labor Day in which I am writing. I have just touched the high spots of my summer, but I have told enough, I think, to let you see how frightfully busy I have been. I have stopped for very little relaxation indeed. One day Rebecca and I ran out to Greenwich, Connecticut, to have luncheon with a new "peace" friend. That too, was a magnificent country place surrounded with immense verandas, on one of which we had our luncheon. Another time I spent the week-end with Anne Herendeen and her husband [Hiram Moderwell] at Croton-on-the-Hudson. They have been spending the summer in a lovely house built by Ralph Waldo Trine, who has made so much money from his books that he had to spend it somehow. The house used to be the dancing school of Isadora Duncan,[24] and is perched high on a hill overlooking the Hudson.

I haven't even mentioned Madame Rosika Schwimmer, who spent over a week in New York, and with whom I spent every hour I could spare from my work. She was, you remember, the woman who induced Mr. Ford to undertake the peace expedition. I had only just met her on the voyage and I was delighted to have the chance to know her well. She rather took a fancy to me, and would call me up if I did not come to her hotel. During her week in New York we spent many happy evenings in her room at the Astor. Mr. Huebsch, Ellis O. Jones, Miss Leckie, Rebecca and I constitute a new committee which Madame Schwimmer has left in America to support her work in Europe.[25] Mr. Huebsch is chairman and I am secretary. I don't just know how I am going to get this in, but I shall try to speed up somewhere.

I think, without doubt, that Madame Schwimmer is one of the greatest women of the century. It is, of course, only historical that few should recognize her worth until a century after she is dead. One afternoon, Theodore Vail, who is one of the chief officers of the Western Union, placed his limousine . . . at her disposal. She invited Rebecca and me to go with her, and we rode for four hours through New York country roads. Then we went back to the Astor where the others joined us for dinner. On the last Sunday night, Mr. Huebsch and I spent the evening with her and then had a little midnight feast in a gay little café. On the night before she sailed, the four of us had dinner together in her room. Our sessions always lasted until midnight, for there was so much to discuss in the limited time. She sailed a week ago yesterday, and I have missed her sorely since she went. I went to the boat with her; we were late in starting, and had a mad taxi race across New York to catch the steamer. It was five o'clock when I got back. Then Caroline, Rebecca and I had a little conference combined with dinner, and at eight o'clock that evening, the executive committee met in our apartment.[26] That is just a fair sample of the way in which the days have flown.

I fear that this detailed account may become tiresome. Still there are volumes more I would write if only I could find the time. Hereafter, I shall try not to let news accumulate to such an extent before getting it down on paper.

Pray don't give this letter any publicity. I'm afraid it would shock the committee.

To Loretta Secor

[September 4, 1916]

Dear Mother,

It is nearly ten o'clock, but I am not going to delay this belated letter another moment. I have just finished the final draft of a sort of "heart" appeal which we expect to send out to thousands of people this week and next. I have put a good deal of time and thought on it, because I wanted to play on people's emotions. It is the only way that one can get money out of folks. From the beginning of our life as a committee I have contended that when the American people themselves were asked for financial support, they would give it. I have contended that we would get a more heart-whole response than we can expect to get from one millionaire in a thousand. So now the next few weeks will be full of anxious waiting for both Rebecca and me, for they will justify or prove false our contention. So far, our own plans have proved wisest on every hand, and I hope to be able to prove justifiable my faith in America.

. . . I worked on the appeal nearly all day yesterday. At about four o'clock, I began to feel so tired and nervous that I could not stay inside a minute longer. So I took an elevated train and went out to Bronx Park. I can't tell you very much about it for this is the first time I have ever visited it, and as it takes an hour to make the trip, you can see it was beginning to get late when I arrived. All I wanted was a place to lie down on the earth alone and just stop thinking for a few minutes. I found a sheltered little spot hidden under the trees and was so happy to stretch out, away from everyone. In just a little while twilight began to settle down; then all the wee creatures of the forest began their night songs, while a little squirrel scampered from limb to limb over my head as though he were having his bedtime frolic. After a time it became quite dark but I still lay there, quiet and motionless. Then a rich yellow moon rose out of a tiny lake at the foot of the hill, and I watched its upward move until it became lost in the treetops. It seemed so like heaven to be alone in my beloved woods that I postponed my return trip as long as I could. By the time I had come back to the city and had my dinner it was so late that I had to go to bed.

Not much has happened since I last wrote to you, except that I have met a number of interesting people. Rebecca and I spent a delightful hour the other day with Mr. Whitehouse, a member of the English Parliament who is in this country for a few weeks.[27] He was simply charming. Baron Waleene, whom we met in Europe, is also in New York and I am going to call him up some day this week if he is still in the city. I am also to meet Mrs. Carrie Chapman Catt this week.[28]

. . . Inez Milholland Boissevain [is] to be in Seattle in a few days. I [am] so sorry I didn't know it before, for I should so much have liked to have you meet her. She rather liked me on the trip, and we got along pretty well together. I hope you went to hear her anyway, for she is an entertaining speaker, though of course I don't agree with her as to politics this time. I am convinced that in spite of the fact that Wilson has been a disappointment in many ways, and has not taken the direct peace action we have hoped for, he is much more to be desired than Hughes,[29] who, I feel sure, is far more belligerent in his attitude. I think also that he much more nearly represents the Wall Street interests than Wilson does. Of course neither of the candidates are much to brag about I think.

I almost believe that if I were to be at home, I would vote the Socialist ticket. They are for women suffrage and they are for peace, whatever else they may stand for. I suppose that I might as well announce now that I am becoming quite strongly Socialistic in my tendencies. I hardly see how one can live in New York with all its bitter strife and struggle for a mere existence, and escape Socialism. I have not yet affiliated with their party, and I am not sure that I ever shall. But I do intend to study the matter somewhat exhaustively as soon as possible.

An interesting change has taken place at the office. We have consolidated with the Crowell Publishing Company, which is the largest competitor of the Curtis Publishing Company. The former publishes the *Woman's Home Companion* and the latter the *Ladies' Home Journal, Saturday Evening Post,* etc. I suppose that we will be moving into the Crowell offices before long. It will not affect us materially, but I think it will offer us greater advantages. It will give us first hand information as to the *Companion,* the *Country Gentleman,* and the other Crowell publications.

It must be lovely in Washington now. I have longed so much lately to be at home again. Yesterday was a perfect day in New York too. The sun shone with a genial warmth, and the country air was filled with all the mellow odors of the fall. But today it was uncomfortably cold. I suppose winter is not far away. It shows its approach most clearly in the parks. I noticed Madison Square, which I pass through every day on my way to work, with particular interest this morning. The grass is still vividly green, but the trees are fading into a brown, hopeless sort of age. There are none of the vivid autumn colors which we see in Michigan, although I suppose we would find them more in the country these days. Water no longer plays in the fountains, and the urns have been emptied of their earth. The poor human derelicts, who crowd the parks even in the early morning, flocked to the benches in the sunlight today and then shivered in their rags.

Since you are finding it so difficult to decide what to do, Mother, I think I shall have to decide for you. I think you might as well begin to plan definitely to come to Michigan. I would not think for one moment of having you remain in Seattle after Lena leaves.[30] That would be one more worry which I quite definitely refuse to accept. I have been looking forward to the time when I could feel that you were much nearer to me. The possibility of getting to see you would seem so much less remote. Besides, as I have so often said before, you will be so much more comfortable and so much happier with the girls, and in the midst of your old friends. . . . I will get the money someway for your fare. I wrote to Ina the other day asking for a complete and detailed financial statement so that I

shall know just how we stand. I also told her that unless there was [some] very pressing debt which has to be met at once, she was to save what she could from week to week to get your clothes in order. That is, I suggested that she pay the actual running expenses, and devote the rest to your clothes. Of course I do not know how much the running expenses are, so I do not know how much will be available for other things. But at all events, the money matter will be managed someway and you need give yourself no further worry about it.
[End of letter missing.]

To Lida Hamm

66 West Ninth St.,
N.Y.C.
October 12, 1916

Dear Lida, and All,

I was so happy to get your good letter after the long silence which has covered the summer months. I am so sorry you were ill, and do hope you are feeling better by this time. How I wish I had money—heaps of it, so that those I love wouldn't have to work so hard.

This is Columbus Day, and the office is closed. However, I have been sitting here at my machine most all day, trying to get a great accumulated mass of correspondence off my hands. It is seven o'clock now, and I have several more [letters] to write before I can have dinner, so this is likely to be rather brief.

Last night I finished an appeal "To the People of America" which I have been writing for the committee. It is the last definite piece of peace work I am going to do for a time, except to attend meetings, etc. I have given so much time and energy, all of which has been infinitely worth while. But now I am at a place where I have got to consider finances a little more, and so I expect to devote my extra time to doing outside literary work. Of course I shall not be able to make any great "killing" in my spare time, but every little bit will help.

I expect Mother will be coming to you some time in November. I shall have to borrow a little money somewhere, but I shall be so happy to get her settled for the winter that I shall not mind that. I know that she will be quite happy with you for a time, and I am sure that you will enjoy Mother. It has been frightfully hard for me to try to keep things together on the Pacific Coast while I have been out here. If only I could have gone home to find out just how matters stand, and to have straightened everything out, I would have been so glad.

I am sending you some of our petitions and the other printed matter to let you know what our committee is doing. I thought perhaps you could get a few signatures among the folks you know.

I spent three days of my brief vacation in the country and it did wonders for me. I had not realized what a serious nervous state I was in. I just lay under the trees in the woods all day long and didn't even try to think. I spent the time with Louise Eberle and her friend, who is secretary to Mr. Page, the man who owns this wonderful estate in New Jersey. Lida, I wish you could meet him. He is a widower—close to sixty I should say—but the livest man you ever saw. I met him by accident on the road and smiled at him. I didn't know who he was, but my smile did the business. He invited us to his palatial home for lunch. I had gone off to the woods to spend the day alone, and was surprised to be discovered by a posse at noon. They had scoured the woods for me, and I was hailed into the august presence of Mr. Page and introduced. We had a delightful lunch, and then he showed us over his palatial home which overlooks the Rappahannock hills and valley.[31] He has a wonderful music room with pipe organ, art gallery, library, etc. The rest of the afternoon we spent riding around the country in his car. We had a jolly time. Louise tells me, since, that I made a big hit with the old chap. Better come to New York, Lidee.

Much love to all,
Lella Faye

TO THE PEOPLE OF AMERICA

IN the frightful holocaust of the past two years, thirty million men have "stood at the door of hell and marched into the furnace." More than five million of these have never returned. Millions more have come out scorched and mutilated, sightless and shattered.

Yet this suggests only a fraction of the human agony which is every day being multiplied. Add a picture of Europe's homes,—that vast Gethsemane where women walk in anguish of spirit. Add the pitiless march of millions swept from their homes without food, without destination or succor at the end of their frantic flight. Add the tragedy of Belgium. Add the unhappy peoples of Poland and Armenia, of Albania and Lithuania who are dying by wholesale starvation no less than by direct assaults of war.

MUST THIS DESTRUCTION GO ON?

Those who sit in high places and direct the carnage have announced a common purpose. Both the Allies and Central powers declare they are fighting to secure guarantees against war for all time to come. With both striving toward a common goal, why should millions more be sacrificed?

BELLIGERENTS WANT PEACE

A few war lords in the belligerent countries do not speak for the whole people. Influential papers in the warring countries avow this, and America knows it is true.

One hundred and fifty thousand Britains have already signed a peace petition asking their government to negotiate at the earliest possible moment. Women of France have urged the allied powers to consider peace proposals, whencesoever they may come. Public utterances, both official and unofficial, have left small doubt of Germany's desire for peace. The other neutral nations of the world look to America for leadership. Yet America, rich in war gold, stands by and raises no hand to check the colossal destruction. Must our government wait for a formal invitation to staunch the flow of Europe's life-blood?

WHAT CAN AMERICA DO?

We can unite in a nation-wide protest against further carnage, and a tremendous plea for official mediation. If in democratic America millions of citizens urge the United States to undertake mediation, even at the risk of being rebuffed, can our government fail to heed the desire of the people?

Appeal written by Lella. See letter of October 12, 1916.

AMERICA'S SOLEMN RESPONSIBILITY

Let the United States, backed by the entire neutral world, attempt mediation on a basis which shall safeguard the just claims of the belligerents, and provide for international guarantees against future wars.

WILL THE BELLIGERENTS LISTEN?

The scourge of war has taken its toll from almost every home in the warring countries. Millions of lives have been lost—neither side victorious. The intense suffering of the winter is at hand. In the face of this universal woe, would the belligerents dare to invite the criticism of the entire world by refusing to consider offers of peace? Would either side dare to assume responsibility for continuance of the carnage when both have so emphatically denied responsibility for starting it?

"Neutral mediation," says a writer in the London *Fortnightly Review* for September, "would save the lives of at least three million human beings, avoid increased misery for those who have already suffered, and untold suffering for those who have not yet come under the shadow."

Perhaps nothing can be done today or tomorrow. But the psychological moment when neutrals can act is inevitable—we must be prepared.

LET AMERICA SPEAK

The American Neutral Conference Committee is urging America to speak. America consists of you and me—100,000,000 of us. It cost money to reach you—we much reach millions more. For stationery, postage, petitions, field workers, we need funds urgently and immediately. One hundred thousand dollars is necessary to carry out our plans.

INVEST YOUR MONEY IN PREVENTION

You have given freely to care for those blinded by the war; to patch up the human wrecks who have come out of the trenches with only a remnant of body to house the war-scarred soul; you have fed the widows and children whose men will never return.

We ask you now to save the eyes of men; to prevent further mutilation; to send a few men back to women and children who wait in tortuous suspense.

Everyone in America however poor or obscure, can aid in hastening the day of peace. Be a stockholder in this gigantic peace enterprise, whether you can give a few postage stamps, $10, or $10,000.

Mail your contributions to the secretary, *Rebecca Shelly, 70 Fifth Avenue, New York City.*

To Loretta Secor

Every Week
95 Madison Avenue
New York

October 28, 1916

Dear Mother,

The dear little waist came yesterday, and you cannot imagine how sweet I think it is. I kissed the collar with the dainty edge on which you spent so many hours. The only trouble is that I shall never want to send it to the laundry, and I am afraid I shall have trouble keeping it white myself. It fits very well indeed. It is a trifle short under the arms, and a bit long in the back, but otherwise it is quite right. Thank you many times.

I dropped you a little letter on the day that your last letter arrived, which I devoted mostly to discussion of your coming trip. So I shall not mention it again here except to emphasize what I have already said. Please do not mention the matter of money to Ellsworth or Lida any more. I am quite able to handle our expenses myself and we shall get along just as we always have. I only hope, however, that you will make your decision soon and let me know.

Lida misunderstood what I said about my peace work I guess. I said that when I finished the Appeal I wasn't going to undertake any definite piece of work for a time, until I had rested a bit and had a chance to do some outside work for myself. Her letter showed how little they understand what I have been doing in New York. It has been my efforts for peace which have given me most of my broadening opportunities so that, while I have spent a great deal of time and energy, I have been amply repaid. I owe the peace cause a great deal just from purely selfish reasons. There will never be a time in my life again when I am not actively engaged in some big work which I think is going to better humanity, unless I am flat on my back.

Even my resolution to take a little respite was broken, however, almost before I had made it. There is so much to be done, and the need is so pressing, that I find myself inexorably drawn into the fight. My spare time this week has been spent in attendance upon a private peace conference of all the existing peace societies. There were about seventy-five people altogether, and Dr. Lynch characterized us as the leaders of thought in America. I felt rather flattered to have been included. We had sessions two days, although I was able to get to only one, and a dinner Thursday night.

Last night I staid all night with Anne because Hiram was away. We got into a shooting fray down in the Italian quarter which was quite exciting. Both of us had all sorts of thrills from our experience.

. . . I forgot to tell you . . . that if you decide to come East, my friend, Mrs. Lloyd, will meet you in Chicago, and see that you are well taken care of. She said in a letter which I received today that she would be delighted to meet you, and that if you wanted to stay over a night she would be happy to take you home with her. She is a wonderful woman. I am quite devoted to her. She has recently had much trouble, having secured a divorce from William Bross Lloyd, the millionaire Socialist, of Chicago. They are wealthy, and a very prominent family.

Much love to Mommer as well as to Lena and the babies.

Lella

P.S. You didn't miss much if you missed Dr. Aked. He's a great bag of wind. I've no use for him, but he *can* rattle off the English language.[32]

To Loretta Secor

Election Day, 1916

Dear Mother and All:

This day has slipped by in such haste that I have accomplished practically nothing at all. Rebecca and I took a rare holiday and slept until nine o'clock. Then I got up and got breakfast at home—something we seldom do—and we chatted until after noon. This afternoon, we came to her office, and have been working on some pamphlets and things, as well as having a conference with Mr. Richards, a conscientious objector from England, whom we entertained last evening.

I must tell you about the wonderful evening we had in our little flat. It was one of those occasions when one feels that something wonderful is certain to result. Rebecca and I invited a little group of radical young people to meet and hear Mr. Richards. The latter is a young chap himself, a Congregational minister of some note, and a big fine young giant both physically and intellectually. Rebecca, Anne, and I each invited a few people, so that a number came whom we had not before met. Our little sitting room was crowded, but we sat all the evening in rapt attention while Mr. Richards told us of the 25,000 and more men in England who have dared to suffer tortures as bad as those of the Inquisition, because they repudiated war and would not under any condition go out to kill their fellow men. Thirty-four of them—ministers, lawyers, the finest type of men—were taken to France and condemned to death. But not one of them flinched or went back on his principles. Their fellow objectors in England heard of the proposed execution and raised such a row in Parliament that the sentence was commuted to ten years at hard labor, which the thirty-four are now serving. There have been no actual executions as far as we can learn, though we have heard that many objectors have been shot in Germany. But we *do* know that any number have died from the hardships and exposures which they have suffered.

Thursday night, and I have not yet gotten this letter off. I have staid at the office on purpose in order to finish and post this tonight. I am sorry for my long neglect, but sometimes I cannot seem to avoid it. I have been feeling especially tired during the last few days—just the usual tiredness which results at certain periods. It was late when I got home from dinner last night, and when I tried to add to this epistle, I simply fell asleep at my post.

I was telling you about the wonderful evening which we spent Monday with Mr. Richards. We got in touch with him when he discovered one of our petitions and came to Rebecca's office. Sunday afternoon we went to a church where he preached, and the idea of having him address a small group of radicals, where he could speak absolutely frankly and confidentially, came to me during his sermon. We asked him afterward, and arranged the little gathering for the following evening. Almost everyone came even on such short notice, which shows the great interest which is felt. I wish I had time to tell you all the experiences he told us—how the conscientious objectors came to be organized, the wonderful "shadow" system which they work so that each officer has his understudy who takes his place as soon as the officer is arrested, and so on. It was inspiring in the extreme, and put new heart into all of us. He is going on a lecture tour as far as Chicago, and will then return to England before Christmas, deliberately walking into the arms of the law again in order to help spread the anti-war doctrine at home. It is wonderful to know that there are yet men who dare to stand by their ideals, and to suffer and die for them if need be. We rather laughed at first when Rupert Hughes[33] wrote quite seriously in *Collier's* that some of "those pacifists" would have to be hung before America would come to her senses. But when the Irish martyrs were so brutally murdered,[34] and when the conscientious objectors have suffered so severely at the hands of England, we have begun to feel that perhaps martyrdom for a cause is not a thing of past ages at all. In time of peace we suffer only the jibes of those blinded and fearful folks who see only the material and never the spiritual side of life. But if we should be drawn into war, I have no doubt that those of us who would preach against enlistment with all the might of our being, would have to suffer. That is wild speculation to be sure, but it is a fine thing to know that in America as well, there are a good many young people who would die before they would sacrifice their principles.

Anne and I had such a wonderful little excursion over the week-end. We decided quite impulsively to take a little tramp Saturday afternoon. We took the ferry across to New Jersey, and started out along the Palisades which skirt the Hudson River. Our objective point was nine miles away at Alpine, where Anne had several times before spent the night at the home of a Mrs. Sickles, who keeps a sort of semi-public place during the summer. We started rather late and had gone only a mile or so before darkness descended. About this time we lost the path, and climbed straight up a cliff so steep that the only way we could get down was to sit on our heels and slide. We found the path again, and had really a wonderful tramp. Finally, when we had both begun to feel pretty tired, Anne turned from the path into the road which she thought led up to Mrs. Sickles. But we discovered that it was a brand new road just being built, and in a little while, Anne confessed that she was absolutely lost.

I rather enjoyed the situation, except that it was rather cold, and the prospect of sleeping out all night in a spring coat did not offer a great deal of comfort. My famous "hunches" had proved their value several times earlier on the trip when Anne had been in doubt about the path, so she suggested that I lead the way on authority of my hunches. So we started out in the opposite direction, and walked for miles along a road which dropped on the one side hundreds of feet to the Hudson, and rose on the other side in a high, formidable cliff. There was not a sign of human habitation, and we began to seriously consider the possibility of remaining out all night. Anne felt sure that we had long ago passed Alpine. Along the road were the implements of the workmen, and among them two sort of dump-carts swung on a pivot. We marked these in our minds, and decided we would return to them if need be, fill them with dead leaves, and enjoy our adventure to the limit for the rest of the night.

Finally, a tiny light appeared on the road ahead. I was delighted for I supposed it to be the light of the Italian workmen's shack. Anne was fearful about approaching, because it was Saturday night, and we had heard loud shouting and carousing from some source a short time ago. But I didn't someway have any fear at all, and so we bravely stormed the citadel. When we came up to the light, we found it was just a tiny shack which could not hold more than two men. I rapped loudly on the door and almost sent the old fellow inside into hysterics. He was much more frightened than we. Finally, shouting through the door, we made him understand that we were lost, and that we wanted directions. Out popped the dearest little old Scotchman you ever saw. You can't imagine anyone more surprised than he to find two girls on a lonely, unfinished road at ten o'clock at night. We found that we had been going in the right direction, and that we were only about ten minutes away from our destination. We routed the lady out of bed, had clam chowder and a

Left, Loretta Secor with daughters Lella (l.) and Ina. Green Bay, Wisconsin.

Below, Loretta Secor with her five daughters. Back row, Lena, Lida, Ina; middle row, Loretta, Laura; front, Lella.

Lella's cabin on her homestead in Coulee, Washington.

Lella Faye Secor, Spokane, Washington.

The *Oscar II* leaves the Hoboken dock.

Official photo from *Oscar II*. (l. to r.) Louis P. Lochner, Henry Ford, Dr. Charles F. Aked.

Opposite (l. to r.), members of the Ford party at a Copenhagen reception. Top row, Judge Ben and Henrietta Lindsey; Miss Florence Holbrook, Chicago school principal; Katherine Blake, New York school principal; Gaston Plantiff, Ford's financial representative; Alice L. Park, California suffragist; John Barry, author; Benjamin Heubsch; Elizabeth Hitchcock and Col. Robert H. Henry, newspaper people; Mr. Leuken, attorney general of Norway. Middle row, unidentified man; Mary [Mrs. Joseph] Fels; Edith [Mrs. Jenkin] Lloyd Jones; Senator Helen Ring Robinson; Dr. Jenkin Lloyd Jones; Mrs. Hamilton Holt; May Wright Sewall. Seated, Louis P. Lochner, Hamilton Holt, Thomas Seltzer.

The Ford peace party landing in Copenhagen. Official expedition photo.

The photograph, taken just before the opening of the peace meeting at Madison Square Garden, New York, on February 2d, shows Mr. Bryan and the committee. Left to right, seated, PROF. EMILY GREEN BALCH, GEORGE FOSTER PEABODY, DEAN GEORGE W. KIRCHWEY, WM. JENNINGS BRYAN *and* MISS LELLA FAYA SECOR. *(Standing),* B. W. HUBESCH, AMOS PINCHOT, MISS REBECCA SHELLY, *secretary, and* LOUIS P. LOCHNER.

O NAV
ARMIES
EDERATION
DEMOCRACY

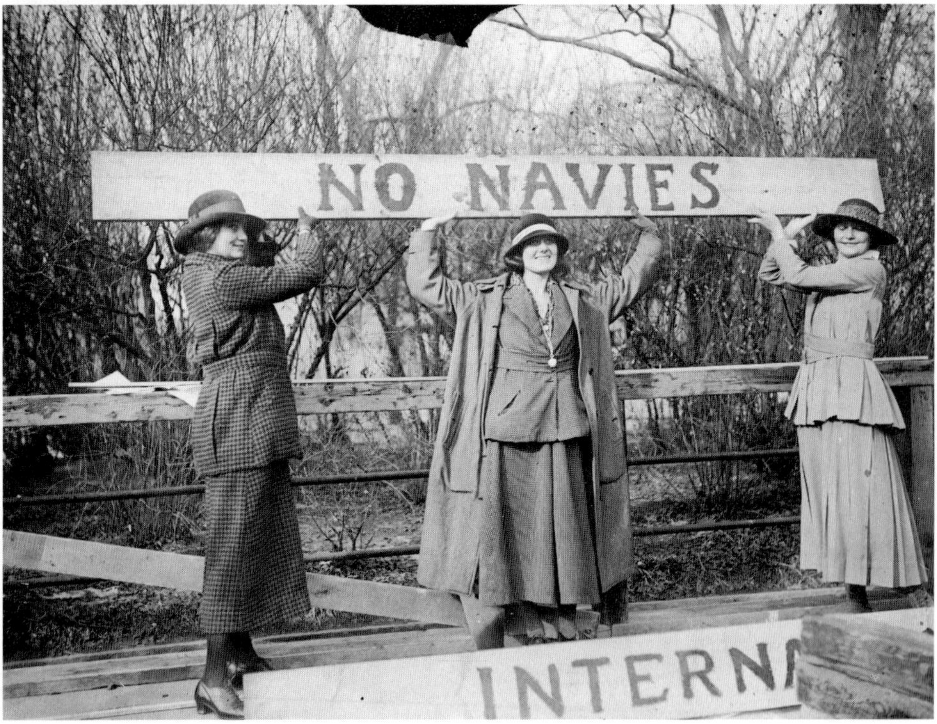

NO NAVIES
INTERN

Photographs courtesy of Brown Brothers.

The Woman's Peace Party prepares for a demonstration. Washington Square, New York. Above, Anne Herendeen, far left; Crystal Eastman, fourth from left; Inez Milholland Boissevain, fourth from right.

Family Photograph, Battle Creek, 1917. Standing (l. to r.), Loretta Secor, Hazel Kelley (wife of Don Kelley), W. Carson Kelley, Laura Kelley. Seated, Lella Secor, Philip Florence.

Long Branch, New Jersey, summer 1917. (l. to r.) Philip Florence, Rebecca Shelly, Miss Ward, Lella, Joseph Cohen.

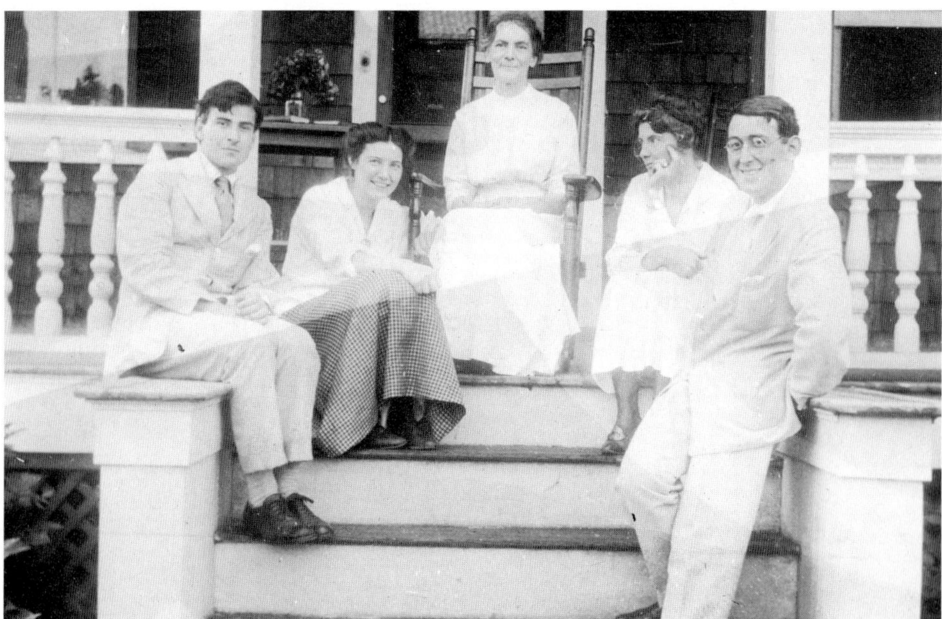

Mary Sargant Florence at Lord's Wood.

Philip's birthplace, 115 Vreeland Ave., Nutley, New Jersey.

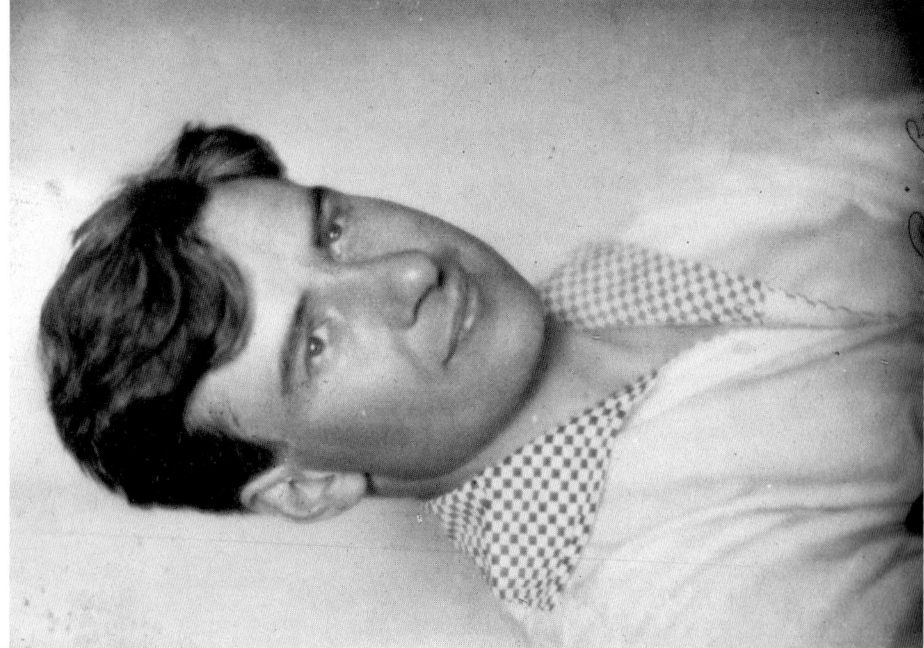

Lella in bed following the birth of Noel on November 9, 1918.

Lella and Noel, New York, 1919.

Laura Kelley, Anthony, Loretta Secor. Nutley, New Jersey, May 1920.

Lella sorting seeds, Nutley. Spring 1920.

oel and Philip at window of Nutley studio.

ella, Philip, Anthony, and Noel, Nutley.

Noel, Lella, and Anthony in Brian Lawrence's motorcar. Lord's Wood, 1922.

Noel, Anthony, and Lella at Waxham, 1923.

Philip and Lella, 55 Chesterton Rd., Cambridge, 1925. (Photo taken by Noel.)

Anthony and Noel with Marthe, their governess. Lord's Wood, 1927.

Lella and Philip in later life. Birmingham, probably late 1940's.

good supper, and then climbed into bed in a complete, but perfectly healthy exhaustion. We slept in a big room overlooking the Hudson; the room had four windows, which was a great treat after the almost windowless flats in which we live. We slept so soundly, and awoke only when a heavy rain storm came up in the night. I tell you we were glad we weren't sleeping in any dump cart on a pile of leaves!

We slept until the middle of the morning and got up feeling prime. We had breakfast, and while we were still eating, a crowd of four young people, soaked to the skin, came in. They had started out for a tramp in spite of the rain. When Anne and I passed through the room to get our things, one of the girls rushed up to greet me. It was Miss Reed—editor of *McCall's* magazine, whom I met when I first came to New York. We were introduced around of course, and joined them for a little while in music and chatter. Anne and I had expected to walk back to our starting point, stopping en route at a little French place for dinner. But it was so wet that we took a little launch straight across the river to Yonkers where we had dinner. Then we took the train into New York, arriving just in time for Mr. Richards' meeting. Afterward, Mr. [Roger] and Mrs. [Madeleine Doty] Baldwin, a young couple just married, asked Anne and me to go home for supper, which we did. So all in all, it was rather a strenuous two days, though one of the most enjoyable week-ends I have ever spent. Not even the rain detracted from the pleasure. There was not one unhappy moment. I feel that it was well worth while though, in deciding to go, I had to struggle as usual against that abominable feeling that I ought not to afford the time or money. I am trying very hard to get over that tendency. The trip cost me the whole sum of a dollar and a half, part of which I would have spent for meals had I been in New York.

By the way, I had a pleasant surprise the other day. My salary was raised to $35 a week without my asking for it. I feel quite pleased, and that extra five a week will really help so tremendously.

I felt so annoyed when your last letter came because you did not state definitely whether you are going to Michigan or San Francisco. I shall certainly look for a definite decision in your next letter. As I have told you in the last half dozen letters I have written, I will attend to the expenses myself, and you need have no concern about them. I would be very pleased indeed if you would just drop the subject of money, decide what you think you would like best to do, and then prepare to do it. If, by the time you get this letter, you have not already written to me saying either that you have decided to go one place or the other, I want you to wire me immediately, collect, giving me your decision. I know you have not made up your mind because you have been troubled over the money side of it, but I wish I could make you understand that that is not worrying me at all, and that the only thing that does worry me is not to know what you are going to do, and what I am to depend on. Please DO do as I ask you in this particular respect. . . .

I can't tell you how sorry I am that you feel as you do about being "turned out of your home." I am afraid we shall never be able to come to any understanding about it, for you will always feel that you alone were wronged, and I shall always feel that there was plenty of room in the house for all the people who occupied it, if all had made liberal efforts to get along reasonably with the others. If you wanted to repeat the conditions that prevailed at the Waters place, you might as well have taken Ina into a nunnery.[35] But there is no use in discussing the matter. Ina and I have suffered quite as much as you have, but we shall all make the best of the situation. You are at liberty, as I have told you before, to do exactly as you wish, and I do hope you will take advantage of your opportunity to make yourself happy. I am convinced that happiness rests with you alone. No one else can make or find it for you. I have worried a great deal about both you and Ina, but I have come to feel that you must both work out your own happiness for yourself . . . it would be feeble folly for me to attempt it for you, as I have often falsely thought I could do, had I gone home.

. . . I am not surprised that you liked Dr. McIntire. I am deeply attached to her. She was such a source of strength and comfort to me when I was in Everett, and I shall never forget her. I remember one night when I was feeling particularly sick at heart, she took me on her lap and cuddled me like a baby. Of course I spilled all over—she has less lap than you, Mother—but it was a big comfort anyway. She is a dear woman. . . .

If you come East Mother, I think, now that you have waited so long, you had better wait until Mrs. Watson comes. It would be pleasant for you to have a traveling companion whom you know. I figure on $75 for the trip East, though I am not sure just what the fare is. I want you of course to travel first class, wherever you go, and to have all the comforts there are to be had. . . . You could spend the time between Lena's departure and your own with Ina, for you would need her to help you get ready for the trip. I am not making any argument of course for the trip East. I want you to decide for yourself. It might be that you would even much more enjoy the winter with Lena, and come East in the spring. That is for you to decide.

If my trunk ever reaches me, I shall want only a few things. I do not want to be burdened with a lot of junk to move around, and besides, I should not want to take anything that Ina might be able to use. The house is barely furnished as it is, and after you go, I shall of course have to buy new linens, silver, etc. to take the place of yours. It's kind of amusing, isn't it, how everything always finally sifts down to me?[36] Anyway, I gets lots of fun out of it, I does. I only want a few books, and I have already given that list to Ina. Ina sent me one outing flannel nightgown today, for which I was very thankful, as I had no nightgowns at all and have not had for some time. In the summer I found it just as comfortable sleeping without any, but it's a bit too cold for that now. Perhaps, when the time comes to have my things sent, I shall think of a few more that I want. With the hangings I borrowed from Anne, and a little stand lamp which I made mostly myself at the cost of a little over a dollar, the apartment really looks quite cheery and cozy. It is certainly better than anything I have ever seen for the money here. Both Mr. Mandel and Anne said it expresses my personality, and I wasn't quite sure whether or not to feel complimented.

Rebecca and I are very happy together, though we see very little of each other because we are both so busy. We get along beautifully, because we allow each other absolute independence. We go off with separate friends at any time we choose, and in fact it is seldom more than once or twice a week that we even have dinner together. We show absolute respect for the individuality of each other. When we do have an evening at home, we feel that it is a rare treat. I am helping Rebecca as much as possible with her work, but I have come, as never before, to a pretty good realization of the limitations of my strength. I find I have very little vitality left, and

REAL PATRIOTS ATTENTION!

Who Starts the Cannon-Balls Rolling?

In 1913 small-arms and ammunitions companies in Germany, Austria and Belgium, backed by French money, were detected in a combination to engineer war-scares to swell their profits.

Repeated instances of such international fraud by munitions makers have come to light.

Josephus Daniels, Secretary of the Navy, has said: **"There is no doubt of an Armor Plate Trust all over the world."**

Are we not drifting into the hands of the same interests that engineered the European War?

America is not without its Professional Alarmists.

During the year of 1915 Hudson Maxim

(1) Published "Defenseless America."
(2) Made début as Movie Star (fully armed with Maxim products) in dramatization of same, under title, "The Battle-Cry of Peace."
(3) Organized $10,000,000 Maxim Munitions Corporation.
(4) Spoke before St. Louis Business Men's League, urging support of National Defense Program.

The Munitions Makers have made us hated in Europe. Now we must buy their products to defend ourselves against that hatred.

President Wilson and his personal representative John Lind have both stated that special interests in the United States are trying to foment trouble between this country and Mexico.

One million rounds of rifle ammunition intended for bandits were confiscated at the Mexican border by American troops, May 10. Who supplied this ammunition? The Eskimos?

Why Not Go After Our Own Bandits?

Nicholas Murray Butler, President of Columbia University, has remarked: "My impression is that somebody makes something by reason of the huge expenditure in preparation for war."

Don't forgot that 2% of the people in the United States own 60% of the wealth. **Note the martial activity among the 2%.**

DO <u>YOU</u> SEE ANYTHING IN PREPAREDNESS THAT LOOKS LIKE PROFITS?

We, the undersigned, hereby petition the Members of Congress from New York State to vote against unusual increase in Army and Navy appropriation during this Session

THE REAL PATRIOTS, 70 Fifth Avenue, N. Y.

for the most part I have to cherish it pretty carefully for my work at the office. I tire out so readily, and then I am likely to be good for nothing for days.

No, Mother, Rebecca has anything but a snap.[37] I have discovered that all people, like Robert LaFollette[38] and those who are giving themselves unreservedly to a cause or to promoting their ideals, do so only at the greatest cost to themselves. I have never seen such magnificent devotion and self-sacrifice as Rebecca has given and is giving to the peace cause. She has organized this big committee—of course I helped a good deal at the beginning—but in the main she may be said to have done everything herself, and she is now the life and spirit of the only movement being made in America to stop the slaughter in Europe. She gets a very modest salary when there are any funds, and when there are none, she goes without. Hers is purely a service of devotion.

At this late hour the election has not yet been settled. Everything hangs on the West, but I feel sure Wilson will win out, and I certainly hope so.[39] I thought of you and Ina and Lena on election day, with your chance to vote. It enraged me when I saw Negroes and half drunk foreigners going into the polls and realized that I was disfranchised. On election night, a little group of us had dinner at the McAlpin, and staid there until nearly midnight. Then we went down on Broadway, but I felt disappointed at the crowds. I usually do, as a matter of fact. I expected so much excitement and found things much more quiet I am sure than they were in Seattle at the same hour.

Now I must go, for it is close to eleven, and I am afraid I will get locked in for the night. . . .

Lovingly your baby,
Lella Faye

To Loretta Secor

[November], 1916

Dear Mother,

I don't suppose I shall have more than ten minutes to dash off this letter in, but I don't want to keep you waiting. Life is steadily growing more and more complex for me, so that I am finding less and less time for myself. In fact I feel now that I am approaching another big crisis, such as I faced when I decided to go to Europe.

We had a very successful luncheon Saturday at which we interested a large number of millionaires, a group of whom have now formed themselves into a finance committee. This committee meets tomorrow and we are fully confident that at last the trying efforts of these past eight months will culminate in success. We expect to have around $50,000 to carry on our work, and as soon as this is assured, I shall be needed to help. I have quite definitely decided now to sever my connection with *Every Week* and go into this larger field the moment the opportunity offers.

It has taken me some time to decide, for I felt that while the peace cause is by far the biggest work of the hour, still it was somewhat uncertain and I confess I was somewhat fearful of striking out. But now I have fully decided that I could not do other than take up the larger line of work and I am thrilled and happy over it. It may be several days before I know definitely, but as soon as I do I'll let you know. I do not know exactly yet what I shall do. There are so many things which depend entirely upon Rebecca and me and we have had hard work to decide where we can best be spared. If it were not for the pressing need in America, I would probably make a flying trip to England, for we need someone to establish lines of communication over there. The probability is that Rebecca and I will divide the office work between us so that while one is on the road, the other can keep things moving here. I cannot tell you what an immense movement this is going to be. It will be one of those things which live in history, and I am so proud and happy to be connected with it.

. . . When I outline my life in the last two days, you will realize how pressed for time I have been. I rushed to the luncheon from the office Saturday, and it was five o'clock before everyone was gone. Then we had a tea engagement with Mrs. Cram,[40] a very wealthy woman, at her club, and rushed up there. We only keep social engagements these days when it seems likely that they can be made useful to us in our work, and we try to keep friendly with all the millionaires. Mrs. Cram is much interested in the working girls, and was preparing a meeting yesterday afternoon to organize. She wanted us to help her hand out invitations as the girls came from one of the big department stores, so we did. By that time the dinner hour had passed, and I had promised to speak to an up-town audience that evening. I rushed back to the club with Mrs. Cram, seized a glass of milk and a chicken sandwich, and then Mrs. Cram took me in her car to my meeting place. It was midnight before I got home, and I tumbled into bed utterly exhausted.

Sunday morning we were roused up rather early by two Chicago attorneys who had come to discuss the Ford trip with us in connection with Mr. Ford's libel suit against the Chicago *Tribune*.[41] They were delightful fellows, and so much enjoyed the peace talk which Rebecca and I handed them that they stayed until half past one. Then we rushed out to get the first mouthful we had had a chance for, and after that I had two conferences with other people and finally spent the evening until midnight outlining and planning with Rebecca our next important moves. So you see I never have a moment even to stop and think.

I have not wired you any advice as to your plans, Mother, because I felt that that was a matter which you must decide for yourself. But it seems to me, with such inducements on every hand, that you ought to divide your time between all three places, and have a lot of fun. Why don't you visit Ellsworth[42] until after Christmas, then take a run down to Frisco until spring, and then come East early in the spring. It seems to me that that ought to offer a very pleasing program. You will have the fun sewing with Mabel and Aunt Lizzie for Christmas, and by the time you are ready to visit Lena and Lew they will be settled and you will not encounter the moving mess. It seems to me that the most delightful thing would be for you just to visit until next fall, and by that time things may have so developed that we shall all be settled together again. I could manage this program financially, without any difficulty.

Don't worry about me, Mother, for I am standing up splendidly under the strain. I shall see that I do not have any breakdown. It is so sad I think about Inez Boissevain.[43] She was a real power and it seems too bad that she should have been cut off in her youth.

I will try to send you a paper containing a front page account of our luncheon Saturday. It is quite a triumph to be able to get on the front page of the biggest newspaper in the United States.[44]

There is so much I would like to tell you, but I really must rush to my work. Miss Lewis has been giving me more and more responsibility until I know she will be pretty sorry to have me go. I have not mentioned it to any of them yet. . . .

Love to everybody and much for Mother from her baby

Lella Faye

To Loretta Secor

Every Week
95 MADISON AVENUE
NEW YORK

December 1916

Dear Mother,

I have thought of you so much since last Friday, and prayed that you might have a safe and wonderful voyage down to sunny California.[45] I have been waiting for several days, hoping Lew would send me a wire announcing your safe arrival so that I would be relieved of anxiety. I am sure you must be in California by this time. It just occurred to me now that I might send you a letter in care of Lew's office in San Francisco. . . .

It is a good thing I guess that I have been so frightfully busy during the past days, for I have not found much time to worry. But the uncertainty about your move, and whether you were happy to go, coupled with the strain under which I have been working lately, has pretty well worn me out. I have not been able to sleep at night, which seldom happens to me. However, as soon as things are a little more settled, I think I shall be quite myself again. I was weighed today, and topped the scales at 118 so you see I am about my usual weight.

I have made a momentous decision since I last wrote to you. I am tonight leaving my place at *Every Week,* and taking up definite work in the peace movement. It is in a measure a leap in the dark, because I do not know what the future holds for me. But having the convictions that I do, I could not do otherwise than take the opportunity. I will have $50 a week, and will carry a tremendous weight of responsibility as publicity manager and executive secretary of our constantly growing committee. You will learn much more about us in California, for the state is wonderfully well organized, under the leadership of Prof. Arthur U. Pope, a splendid young fellow who is professor of philosophy in the university. We met him when he came East this summer to go on the visit to the president. I hope you and Lena will have a chance to meet him, and that you will both do everything in your power to help him in the tremendous work he is doing out there. We have had a good deal of publicity lately, and our work has even been discussed in the English newspapers so that we feel we are getting on. Of course we shall receive much criticism and much ridicule—every big movement starts that way. But I neither fear nor mind it.

Mr. Barton and Miss Lewis feel very badly about my leaving the office, and both have been almost extravagant in their appreciation of my work. Mr. Barton said that with my ability and experience, I could get an editorial position in New York any day I wanted to. And so I really do not fear for my material future at all. But I have a feeling that the step I am taking now is but one nearer to that goal of internationalism toward which I am striving, and in which I hope someday to be a person of weight and influence.

Rebecca called me on the telephone this morning to say that a labor leader in Jamestown had wired for an *ABLE* speaker for the evening of December 24, and that she had wired them at once that I would go. There is to be a large labor gathering. I am feeling the weight of that a good deal at this moment, but perhaps I can "get away with it." Jamestown is over near Buffalo, and I was anticipating rather a lonely Christmas, alone in a strange city. But the most delightful thing has happened unless something intervenes. I was telling Anne about it and she cried, "Come to Rochester." That is where her mother lives, and she and Hiram are going home for the holidays. When we got back to the office, we looked at the map and found the two cities far removed, but in looking up railroad connections, I find I have to pass through Rochester, which is only about six hours' ride from Jamestown. So it is possible that I can take a night train or an early morning one from Jamestown, and get into Rochester in time for Christmas dinner. . . .

As soon as I know your address, I will send you a little money to start your Christmas things. I had no idea that December had arrived.

I have a new dress—a bright green crepe de chine which is really quite pretty. I was down to the last shred. Anne also sold me a beautiful dark blue skirt and a little velvet blouse, which she could no longer wear because she is too fat, for $5. So I shall be quite comfortably fixed. This sort of life requires so many more clothes. The little blue frock which I got this summer is practically worn out, I have worn it so steadily.

I am going to have dinner with Anne, and then for the first time in weeks I am going to indulge in a bit of relaxation, for tomorrow I shall have to begin on another strenuous job.

Anne has come. Love . . . from your baby daughter.

Lella Faye.

To Loretta Secor

WESTERN UNION
TELEGRAM

JAMESTOWN NY
DEC 24 [1916]

MRS L E SECOR
1815 SHORT ST BERKELEY CAL
XMAS GREETINGS AM SPENDING XMAS EVE IN JAMESTOWN EXPECT BE ROCHESTER TOMORROW SHALL THINK OF YOU ALL TOO BUSY PREPARING GREAT NEW YEARS EVE DEMONSTRATION[46] TO EVEN WRITE CARD PROSPECT FOR PEACE BRIGHTER THAN EVER BEFORE LOVE TO CHILDREN LENA LEW MUCH FOR MOTHER FROM HER DAUGHTER

LELLA FAYE

To Lida Hamm

WESTERN UNION
TELEGRAM

JAMESTOWN NY
DEC 24 [1916]

MRS LIDA HAMM
158 GROVE ST BAT CREEK MICH
XMAS GREETINGS TO ALL LOVED ONES AM SPENDING CHRISTMAS EVE AT JAMESTOWN EXPECT TO BE ROCHESTER TOMORROW HAVE NOT WRITTEN EVEN CARD SO BUSY PREPARING GREAT NEW YEARS EVE DEMONSTRATION AM SPENDING ALL STRENGTH TO MAKE XMAS BRIGHT WITH HOPE FOR MEN IN TRENCHES PROSPECT FOR PEACE SEEMS ENCOURAGING LOVE

LELLA FAYE

To Loretta Secor

AMERICAN NEUTRAL CONFERENCE COMMITTEE
70 FIFTH AVENUE
NEW YORK

January 5, 1917

Dear Mother:

I am so sorry that I have had to neglect you for such a long time when I know you look forward so much to my letters. . . . It sounds like exaggeration to say that I have been working every night until midnight for days and days but it is quite true. I thought that after the New Year's Eve celebration we would have more time but these days, when events are happening so rapidly, there is no rest for those who are giving themselves body and soul in an effort to bring about peace.

I do hope you are not worrying about me. I am really feeling much better. I have been able to get the offices pretty well organized. Now that the strain of the New Year's Eve demonstration is over I shall not be carrying quite such a heavy mental load. Miss Balch and Rebecca have been insistent that I take a week for a rest and I did for a time consider going to the Sanitarium just to make a business of building up a bit, but now that I am feeling so much better I think I will postpone it until I can better be spared.

When Dr. Kellogg was in Washington this fall he urged me to come to the Sanitarium whenever I wanted to, so I think the first opportunity I have I shall just go over for a couple of weeks to have a complete rest. However, there is now no occasion for worry on your part. You must know that I am feeling pretty well or I would not be able to stand the strain of my work.

I am so sorry I was not able to get my check to you sooner. I had fully intended sending you money for Christmas shopping and it was simply press of time that kept me from doing it. I do hope you will enjoy spending it and I am especially anxious to have you use it for your own pleasure.

I was delighted with the little gifts you sent. I had so many pretty things, not one of which I have yet acknowledged. Except for your check and a little check for Ina, I did not attempt to buy a single gift. Ina sent me such a dear little lavender blouse and Mabel a wonderful white embroidered collar and cuff set. . . . From Lida came a dear little jeweled purse and a lovely handkerchief, while Laura sent silk hose. In addition there were a dozen dear little remembrances from my new friends including an exquisite basket of fruits and bonbons from Mr. Huebsch.

I finally went to Jamestown to keep my lecture engagement but my train was six hours late so that I missed my audience.[47] However, I had a fine rest on the train and overnight in Jamestown, so that it was well worth while. I spent most of Christmas day on the train and dropped off at Rochester at four o'clock to have dinner with Anne and Hiram.

The New Year's Eve demonstration was a fine success. The work of our Committee is really growing to tremendous proportions. I do not think anyone will be able to estimate just how large an influence we have had on public affairs during the last few months. . . .

I cannot tell you how sad it makes me to know that all of the family feel as they do about preparedness. Of course I know that I shall speedily be able to convince them if ever I have an opportunity. At all events, you and I see the light and we shall try to do our part. I hope that you will seriously undertake to be of help there in California, even though Lena does not feel inclined to lend herself in this way.

I am glad that you find the climate there agreeable and that you are less discontented than in the beginning.

I hope that this year will be filled with much happiness for you. . . .

With much love,
From your little daughter,
Lella Faye.

. . . I'm sending our latest pamphlets.

[Prof.] Pope is arranging a big peace mass meeting [in Berkeley] in the middle of January. Be sure to go!

To Loretta Secor from Dorothea Ziegel

AMERICAN NEUTRAL CONFERENCE COMMITTEE
70 FIFTH AVENUE
NEW YORK

January 16, 1917

My dear Mrs. Secor,

Miss Secor has requested that I write you this little note, to let you know that she is well but very busy. Such a great mass of work has accumulated during these busy days, that it is very difficult for Miss Secor to handle it all. She is feeling much better now, and will write that long promised letter, in a very few days.

Very truly yours,
Dorothea Ziegel
Secretary to Miss Secor

To Loretta Secor

AMERICAN NEUTRAL CONFERENCE COMMITTEE
70 FIFTH AVENUE
NEW YORK

January 18, 1917

Dear Mother:

I am not going to eat or sleep, or do anything else ever again until I write to you. I wonder if it comforts you any to know that I am thinking of you many many times every day even when I do not have an opportunity to write. This work, to which I have devoted my soul, has swallowed me up, and I sometimes fear I shall never see beyond it until after this awful war has stopped. For several days I have not read the papers at all. Quite often I just have to stop for a while, in order to keep my balance at all. When I see before me on the printed page the accounts of the frightful madness, the horrible, the futile, the inexcusable carnage which men are engaged in, I can neither eat nor sleep. Nothing in my life before has so burned itself into my soul.

I was so happy to receive your good letter this morning, and to know that you are feeling better. I too am much better, but I do not suppose I shall gain very much as long as I am working so hard. Today I had such a charming letter from Dr. Kellogg inviting me to come to the Sanitarium for two or three weeks. I do not see how I can get away to go now, but perhaps I shall a little later. I shall have to take the advice somewhat of Miss Balch, who wants to pay my railroad expenses. I had thought I could keep up until after the war is over, but no one knows how long that will be. You may be sure, Mother, that I shall come to see you when you are in Battle Creek, whether I go to the Sanitarium now or not. I am planning already on the wonderful time I will have this summer with you.

I had such a lovely dream about you the other night. I seemed to be in California, for the place was strange to me, and everywhere flowers were blooming. I seemed just to have arrived, and inquired eagerly for you. Lena said you were in the hammock sleeping. I ran around the house to a side veranda, and there you were, sound asleep. I kissed you, and you woke up smiling, and as pink and fresh as a baby, from your nap.

I do hope you have seen a doctor or that you will take your treatments, or whatever precaution seems necessary to get yourself in better health. I only wish that the chance to be at the Sanitarium could be transferred to you.

We are planning now a great mass meeting in New York. I have Bryan on the string, and think I shall be able to close a date with him for the middle of February.[48] Then we shall start a tour of speakers across the continent to touch at all the big cities. We are also beginning a whirlwind campaign to get petitions signed in New York.

Yesterday I had a meeting with the heads of settlement houses, and lined up a lot of volunteer workers.[49] Tomorrow we are to have a little tea for some of the university students, in order to get them lined up.

We have a new chairman, George Foster Peabody,[50] who is one of the most charming men I have ever met in all my life. He lives at Saratoga Springs, and is not always in New York. Every time he comes to the city he has Miss Balch, Rebecca and me to dinner at his hotel. Your little daughter has gotten to be quite worldly-wise, Mother. The prospect of eating at a magnificent hotel doesn't excite me at all any more. I wash off a little office grime and trot along. When I think of the magnificent feasts I have attended, and of the elite company in which I have traveled, I can hardly believe that this is any of me. But all the feasting has been secondary to the work at hand, and usually at the luncheons or dinners I have been so keenly alive to the issue which Rebecca and I wanted to force through, that I have not been able to eat any of the fine food. Clothes and food and everything else, even friends, have become secondary to this one great passion.

I have been going out very little indeed of late because I have been working night after night. Each week I determine to take some relaxation, but the next week things pile up again so that I cannot. I have met a young Englishman who came over recently.[51] He is a Cambridge man, and came to this country to study industrial fatigue. He smuggled though the censors two remarkable pamphlets.[52] I am not certain that I have ever sent these to you. I'll try to have my secretary do that tomorrow. I have found him somewhat interesting, although the only time we have spent together has been at dinner. He drops in whenever he comes to New York, and we usually have a feast together at some nice place.

I asked my secretary to write you a little note early this week, because I hadn't a moment to write myself, and I didn't want you to be worrying about me. I have such a competent little secretary. I hardly know how I should get along without her. . . .

I am sending you a clipping of a little story a reporter wrote about me at Jamestown. It is frightfully extravagant in its commendation, but perhaps you will enjoy it. . . . Rebecca and I do not generally appear in the open—at least so far as names are concerned. Few people get into the New York newspapers except those who have big reputations, or commit a murder. We do not expect fame or anything else out of our efforts, except the consciousness that we have done a big thing. I think I may say without being accused of egotism, however, that we have accomplished a tremendous thing, and that many people here in New York recognize the fact. We have been able to build up this very strong committee which now has an international reputation. It has brought us into contact with some of the big people of the world, and that has been so broadening and so very much worth while.

Now I must stop and hurry on, for I have an article to write tonight which I have been promising for days and days. I want you to spend the money I sent you entirely on yourself. I love the little gifts you sent, and they are quite as acceptable as though they were worth many dollars.

I know you must be enjoying the lovely weather there. New York has not been as disagreeable as I had expected. But there is still plenty of chance. We have not begun to have as much snow yet as we had last year after I got back from Europe. A year ago today we were lying at anchor off the coast of Falmouth, England. It all seems like a dream to me now. I had such a wonderful letter from Christian Sorensen yesterday. He, too, was so filled with remembrances of the trip that he could hardly write. . . .

Rebecca has just come in all thrilled with an interview she had with the Baroness de Sidlitz and some charming young French people. Rebecca and I often smile as we realize that sometimes we have to play second fiddle when in reality the whole orchestra depends on us. They are friends of Mr. Peabody, and he had invited Miss Balch, who is, to be sure, a distinguished professor, and very wise as well as very delightful and sweet and simple, to meet them. But we had wired to Miss Balch that she must stay in Philadelphia to attend a big mass meeting there, so that she was not in town and Mr. Peabody invited Rebecca as substitute. They talked about the wonderful young people's movement which is really the thing for which Rebecca and I have been planning these many months, and which will be the big thing of our lives. The Baroness and her friends are to be our guests some evening next week, together with a dozen other young radicals. We have just been debating whether we should ask Mrs. Villard to open her exquisite town house, or whether we should invite them to our own simple little apartment, where there have been held so many memorable little gatherings. I rather fancy that on this occasion we shall go to Mrs. Villard's, for we love her so much and she is such a delightful hostess. . . .

. . . I WILL try not to neglect you so again, but if you do not hear from me, you will know it is only because I am giving my heart and my soul to my work.

Much love . . . for my Mother from her baby daughter

Lella Faye.

Philip Florence, the "young Englishman" who had entered Lella's life and whom she was to marry before the year was out, was actually an American, born in Nutley, New Jersey, to an English mother and an American father. His father had died when Philip was two years old and his mother had then returned to England with her two children.

Educated at Rugby and Cambridge, where he studied economics, Philip was primarily interested in industrial research and had worked for the Lloyd George government on its "Health of Munitions Workers" committee. He was in America to complete work for a Ph.D. at Columbia University, for which he had been awarded the Garth Fellowship, and was soon to begin work with the U.S. Public Health Service, doing research on fatigue in industry.

He and Lella were introduced by Caroline Cumming, New York representative of the British Union for Democratic Control. Philip was "knocked for six" by Lella's bright blue eyes and flaming hair, but she was businesslike and rather cool to his overtures of friendship. During the next weeks, however, while he established himself at Furnald Hall, Columbia, he telephoned her often and bought her late dinners at Greenwich Village restaurants.

To Loretta Secor from Dorothea Ziegel

AMERICAN NEUTRAL CONFERENCE COMMITTEE
70 FIFTH AVENUE
NEW YORK

January 31, 1917

My dear Mrs. Secor,

Miss Secor has requested that I write to you again, as she really has no time at the present to do anything but attend to the great mass meeting which we have under way. We expect to have a mass meeting at which Mr. William Jennings Bryan will be the chief speaker this Friday night.

Miss Secor is well and very busy and truly will write at her first opportunity.

Very sincerely yours,
Dorothea Ziegel
Secretary to Miss Secor

William Jennings Bryan had resigned as Secretary of State after the 1915 sinking of the Lusitania *because he believed the President's strong protest to Germany might lead the United States into war. Bryan was much in demand as a pacifist speaker and Lella was proud to have secured him for the key oration at the February 2 mass meeting.*[53] *In a stirring peroration he declared: "If any nation ever attacks this nation . . . I believe we ought to fight until the last man is dead, but I am not willing that one single mother's son shall be carried across an ocean three thousand miles wide to march under the banner of any European monarch, or die on European soil, in the settlement of European quarrels."*

As Lella reported, "The enthusiasm reached such a pitch of excitement that the audience rushed the platform to shake his hand, and poor Mr. Bryan was hurried off under police escort just as the platform began to collapse. The collection amounted to less than half the sum we had anticipated, but it was useful to have had that lesson early on in our experience. Thereafter we [would take] the greatest care to see that anyone helping to take the collection at meetings had credentials above reproach."[54]

There was a reception for Bryan at the Ritz-Carlton Hotel later in the evening. High city and state officials had been invited and at least some of them came.

To Loretta Secor from Dorothea Ziegel

AMERICAN NEUTRAL CONFERENCE COMMITTEE
70 FIFTH AVENUE
NEW YORK

February 6, 1917

My dear Mrs. Secor,

Miss Secor has again requested me to write you with the promise that she will write real soon herself.

Of course, considering the events which have occurred within the last few days, you can just about imagine how rushed she is. Our Madison Square meeting was a splendid success, as you have probably read in the papers. Just now we are arranging successive meetings to take place in New York City and Miss Secor is just overwhelmed with work. Considering the strain that she is working under she is feeling very well.

Very truly yours,
Dorothea Ziegel
Secretary to Miss Secor

Lella was jubilant. If all these well-known Americans wanted peace, how could the country go to war? But on February 6 the United States broke off diplomatic relations with Germany after German submarines had sunk a number of American merchant vessels without warning.

Lella had kept a luncheon engagement with Philip Florence that day. She told him breathlessly that she had no time to eat but must go back to the office to stop the war. She and Rebecca hastily summoned their executive committee; to their surprise most of its members resigned, saying they must back their country right or wrong.

The two young women were now more determined than ever to keep America out of war. Through their efforts, the American Neutral Conference Committee was reborn as a militant peace organization christened the Emergency Peace Federation. For the next two months, as Lella remembered it, the "E.P.F." was in

> *. . . the centre of the picture as the militant leader of the anti-war forces. We managed to get a few more rooms in the same building to cope with our increasing volume of work. During those hectic weeks I seldom slept more than four hours a night. Once or twice I didn't leave the office at all—just worked through a 36-hour shift. We had a loyal band of supporters who often helped half the night and then turned up at their jobs the next morning. The loyalty, enthusiasm, and devotion of those workers created an atmosphere which cannot be described. I have never lived through such a vivid and buoyant emotional experience. The work was exacting and exhausting, yet one never felt tired.*
>
> *We had continuously to make quick and important decisions. The newspaper men were constantly at our door—what was our view of the latest step in Washington, and what were we going to do about it? We began to subscribe to a newspaper cutting agency, but this became rather a white elephant, for we had to pay for another small room to house the great sacks full of cuttings which we seldom found the time to read. . . . Letters and telegrams were sent to congressmen by*

KEEP OUT OF WAR MEETING

Carnegie Hall, February 5, 1917

THE RESOLUTIONS TO BE PROPOSED

In view of the expressed desire on the part of both groups of warring nations to retain the friendship of the United States.

And in view of the fact that the losses suffered by this country through the war are not wilfully inflicted upon us, but result from the ruthlessness inherent in warfare.

This mass meeting at Carnegie Hall solemnly protests against America entering this war with the immeasurably greater loss involved in blood and treasure, protests against the proposal to send abroad American soldiers pledged by oath to the prosecution of alien quarrels; and protests against the proposed conscription of the youth of America and against all other encroachment on our traditional rights and liberties, and this meeting enjoins Congress which has exclusive power to declare war, to submit this declaration by referendum to the people who alone bear its burdens.

This meeting is unwilling that America should abandon her great stand against the conventional dogmas that shame governments into precipitate war and thereby surrender her truly patriotic task of leadership in the cause of the world's peace.

If you are in sympathy with the above resolutions please write your name and address in the space below and hand slip to an usher. We need your co-operation

Other mass meetings were held after the successful February 2 demonstration.

> *the thousands. But the militarists were gradually sweeping the country into acceptance of war. . . .*[55]

Philip Florence's studies at Columbia were not to begin until the fall semester. He worked closely with Lella in the E.P.F. between January and June 1917, when his job with the U.S. Public Health Service began.

After the Madison Square Garden mass meeting Lella planned an anti-war demonstration to be held in Washington on February 12 under the auspices of the Emergency Peace Federation. Jane Addams wired that she would organize a Chicago contingent and delegations were expected from a number of other cities. It was hoped that Bryan would be principal speaker.

In the end Bryan did not join the delegation, but Mrs. Henry Villard, Mrs. May Wright Sewall, and Dr. John Harvey Kellogg did. The gathering impressed a reporter for the New York Evening Mail, *who wrote on February 14:*

> *I think a certain young woman named Rebecca Shelly stirred up her congressman to a consideration of whether "democracy," so frequently and glibly quoted, is compatible with compulsory military service. In fact, little Miss Shelly woke things up in a good many directions. I doubt if Washington, D.C., ever saw quite as much energy concentrated in so small a compass as that represented in the 98-pound person of Rebecca, field secretary of the Emergency Peace Federation.*
>
> *If Miss Shelly has a rival in dynamic force and propulsive power it is her orange-haired associate worker, Lella Faye Secor, who in the brief space of four days shook together this Emergency Peace Federation and arranged its Lincoln's birthday visit to the capital.*

To Loretta Secor from Dorothea Ziegel

EMERGENCY PEACE FEDERATION
70 FIFTH AVENUE
NEW YORK

February 17, 1917

My dear Mrs. Secor,

As you will probably note our new stationery, you can judge how busy she has been, helping to organize this new organization.

Miss Secor is secretary of the Emergency Peace Federation, and with her splendid untiring efforts is helping to bring it before the public.

You probably have read of the great success we achieved at the demonstration at Washington, which I am sure was also due to Miss Secor's plans. At her first leisure moment Miss Secor will write the long promised letter.

Very truly yours,
Dorothea Ziegel
Secretary to Miss Secor

To Loretta Secor

Braewold [the country home of
Quaker friends, the Woods]
Mount Kisco, N.Y.
[February 1917]

[Fragment]

Since I last wrote to you, I have twice been to Washington, taking with me the first time a deputation of 104 people, and the second time nearly a hundred collegiates.[56] Both demonstrations were

Emergency Peace Federation

OBJECT: To defend American ideals of liberty and democracy in war time and to work for an early and lasting peace.

MEMBERSHIP: Any American citizen in sympathy with its object may become a member of the Emergency Peace Federation by signing the membership card. The membership fee is $1 per year. Inability to pay the fee is no bar to membership.

IMMEDIATE PROGRAM:

1. To defend our constitutional rights of free speech, free press, peaceful assemblage, and the right to petition the government.
2. To assert the right of the people to know and discuss the aims, scope and method of our participation in the war, and their right at any time to advocate terms of peace.
3. To oppose the adoption of any treaty, alliance or policy which would prevent the United States from making an independent decision as to when and on what terms it shall make peace.
4. To urge our government to seize every opportunity for bringing about peace negotiations and establishing international organization as a guarantee against future wars.

EXECUTIVE COMMITTEE: The governing body of the Emergency Peace Federation shall be an Executive Committee consisting of not less than eleven (11) members. It shall meet as often as occasion demands to conduct the business of the Emergency Peace Federation and to determine its policy. The Executive Committee shall be elected at the annual meeting of the Federation. Vacancies are to be filled and other officers to be appointed by the Executive Committee.

ADVISORY BOARD: The Advisory Board shall confer and advise with the Executive Committee at such times as shall be mutually determined upon.

FEDERATED ORGANIZATIONS: Groups organized for other purposes, expressing themselves in substantial sympathy with the object of the Emergency Peace Federation, shall, at their request, be admitted to affiliated membership in the Emergency Peace Federation. Representatives from such federated groups shall have representation on the Advisory Board of the Emergency Peace Federation.

BRANCH ORGANIZATIONS: Individuals are invited to organize local branches on the general plan herewith indicated, and to appoint a corresponding secretary, whose duty it shall be to remain in intimate touch with the work of the Emergency Peace Federation.

HEADQUARTERS: The administrative headquarters of this organization shall be in the city of New York and Legislative Headquarters shall be maintained in Washington, D. C.

EXECUTIVE COMMITTEE

Emily Greene Balch	Joseph Cannon
Chancellor David Starr Jordan	Prof. H. W. L. Dana
Philip Sargent Florence	Elsie Borg Goldsmith
Louis P. Lochner	Prof. Harry Overstreet
Rabbi Judah L. Magnes	Tracy D. Mygatt
Prof. Simon N. Patten	Dr. Henry Neumann
	Fannie M. Witherspoon

Secretary
Lella Faye Secor

Field Secretary
Rebecca Shelly

Treasurer
Dr. Frederick Lynch

Legislative Secretary
Elizabeth Freeman

HEADQUARTERS
70 Fifth Avenue, New York

LEGISLATIVE HEADQUARTERS
Room 648, Munsey Building, Washington, D. C.

From the Organization Plan of the Emergency Peace Federation.

MOTHERS, DAUGHTERS AND WIVES OF MEN--

Have You No Hearts? Have You No Eyes? Have You No Voice? We Are Being Rushed to the Brink of War--and

YOU DO NOT WANT WAR

On April 2nd, Congress will meet to face the question, "Shall this country be plunged into war?" The war which has already sacrificed five million lives, desolated millions of homes, orphaned many millions of children, robbed a million mothers of their sons.

Your men are to be sent into this horrible butchery—your husbands, your fathers, your sons.

We have no REAL cause for war. The provocation is great—but we have not yet exhausted all the reasonable alternatives to ruinous war:

A JOINT HIGH COMMISSION, in accordance with agreements adopted at The Hague Convention.

A CONFERENCE OF NEUTRALS.

THE DECLARATION OF LONDON, regarding the laws of naval warfare.

AN APPEAL TO THE BELLIGERENTS for a Congress to discuss a basis for permanent peace.

This the U. S. Congress has actually authorized our President to do.

$200,000

is needed to arouse them to the danger. This sum spent within next week may

KEEP AMERICA OUT OF WAR

The President and Congress are waiting to hear the voice of the people. It is not up to Congress to make war—it is up to the people. If the people are heard from there will be no war.

Money is needed to make the voice of the people throughout the land HEARD. Advertisements inserted in the leading newspapers throughout the West and Middle West will liberate the overwhelming peace sentiment there. Tens of thousands of telegrams, hundreds of thousands of letters will pour into Congress from the men and women who re-elected President Wilson because "He Kept Us Out of War."

This pitifully small sum may save countless thousands from a horrible death, save many thousands from a living death, crippled or blinded for life.

Send in what you can NOW. Don't delay. We must act at once. Send money by wire or messenger—we want to know TODAY how many papers are to be included.

Mothers. save your sons. Daughters, save your fathers. Wives and sweethearts, save your husbands and lovers. Write a message to Washington. Go to Washington, if you can, with the great peace delegation on April 2nd. Help us get that $200,000 within 12 hours. We are fighting your fight.

THE WOMAN'S COMMITTEE,
Mrs. Henry Villard, Chairman,

EMERGENCY PEACE FEDERATION

70 Fifth Avenue, New York

Telephone [illegible] 5458

Advertisement placed in New York newspapers, March 29, 1917.

wonderfully successful and made a very definite impression on Washington. We now have a representative in every congressional district in the United States and are sending out thousands of letters asking people to wire and write to Congress and the President to keep us out of war. I am not sure what the ultimate result will be, but I do feel much more hopeful now than a week ago. If we can be kept out of war now, there is some hope for the future. If we are drawn in, I see no hope for my generation or those to come for many years. I feel this thing so keenly that I have been willing even to sacrifice my beloved mother on the altar for the time being if I could help to maintain peace. . . .

I feel that I have lived years in a few days. I guess I never told you either what a triumph our Madison Square meeting was. I shall try to have my secretary send you some clippings. Of course you must always remember that the N.Y. newspapers never report peace news accurately or fairly, with the exception of the *Call,* a Socialist paper, and the *Post,* Mrs. Villard's paper.

I have so missed hearing from you, but I suppose I have no right to expect letters when I can't write them. But I have felt certain during these trying days that you would know how wholly I was giving myself to this great work which means so much to all the world, and that you would be glad. These past weeks have been rich in experience for me, and I feel years older. I have suffered much, and worked beyond all human endurance, yet I have found a supreme sort of happiness in my work—the happiness which comes from complete self-forgetfulness. I have met many splendid people who have rallied to the cause and stood splendidly by the ship. Mr. Florence, a young American who has lived all his life in England and was educated at Cambridge, has spent every day at the office, and has stayed with me innumerable times until three or four o'clock in the morning when that was necessary. Dr. [H.W.L.] Dana of Columbia, the grandson of Longfellow, has been another faithful cohort.

To Loretta Secor from Dorothea Ziegel

EMERGENCY PEACE FEDERATION
70 FIFTH AVENUE
NEW YORK

March 21, 1917

My dear Mrs. Secor,

Miss Secor has asked me to send you the enclosed money order for twenty-five dollars. It is quite impossible for her to write at the present time. Conditions are at such a critical stage and things are developing that make it necessary for Miss Secor to devote herself entirely to her work.

She is very well, however, and we have persuaded her to take a few days off, which I trust she will do in the near future. With Congress meeting the second of April it is hard to tell what she will do.

Very sincerely yours,
Dorothea Ziegel
Secretary to Miss Secor

With the demise of the American Neutral Conference Committee, Lella and Rebecca had lost their solid financial backing. Now they desperately needed funds to finance an Emergency Peace Federation convention in Washington, planned to coincide with the April 2 special meeting of Congress. According to Lella:

> *Courage was about the only thing we had left, and so with that we bought a page in the New York* Times.[57] *We wrote the advertisement ourselves. . . . We appealed for money and for help. The next morning, postmen began to struggle in with mail-bags full of letters—thousands of them. We had to dump them on the floor in a corner until we had time to open them.*

> *As soon as our office was opened, hundreds of people came in person. The corridors were clogged and the lifts jammed. We worked all day long enrolling people under our militant banner and taking their freely offered money. Dawn was breaking the next morning before we finished counting the money that had poured in that day. We had $35,000.*[58]

Lella at once hired two special trains to carry delegates to Washington. On April 2, while the entire Emergency Peace Federation membership was meeting in the Willard Hotel, Woodrow Wilson delivered his famous war message to Congress, asking America to enter the hostilities that the world "be made safe for democracy."

Back in New York, Lella hired Madison Square Garden on four days' notice for another mass rally. This time her principal speaker was Rabbi Judah L. Magnes, "with a golden voice and such powers of persuasion that women had been known to throw their jewels into his collection plate. . . ."[59] *The Garden was packed, with thousands unable to get in, so that four street meetings took place simultaneously.*

On April 6 the United States formally declared war on Germany. But the Emergency Peace Federation's efforts had not been entirely wasted, for when the war vote was taken, almost fifty members of the House of Representatives voted "no." Jeanette Rankin, the only woman in the House, whispered, "I cannot vote for war."

To Loretta Secor

WESTERN UNION
TELEGRAM

NEW YORK NY
APR 6 1917

DEAREST MOTHER LOVING WISHES ON BIRTHDAY WOULD SO LOVE BE WITH YOU FORGIVE LONG NEGLECT CRITICAL DAYS LEAVE NO TIME LETTERS DEEPLY DISAPPOINTED WAR DECLARATION BUT FEEL FIGHT WORTH WHILE SHALL KEEP UP EFFORTS TO BRING PEACE PRAY YOUR HEALTH MUCH BETTER EXPECT LETTER AND GIFT SOON DEEPEST LOVE

LELLA

To Laura Kelley and Lida Hamm

EMERGENCY PEACE FEDERATION
70 FIFTH AVENUE
NEW YORK

April 13, 1917

Dearest Sisters and all:

I hardly know how to begin this letter after my long neglect of you. These past months have been such critical and strenuous ones that I have not been able to write to anyone, even to Mother. . . .

I want to thank you all first . . . for the dear Christmas gifts which you sent. Christmas this year and in fact the past four or five months have seemed like a dream to me. I have been devoting myself soul and body to this great cause which has enlisted my complete devotion; everything else has been set aside for its sake. . . . Perhaps I can better make you understand . . . when I see you, which I hope will be soon.

I expect to leave for Battle Creek about April 18. I am completely worn out in body and spirit after the strenuous labor of the last few months. Dr. Kellogg has invited me to spend some time at the Sanitarium, and though I should love to come directly to you I think it will be better for me to go immediately to the Sanitarium until I have gotten a little rest. I hope this announcement will not give you any cause for alarm. I am not ill at all; in fact I have stood up splendidly under almost superhuman efforts. But now I have reached the limit of my endurance and realize I must make it a definite business for a time to build up for the struggle which is ahead. I am not ill at all and there is absolutely no cause for worry. I am looking forward more than I can tell you to seeing you all. Now that I have actually decided to come I can scarcely wait. . . .

It is possible that Mother will also come within the next two weeks. She is very anxious to be in Battle Creek while I am there. . . . I have wired her to start right away if she wants to come so we shall perhaps have a little jollification together.[60]

Lovingly,
Lella Faye

When Lella left New York for the Kellogg Sanitarium her absence was keenly felt by Philip Florence. He had fallen deeply in love with her and in March had proposed, but she had put him off, saying she was too busy even to be engaged *until the war was over. In fact, marriage to anyone was not in Lella's plan. She treasured her independence, thought of the future only in terms of a career, and had absolutely no wish to enter the domestic arena.*

Lella's friend Anne Herendeen had taken up Philip's case and favored the marriage. But Lella had departed for Battle Creek still undecided.

Fate stepped in when Philip's research into industrial fatigue took him to the Ford plant in Dearborn, Michigan, close enough to Battle Creek to permit frequent visits to Lella in the Sanitarium. For the first time, they had leisure for long talks as they sat on the ve-

"To Defend American Ideals of Liberty and Democracy in War Time and to Work for an Early and Lasting Peace"

Our country is at war. Events are moving rapidly. Each day brings new threats against American liberties, new dangers to our democracy. In the heat of war, measures are being proposed which would curtail or abrogate the most fundamental of our constitutional rights. Certain elements are trying to entangle the United States in the quarrels and ambitions of Europe.

LET US REMAIN A FREE PEOPLE

The Espionage Bill was supposedly aimed against alien spies, but contains clauses which would kill free speech and muzzle the press. Meetings to protest against conscription have been and are still being suppressed. Speakers have been jailed for criticising the war, and in some cases the police have stopped the sale of peace literature. A campaign of threats and "frightfulness" is conducted in the press against those who refuse to bind their consciences.

SHALL WE ADOPT CONSCRIPTION?

If this were a people's war there would be no need to talk conscription. If free Americans are failing to rally to the cause, may the fault lie not in their loyalty but in the cause itself? Is it American, is it democratic, to force the plain people to fight the war on which they had no opportunity for consent or opposition?

The Canadian Parliament refused to adopt conscription. In Australia conscription for European service was submitted to a referendum vote of the people and overwhelmingly defeated. Shall the United States send a conscript army to the battlefields of Europe when the British Colonies send none but volunteers?

NO SECRET DIPLOMACY

Secret diplomacy in Europe is admitted to be one of the chief causes of the war. The American nation does not want to be blindfolded. We have the right to know and fully discuss the terms of any agreements or policies discussed between our government and the representatives of the allied powers. It is our duty to demand complete publicity in all our foreign dealings. No secret diplomacy, no secret treaties, no secret agreements.

From an Emergency Peace Federation flyer written after the war declaration of April 2, 1917.

LET AMERICA CONTROL HER OWN FOREIGN POLICY

Let America control her own foreign policy. Each of the Entente Allies has bound itself to make no peace until the war aims of all shall be satisfied. The Sherman Resolution, just introduced in the Senate, would "bind the United States not to make a separate peace with the German Government—nor with any of the Allies of the German Government." It demands that no peace be concluded save by the "joint action of the United States and the governments with which it wages war against Germany, and any other governments which may be joined with Germany as an ally, either now or hereafter."

This would make it absolutely mandatory that America continue the war even though Germany abandon her submarine warfare. It would mean that our American boys must die on European battlefields in order to secure Albania, Dalmatia and the Greek Islands for Italy, or to win for Great Britain Mesopotamia, or to acquire new Asiatic possessions for Japan.

Shall we sacrifice the flower of American youth to serve the imperial ambitions of Europe?

WHAT THE EMERGENCY PEACE FEDERATION DOES

The Emergency Peace Federation maintains a strong legislative committee in Washington which examines and reports especially dangerous war bills. It demanded and secured public hearings on the Espionage Bill, which exposed its pernicious features. At this writing it is watching sharply to prevent any clauses being slipped in which would endanger free speech.

The Emergency Peace Federation also induced the Committee on Military Affairs to hear opponents of conscription in executive session. By letters, telegrams and newspaper publicity it is organizing the vast though inarticulate opposition to conscription. It is sending out hundreds of letters warning against the dangers of binding ourselves to continue the war until the ten Allies agree on terms of peace.

PREPARE FOR PEACE

An immense mailing list is also being built up. The Federation is trying to get in touch with all persons and organizations who will courageously stand with us when the psychological moment comes for a strong, concerted demand for peace negotiations.

The war fever caught the peace forces unprepared. The Emergency Peace Federation is determined thoroughly to equip itself, organize and PREPARE FOR PEACE.

STAND WITH US!

randa or strolled through the grounds. Philip was intrigued by Lella's Midwestern background and she was similarly fascinated by tales of his British boyhood. After a month's rest at the Sanitarium, she was pronounced fit.

On May 22, Philip proposed again and this time Lella accepted him. The two spent a few days visiting Lella's family in Battle Creek; then they traveled to Long Branch, New Jersey, where Philip had taken a house near the beach for the whole summer. Rebecca Shelly and another friend, Joseph Cohen, would make up a foursome and share the rent. Philip had hired a housekeeper, Miss Bridget Ward, who would also act as a chaperone, for the proprieties were strictly observed by the four young people.

Lella eagerly resumed her work for peace. The Emergency Peace Federation continued with new goals: "to defend American ideals of Liberty and Democracy in Wartime, and to work for an early and enduring peace." Meanwhile Rebecca Shelly and Louis P. Lochner had launched a new organization, the People's Council of America, headed by Rabbi Magnes with Lochner as executive secretary. Lella was employed as organizing secretary: her function was to try to enlist liberals throughout the United States in the group whose object was "an immediate, general and democratic peace, and . . . world reconstruction on democratic principles."

Membership in the "P.C." grew rapidly, and Lella and Rebecca soon found it taking much of their time. On June 29, the E.P.F. membership voted to merge its organization with the People's Council, which shared its goals.

Philip's summer letters to Loretta Secor, whom he had met in Michigan, suggest how seriously he took the campaign to build up Lella's health:

> *Please do not worry about Lella. . . . I am doing all I know to lead her back to civilized meal-times. . . . The air down here is certainly doing her good and she is usually able to stay the whole day* [*in Long Branch*]*, dictating letters, once or twice in the week. . . .*
>
> *It is quite true that she is busy—some busy, you might say. When she gets home all I can do is to push food down her*

mouth and put her to bed. In return she wakes me up next morning, but MUCH too early. Then she disappears to the city while I make the best of it by the sea. Sometimes I go off on a personal visit to my factory[61] *and stay two or three days and then it's Lella's turn to see me home.*

. . . I make her give a full account of her meals every time I have to go away and sometimes I have to be severe; but very often she is found to have been quite reasonable and to have eaten almost as much as a normal human being should!

She is sleeping very very much better and is not nearly so worried by her work. Our housekeeper, Miss Ward, is an absolute wonder and does all our mending and laundry as well as tidying. . . .

We really must keep on Miss Ward to look after us when married, as I won't have Lella bothered with domestic duties on top of all her work. . . . She is not even to choose her own clothes. I see to that. . . .[62]

The People's Council of America was by far the most radical group Lella had ever been involved with. In one Council publication, Tract, *Dr. Magnes exhorted his readers to "stand shoulder to shoulder with the Russian people," and a full-page announcement very much in Lella's style appealed to the "Mothers of America." "A dollar now may mean years of joy and comfort with your boy at your side. . . . In Russia the workers are leading the way. . . ."*

Louis P. Lochner had conceived the idea of holding a huge People's Council convention in some Midwestern city, with delegates coming by train from all over America. Much of the organization of this grandiose scheme fell to Lella. Letters were written to affiliated groups, tentative schedules were drawn up, and—most important of all—queries were sent to the mayors of several large cities requesting permission to converge there. Eventually, the meeting was fixed for September first in Minneapolis, Minnesota, and Lella arranged for a special train to carry the New York contingent.

To Loretta Secor

[Late August] 1917

Dear Mother,

This is Sunday afternoon. I have just had dinner after spending the morning in bed. I came home for the first time in a week last night but it was after midnight when I got back from the city. I have never experienced more strenuous times, but I am keeping up splendidly. I am taking a special train from New York to Minneapolis. It leaves N.Y. Thursday at 2:30 p.m. We arrive in Minneapolis at 7 a.m. Saturday. My plan now is to return to B[attle] C[reek] the last of the following week, so that I shall probably be with you two weeks from today. Does it seem possible? I shall probably not be able to stay long, but I do so want to spend a little time with you. It all depends on the developments at Minn[eapolis]. If I go on with the organizing work, I shall have to get back to N.Y. soon so as to get things under way. Philip and I have tried to plan someway so that we could be married in B.C. but I'm afraid we can't manage it. He will be very busy with his work in Detroit for several weeks after we return from Minn., and I shall have to spend some time in the office again before I can get away. We are both tired, and feel the need of just running away for a couple of weeks when we are married. We shall probably be married some time late in October. . . . Then we shall go up to the Adirondacks or to some country place for a couple of weeks before settling in the city for the winter.

Philip made me a gift yesterday of five hundred dollars which is to be used—as much as need be—for my clothes. Considering the fact that I have only one dress and absolutely nothing else, I guess it will take a good deal to fit me out. And for once, I'm going to make a good beginning and have nice things.

I shall want you and the girls to help me buy a good deal—linens, bedding, etc. as well as some underwear. However, I shall not let you try to do much sewing because I don't want you to be tied down. I'm going to send you some money in this letter. It is for you, but if you want to use it to buy some materials for me, you may, and I'll send more later in the week. . . . I'd like to have three or four crepe de chine nighties, and I thought you might make these for me. Can you? Perhaps you can buy the material before I come; then we can decide on pattern, etc. when I arrive. I want one lavender, one light green, one bright yellow and one cream color. I'd like the colors as bright as possible.

I think if you do these and some linens, and help me buy loads of other things, you will be quite busy enough. I think I'll have a woman in N.Y. make me a couple of combination suits or else buy some. She's going to make a dress for me too, but I fear I'll have to buy one ready made in order to be presentable at Minn. I only wish I had weeks to spend in shopping, but I'm afraid it will all have to be very hurried.

None of us knows what is going to happen in Minn. There are vague rumors that we are to be suppressed, arrested, and otherwise persecuted, and it would not be surprising. However, there will be many exaggerated newspaper accounts and I do not want you to worry, whatever you hear. If anything *should* happen—and I doubt it very much—I'll wire you. . . .

Much love to all but most for Mother from her baby,

Lella Faye

Philip sends his too.

Thursday—I've waited all week about mailing this to get a money order and now I'll just slip in a bill. This money is entirely for you. Anne wanted so much to do something so I let her buy the material for nighties. I'm bringing it with me. Rushed to madness with special train which leaves 2:30 this p.m. Minn. gov[ernor] keeps us out of state; N[orth] D[akota] gov. invites us to Fargo. Much love.

On August 30 the special train carrying New York delegates to the People's Council convention set off, ultimate destination still unknown. "We didn't know where we were going, and the delegates traveling from the far West didn't know where they were going to

Mothers of America

We Need Your Help and YOU Need OURS

The President said in his Flag Day speech:
"We are about to bid; . . . it may be millions of our men—the young, the strong, the capable men of the nation—to die . . . on fields of blood far away."
This may mean that your boy, brother, sweetheart, husband, may soon be added to the

SEVEN MILLION DEAD

lying in unmarked graves on the bloody fields of Europe. It will be too late to bring your loved ones back if you neglect this **call for** immediate action.

Put aside any ideas you may have of who is right or who is wrong. General Grant said no war was ever fought where the dispute could not have been settled by other means. ***We want***

TO SUBSTITUTE *THINKING* FOR KILLING

We Need $50,000

We want all readers of FACTS to respond. We want their financial help. We want them to carry our message to the MOTHERS OF AMERICA whose boys will do the fighting, the bleeding, the dying.

Claude Kitchin says: "This is a rich man's war and a poor man's fight."

The Men Who Make Wars Do Not Go To The Trenches

They are TALKING! And, REMEMBER, it is the MONEY THAT TALKS. "Money Talk"—commercial interests—helped **to make the war.** AND NOW—YOUR money—a little here, a little there, MUST BE COMBINED to spread the program of the PEOPLE'S COUNCIL OF AMERICA for an early GENERAL and democratic peace.

IN RUSSIA THE WORKERS ARE LEADING THE WAY

The Russian Council of Workmen and Soldiers' Delegates, fresh from the bloody trenches and the busy mills—men who have bled and sweated in a war which was not of their will or their making—these men are demanding

AN EARLY GENERAL AND DEMOCRATIC PEACE; FREE DEVELOPMENT FOR ALL NATIONALITIES; INTERNATIONAL COOPERATION TO MAINTAIN PEACE; THE END OF MILITARISM; SAFEGUARDS FOR LABOR STANDARDS

To All of This Programme the PEOPLE'S COUNCIL OF AMERICA is Unqualifiedly Committed

with the addition that

We Urge Our Government to State Concretely Upon What Terms It Is Willing to Make Peace

THE PEOPLE'S COUNCIL OF AMERICA

is to be a great body of delegates sent from the masses all over the country—farmers, laborers, industrial workers, Socialists, single taxers, teachers, Churchmen—any and all who are ready to concentrate their forces for *Democracy and Peace.*

The People's Council will be the mouthpiece through which the voice of the people will be expressed, as the voice of the Russian people through the Council of Workmen's and Soldiers' Delegates.

The first session of the PEOPLE'S COUNCIL OF AMERICA will be held August 4, the fourth anniversary of the commencement of this bloody, futile war.

Before this day we MUST raise $50,000. We must have the moral and financial support of individuals and organizations.

We have no endowment, no special source of income. We depend on the MOTHERS OF AMERICA TO HELP SAVE THEIR BOYS FOR BETTER THINGS THAN WAR.

A dollar NOW may mean years of joy and comfort with your boy at your side instead of mourning his death on a foreign battlefield. A few dollars may help some mother less fortunate in worldly possessions to keep her boy at home and alive.

WE MUST HAVE MONEY AT ONCE

There is no time to lose. Organization and advertising cost money. We need both. Our plans are held up this very minute **for lack of funds.**

The Organizing Committee

PEOPLE'S COUNCIL OF AMERICA

For Democracy and Peace

No. 2 West 13th Street, Corner Fifth Avenue

Officers and Committee:

James J. Bagley
Emily G. Balch
Joseph D. Cannon
Mary Ware Dennett
Crystal Eastman

Morris Hillquit
Lindley M. Keasbey
Daniel Kiefer
Algernon Lee
Judah L. Magnes

James H. Maurer
Howard Mellish
Benjamin Schlesinger
Gilbert E. Roe

Treasurer: David Starr Jordan

Secretaries:

Louis P. Lochner, Executive
Lella Faye Secor, Organizing
Rebecca Shelly, Financial
Elisabeth Freeman, Legislative

DAVID STARR JORDAN, Treasurer,
2 West 13th St., New York.

I am in sympathy with the aims of the PEOPLE'S COUNCIL COMMITTEE OF AMERICA for Democracy and Peace. Enroll me as a constituent. I send herewith $ .... for the support of the Council.

NAME ....

ADDRESS ....

STATE ....

WHEN ANSWERING PLEASE MENTION "FACTS"

A magazine advertisement for The People's Council.

meet us. . . . We tried to keep in touch with our agents by wire as we went on.

"Occasionally the train would stop, the engine driver would come to us very puzzled and sympathetic. 'Well, where do you want to go now?' It was difficult sometimes to answer that question."[63] *The press dubbed the train "the rabbit special," after its tendency to "freeze" between bursts of movement.*

In contrast with the glorious days of the Emergency Peace Federation when peace still seemed possible, the country was now at war and the People's Council was regarded with hostility and suspicion. The farther west they traveled, the more war hysteria they encountered. Several of their advance agents had been threatened; one of them had been escorted out of town at gunpoint.

To Loretta Secor

WESTERN UNION
TELEGRAM

CHICAGO ILL
AUG 31 [1917]

SPENDING NIGHT IN CHICAGO PLANS UNCERTAIN FOR TOMORROW MAY GO MILWAUKEE OR MINNEAPOLIS PHILIP HERE TOO DONT WORRY EVERYTHING WELL WITH US MUCH LOVE FROM US BOTH GET CHICAGO NEWSPAPERS

LELLA

On the morning of September first, they started out again. A convention site still had not been secured. The governor of Min-

nesota barred delegates from his state. In Wisconsin the Council members were accused of being pro-German and sent away. Finally the train turned back to Chicago whose mayor, Big Bill Thompson, was said to be sympathetic to their undertaking.

Lella's room in the Fort Dearborn Hotel in Chicago quickly became convention headquarters. "Soon the corridors were jammed with people each asking the other what we were to do. . . . Finally, we got a hall and hastily organized the People's Council of America [Convention]. . . ."[64] But the governor of Illinois, deeming their activities disloyal, announced he was sending state police to break up the meeting. According to Lella, "We never did, or intended to do anything unconstitutional . . . but the organisation was too young and confused to stand the heavy strain imposed upon it both from the police and federal authorities outside, and from timid people inside who were frightened of going to jail for their principles. . . . The People's Council never did any effective work after the Chicago debacle."[65]

While worried delegates scurried to catch the next train home, Lella and Philip went to Battle Creek for a visit with her mother and sisters.

To Loretta Secor

N.Y.
September 1917

Dear Mother and All—

I am sitting in Anne's gay little apartment on a wonderful, cool Tuesday morning. I haven't yet been to the office, or to Long Branch either. But I have rested wonderfully, and feel more like my old self this morning than I have for years.[66]

Rebecca met me at the station yesterday morning, and we went to our former room in New York to have a long talk. We went over the whole situation in detail, and as a result of our talk I have about determined to give up my work for the present. I am sure you will be glad of this. Of course, I am not absolutely certain yet that this is the best thing to do, but I have felt so supremely happy since I arrived even at this state of thought that I cannot help feeling it is the wise thing to do. I feel like a squeezed lemon. For two years I have been giving continuously and lavishly of myself, and I honestly feel that I shall not be of much service to the cause until I have had an opportunity to renew myself in body and spirit.

I am bitterly disappointed in the Council. I doubt very much whether it can now accomplish even a fraction of the good which I had hoped would come from it, for it is in the hands of selfish and reactionary people. To work with them would mean constant friction and unpleasantness, and I am in no condition to undertake such a strain, especially in view of my approaching marriage. If it is a truly great movement, as I had hoped, it cannot depend upon any one or any dozen individuals. It will go on of its own momentum. If on the other hand it cannot stand alone, then it is not worth slaving for any more. I have the same fervid devotion to the cause of peace and democracy that I have had before, but I think I can make a greater contribution through writing, speaking, and developing new ideas than I can through routine organization work.

Philip and I have had almost no opportunity to talk this matter over. . . . But he has wanted me to take several months in which to read and study and renew my energies, and I am now convinced—though this is quite different from my original plans—that the most propitious time for this is the present. There will be many stirring needs within the next year, when fresh minds and steady nerves will be needed, and I shall be able to accomplish much more then, and contribute much more to the cause.

Rebecca may or may not remain as financial secretary. . . . She too is seriously in need of a rest and of a new spiritual vision, but she will have to decide for herself. *Every Week* has an opening for me, but I shall make no decision on any point until Philip returns. It is probable that we will be married sooner than we expected—perhaps within a week or so. We shall be able to decide this when he returns the last of this week.

As for me, in spite of my bitter disappointment in the People's Council, I cannot help feeling that a colossal responsibility has rolled off my shoulders. I did not realize until yesterday how heavy the burden has been. I only wish I had been able to see Rebecca and go over the entire situation in the light of more recent events,[67] before I left Michigan, for I should then have been able to remain [in Battle Creek] during this week. But I shall be coming back again another time, and it is perhaps better for me to be here and get a great many things off my hands which have been hanging over my head for months.

. . . Anne insists that she is having all the sensations of one whose long dead friend has suddenly risen from the grave. I have indeed been buried in my work to the utter exclusion of everything else.

I am already feeling so rested that I can hardly wait to begin my studies.[68] I have never had such a wonderful opportunity before, and I want to make the very most of it. It would be wonderful enough to be able to study for a few months, but to have one's studies directed and supervised by a Cambridge instructor who is at the same time one's own dear Boy, is quite too wonderful for belief.

After I had my talk with Rebecca, I came directly to Anne's little apartment, and I have camped here continually since. Freddie came up to see me as soon as he knew that I was in town. We both took Rebecca out and tried to buy her a hat, but we gave it up as a hopeless task. Anne and Hiram joined Freddie and me at dinner, and afterward we went to a silly little show just to celebrate my emancipation. I was so grateful to them, for I miss Philip frightfully when he is not here. He will not be back until Saturday morning, which seems an eternity away. . . .

Everyone admires my new clothes tremendously. Freddie quite went into raptures over the green dress, and everyone "falls" immediately when he sees the belt and bag. My brown dress is not yet finished. . . . I'll try to give you a true description as soon as I see it myself. It is to be mailed to me tomorrow.

I am so glad that I had the chance to spend those few days at home. They have meant so much to me, and our little shopping tour together will always remain as such a jolly memory—a sort of link between my strenuous work-filled days and the new life into which I am about to enter. My only regret is that I did not know the full situation [here] as I know it now, for I should not then have been constantly tormented with the weight of things hanging over my head as I was. However, my next visit may be different.

I hear Anne coming up the stairs, and I want to get this off before lunch. My love to all the dear ones, and heaps and heaps for Mother from her

Baby Daughter.

Notes

1. Public opinion in favor of preparedness was growing, in response to pressure from militarists at home and allies abroad. Wilson, at this time, still maintained his neutral stance, but in June Congress would increase the size of the U.S. Army and several months later vote more than seven million dollars for national defense.

2. A short knitted or crocheted jacket, often sleeveless.

3. See also Lella's letter of September 14, 1916, to her sisters in Battle Creek for a further discussion of the events described here.

4. Rebecca's idea was to set up an American committee which would support a conference of neutral nations, to persuade the belligerents to end hostilities and work toward a negotiated peace.

5. Jane Addams had been named one of the original delegates to the Stockholm Neutral Conference but could not attend because of ill health. She had agreed to serve as vice-chairman of the newly organized American Neutral Conference Committee.

6. George Kirchwey was Dean Emeritus of Columbia Law School; Stephen S. Wise, a liberal Jewish leader and rabbi of New York's Free Synagogue.

7. The 1916 Democratic Presidential Convention was held in St. Louis.

8. Secretary of War Newton D. Baker.

9. Lola Maverick Lloyd, delegate to the Hague conference and Peace Ship official.

10. Lella was now an associate editor at *Every Week*.

11. Where she had been visiting Anne Herendeen.

12. Bertha K. Baker, member of the executive committee of the American Neutral Conference Committee.

13. A family friend.

14. The British had intercepted a message from Germany to Mexico, offering to help Mexico regain land lost to the United States in the Mexican War if an alliance could be formed. The offer was rejected, and the United States was able to step back from the brink—at least for the time being.

15. The Neutral Conference in Europe was still looking to Ford for guidance. On his instructions the five delegates per nation were reduced to two, and the sessions were transferred to The Hague.

16. Chautauqua, in central New York, held annual summer series of lectures, concerts, and plays.

17. Lella was devoting her evenings to work for the American Neutral Conference Committee, using her *Every Week* office and typewriter for the purpose.

18. See illustration on p. 91.

19. Oregon, Washington, California, Montana, Idaho, Nevada, Utah, Arizona, Wyoming, Colorado, and Kansas allowed women to vote in presidential elections. The state of Washington had given women full suffrage in 1910.

20. The country was on the verge of a great railway strike with unions threatening a walkout if denied an eight-hour day.

21. Mary Woolley was president of Mount Holyoke College; David Starr Jordan, chancellor emeritus of Stanford University.

22. Hamilton Holt was chairman of the American Neutral Conference Committee.

23. The New York *Times* of August 31, 1916, reported this meeting, but Wilson's words to the committee were not quoted in the story.

24. The school had actually been run by Isadora Duncan's sister Elizabeth.

25. At the conference in Stockholm, Mme. Schwimmer's autocratic manner and taste for intrigue had not gone down well with the Americans. Her power had been curtailed by Ford's representatives and she had finally resigned to form her own organization, the International Committee for Immediate Mediation. The American branch, in which Lella was involved, held only two meetings.

26. Lella and Rebecca had moved to a small apartment at 66 West 9th Street in Greenwich Village.

27. John Howard Whitehouse, Liberal Member of Parliament from 1910 to 1918.

28. Mrs. Catt was president of the International Woman Suffrage Alliance; her "Winning Plan" was an important factor in gaining women the vote in 1920.

29. Charles Evans Hughes was the Republican candidate for President.

30. The Cases were moving to San Francisco.

31. The Rappahannock River is in Virginia. Perhaps she meant the Ramapo, which is in northern New Jersey.

32. Lella's high opinion of Dr. Aked had altered since the Ford Peace Ship days.

33. Popular American journalist.

34. In the Easter Rebellion of 1916, members of the Sinn Féin had tried to free southern Ireland from British rule. Many of their leaders were shot by British soldiers.

35. Lella refers to an earlier family home. Loretta Secor enforced a rigid code of behavior even upon her grown-up daughters.

36. A flash of bad temper. There is no reason why Lella would have *had* to replace linens and silver in the Bellevue house.

37. Loretta Secor must have written that Rebecca's job sounded like a "snap," i.e., easy.

38. Pacifist Senator Robert LaFollette of Wisconsin

39. Using the campaign slogan, "He Kept Us Out of War," Wilson's Democratic party won by a small margin.

40. Mrs. J. Sergeant Cram.

41. Ford, who had abandoned his pacifist position and was turning his industrial might toward the manufacture of war matériel, was suing the *Tribune* for publishing inaccurate and libelous reports of his pacifist activities. (See Appendix C.)

42. Lella's half-brother, who lived in Spokane with his wife, Mabel.

43. Inez Milholland Boissevain, lawyer and suffragist, had recently died at the age of thirty.

44. The New York *Times*.

45. Loretta Secor had finally left Bellevue, by ship, to visit her daughter Lena Case and family in Berkeley, California.

46. Emily Greene Balch was organizing a large peace rally in Washington Square for New Year's Eve.

47. See Appendix B.

48. William Jennings Bryan, Wilson's former Secretary of State, was a strong believer in neutral arbitration and was using his considerable influence to keep the United States from entering the war.

49. To serve as ushers at the mass meeting. The Socialist newspaper *Call* (February 2, 1917) ran a notice asking for "Socialist girls who want to assist in the collection. . . ."

50. Banker and philanthropist.

51. Philip Sargant Florence.

52. *Why Must the War Go On?* by Arthur Ponsonby, M.P., liberal diplomatist and *Peace*

This Winter: A Reply to Mr. Lloyd George by Charles Roden Buxton. An even more important document smuggled out of England that winter was an "open letter" to President Wilson from Bertrand Russell, who was to go to prison for his pacifist beliefs. It contained an urgent plea to America to act as arbitrator rather than throw her military forces into war. Lella arranged for it to be read at an American Neutral Conference Committee dinner at the Astor Hotel on December 22, 1916. "The ante-room was full of restless reporters. . . . When the famous philosopher's letter was read (his stock was very high in America) there was a grand scurry for copies. . . . The next morning every newspaper in America carried Russell's letter." Lella Secor Florence, "The Ford Peace Ship and After," in *We Did Not Fight: 1914–18 Experiences of War-Resisters,* ed. Julian Bell, London, Cobden-Sanderson, 1935:117.

53. Other speakers were George Foster Peabody, Rabbi Stephen Wise, and the Reverend Frederick Lynch.

54. Florence, "The Ford Peace Ship": 118.

55. Ibid.: 122–23.

56. On February 12 and February 22, respectively.

57. Of March 29, 1917. See illustration on pp. 134–35.

58. Florence, "The Ford Peace Ship": 119–20.

59. Ibid.: 121–22.

60. Loretta Secor did travel to Battle Creek for the long-awaited reunion with Lella.

61. Philip had a summer assignment with the U.S. Public Health Service, studying fatigue at Scovill's Brass Works in Waterbury, Connecticut, which was manufacturing shell cases in ten-hour day and twelve-hour night shifts.

62. Philip's conviction of Lella's right to pursue a career, while unencumbered with domestic duties, was to underlie decisions made throughout their married life. Philip's artist mother had always devoted herself to her work and he had grown up taking servants very much for granted.

63. Florence, "The Ford Peace Ship": 123–24.

64. Ibid.: 124.

65. Ibid.

66. Lella had traveled from Battle Creek alone; Philip was in Detroit. After Lella left, her mother wrote her, "I certainly am supremely happy to know you have picked up so fast. . . . I am sure it was the chicken that started you on your way to be well and strong, and the good molasses cake. . . . I know you were a swell looking little girl when you left me on Sunday. . . ."

67. The People's Council had run into new difficulties: the Post Office had refused to deliver its publications and local offices were being raided by the police and forced to suspend operations.

68. She had signed up for two courses at Columbia University.

IV

Marriage and Motherhood

To Loretta Secor

127 Matilda Terr.
Long Branch, N.J.
October 1, 1917

Dear Mother and All the Loved Ones,

And so they were married, and lived happy ever after—more happy than either he or she had dared to dream. But I suppose I had better begin at the beginning of this romance, though I'm not just certain where the beginning is. Philip and I decided scarcely a week in advance that we would be married on Saturday.[1] The P.C. [Peoples' Council] convention was still in progress, and lasted until Tuesday afternoon, so that there was not a moment to write.[2] Instead I telegraphed you.

Our real adventures began on Tuesday afternoon when Philip and I set off in one of those darling hansom cabs driven by some mysterious tophatted person whom one never sees at all. We made a tour of the shops, and within two hours had selected my wedding dress. (There was no time of course to have one made.) It was Philip's choice. It's a curious shade which might be brown or taupe or smoke, or half a dozen other colors. The material is soft messaline, and its only decoration is a lovely short tunic embroidered in yellow beads. It was nine o'clock before we reached Long Branch, and both of us were frightfully weary. For tne next few days we tried to rest and to crowd in as well all the preparations for our wedding.

Freddie, Rebecca and Joseph had in turn taken over the responsibility of getting us married, but finally at the eleventh hour we just went merrily off without speaking to anyone and conducted the whole affair ourselves. First we planned to be married in New York. Then we thought it would be rather nice to have our five friends, including Anne and Hiram, come to Long Branch for the service. Both Philip and I agreed that it should be just as simple as possible, and that we should have no minister who was not a pacifist and in accord with our views. We could not endure the thought of being married by a hypocrite such as most ministers are.[3] There was not a very great selection—John Haynes Holmes whom we both adore, and who is pastor of the Church of the Messiah, a Unitarian church, and Norman Thomas, a Presbyterian and a fine young fellow who has often helped me to bring some of my undertakings to a successful conclusion.[4] Then there were Dr. Lynch of the Church Peace Union; Gordon, a young minister who has been doing organizing for us; and Richard Hogue of Baltimore.

We suddenly discovered on Friday that we had neither minister, license, wedding ring, or anything that goes into the making of a marriage. Long distance revealed the fact that John Haynes Holmes was in Maine, that Dr. Lynch was unavailable, and that Gordon, as we supposed, had gone to New Hampshire. Mr. Thomas promised to come, however, and we congratulated ourselves that our wedding was as good as over when Philip discovered that one must apply for a license three days in advance in New Jersey, and then wait for it to cool twenty-four hours before using. So we scratched New Jersey from the map, and turned our attention to New York.

We decided to have a wedding at Anne's. I wrote her a hasty note telling her that a wedding was going to take place at her house at twelve-thirty. She did not receive my letter until Saturday morning, an hour or so before the time set for the event. So you see we were not actually certain ourselves until we arrived. In fact, I did not know Friday afternoon whether or not I would have any nighties or any underwear to take on my honeymoon. All our arrangements were like a fleet of kites flying hither and thither, and it was not until Friday evening that we began to gather them in.

The first to come in was the package from you, which we got from the post-office a few minutes before it closed. I found difficulty in restraining myself until I got home to open the box, and when I did finally get a peep, I danced with delight. I have never seen such adorable nighties. I really hadn't expected them to have any decorations, because the time was so short, and I was simply overwhelmed. I show them to everyone who comes near me, and there is unanimous agreement that no one ever had such charming nighties before. I wish I could see you to tell you how much I love them, and how grateful I am for all the tender stiches woven into them. I have never enjoyed any garments quite so much.[5]

After this kite had been drawn in, we went to the jewelers for the wedding rings. Both Philip and I wear one. They are very fine—so much smaller than the ordinary wedding ring that we had to have them made to order. I did a bit of hasty shopping for little odds and ends and we went back to Matilda Terrace late at night, frightfully weary but beginning to feel that our wedding was almost an assured reality. We went to New York very early the next morning.

We trudged up to the City Hall immediately to get a license. We tried very hard to look unconcerned, but evidently we did not succeed, for while we were wandering about the hall, trying to find the proper department, a saucy man walked up to us with the pert announcement, "Second floor, Municipal building." I jerked off my white gloves in an effort to look less bridey. We found a dozen or more couples ahead of us, mostly little Jews and Italians from the East Side who stood in a long line, two by two, trying to appear nonchalant or just looking silly. We rather hated to join the queue, although we both agreed that it was very democratic and quite all right. As soon as we had filled out our application, however, a man in a side window beckoned to us, and whispered that he would fix the license for us at once so that we would not have to stand in line.

Philip has certain ideas about one's duty to the State, in consequence of which we had a civil as well as a religious service. . . . I was terribly worried lest the justice should be fat and pudgy. But he wasn't. He was young and rather nice, and I could almost have forgiven him for rattling off the service from a pasteboard on which he had his notes pasted, except for the nonchalantly gay fashion in which he commanded Philip to "kiss his wife as any good husband should do."

Finally we escaped, feeling no more married than I feel at this moment, which isn't much. We decided that the proper thing for a young married couple to do was to get drunk, and we rushed up to a soda fountain where I steadied my nerves with a malted milk. Then we dropped casually into Freddie's office and announced that we were married, and that it had been so pleasant that we expected to repeat it. There was only half an hour left until our other service at Anne's, and, as neither Philip nor I had fully connected with our bridal clothes, we rushed off. Philip put on his new dark blue suit, which is astonishingly becoming, and I donned my lovely light green B.V.D.'s [underwear] which the dressmaker had also delivered to Anne's. One by one the kites were pulled in. Anne had ordered a lovely bridal bouquet of lilies and orchids. Joseph and Rebecca arrived, each announcing that he had secured a minister—Joseph had found Mr. Hogue in New York, and Rebecca had discovered that Gordon was still in the city, and eagerly waiting to perform the service. Mr. Thomas arrived, however, and being the man on the scene, was the one elected. The hour for the service arrived, and the host and hostess had not yet put in an appearance. It was also discovered that Freddie had left the second marriage license in his office. So while host, hostess and license were being gathered in together, Philip rose wonderfully to the occasion and related entertaining stories to amuse the minister. Also we went over the marriage service and eliminated most of it in advance. It was very sweet and simple when we had finished with it. Anne arrived finally, looking very happy to find herself the sudden hostess of a wedding party. She strewed some yellow crysanthemums on the mantel shelf, and Philip and I took our places before the fire-place. Just as the minister was about to begin, Anne bolted across the room and begged to be matron of honor. She hastily crammed a crysanthemum in her belt to attest her qualification for such an important post, and I accepted her at once.

Then Mr. Thomas began. I am afraid this all sounds rather flippant, and the whole affair WAS delightfully informal and unconventional. But it was nevertheless sweet and impressive. I realized then, as I had not done during the civil service, how great was the step and how full of significance. But I have never done anything more joyously or with more certain assurance of its wisdom.

Anne and Joseph had suddenly become a committee of two to arrange a luncheon at the Lafayette Hotel.[6] We had a little private room, and everything was as gay and jolly as could be. Philip and I still had some shopping to do before the boat left, however, so the party was cut short and we started off. We took [the] night boat up the Hudson River and landed at Catskill Landing early in the morning.[7] It was a crisp Autumn day, which, as it merged into the rest of the week, grew warm and mellow and sunny. A little narrow gauge train whisked us through green and crimson forests and over rocky streams until it plumped us out at the very foot of one of the Catskill peaks. Here we got into a little mountain cablecar which crawled slowly but persistently up the almost perpendicular face of the mountain. We had expected to stay at the Catskill Mountain House which is a great white hotel at the very top of this mountain, commanding a view of the entire valley below. Luckily we soon discovered that it was closed for the season, and were able to catch an outgoing railroad train by catapulting down the hillside at terrific speed. We didn't know where we were going, but we were on our honeymoon and it didn't much matter. The conductor thought Haines Falls would be a suitable place, and after we had been settled in the charming Twilight Inn nestled among the hills, we were in full accord with him.

Our wonderful stay in the mountains is a memory which will always fill my heart like a flood of warm sunshine. There was only one shadow to mar our entire stay, and that was a near-tragedy as the result of my own unbelievable stupidity. The mountain air gave me a tremendous appetite, and I ate more than I had done in weeks before. Tuesday night I felt symptoms of the gastritis with which I suffered so at the Sanitarium, and decided to follow their course of treatment.[8] I rang for hot water which wasn't very hot, and I was rather afraid to use it for fear it had not been boiled. Philip happened to have along some antiseptic tablets which the doctor had given him when he had his bad leg, and I thought it might kill the germs if I dropped one in the water. I read on the bottle that they were poison, and I [would] never have swallowed one, of course.

But like an idiot, it did not occur to me that it was quite as bad to inject poison into the intestines. I suffered frightful agony which was only relieved when my frantic husband, rushing about the hotel in his bathrobe, succeeded in getting a physician from the nearest village.

This trying experience left us both rather fagged, and the next day, instead of trying to walk as we had done on previous days, Philip got an automobile, and we rode in and out among the hills for a wonderful two hours.[9] Each day that we stayed, the sun was brighter and the air balmier, to say nothing of our accumulated happiness. We had but four short days in the mountains, and we made the most of every moment. It was the first time Philip and I had ever had an uninterrupted bit of leisure, and we agreed not to do any work or to carry into our honeymoon any responsibilities from the outside world. It gave me an opportunity to get acquainted with the most charming, tender, thoughtful and delightful person in the world. I had always thought that marriage represented a distinct change in one's life, with always the lurking possibility that one might suddenly awake to the fact that the change was not agreeable at all. Instead I have found it just a delightful continuation of a rare and beautiful comradeship. I am convinced that there are not many marriages such as ours. I suppose every bride thinks so. But my belief is based on something more than love for my husband. I have seen much of married people, and I have known much of marriage, but I have never known any union so sweet and beautiful, so spiritual and soul-satisfying as ours. I dwell in the sunshine of Philip's great soul, and my heart sings with happiness.

I cannot tell you how sorry I am that we could not arrange our wedding so as to have you all here. When we had to attend to every detail ourselves, I thought of you pretty often, and wished I were near. Especially I missed Ina so much. I am sending you all a bit of the wedding cake. We had for lunch fruit compote, creamed chicken with mushrooms, rolls, potatoes, salad, fruit punch, baked ice cream [baked Alaska?] and the fruitcake, as well as other little wafers.

I am sending you . . . a little book showing some of the things we saw on our wonderful trip down the Hudson. . . . We left the mountains early Thursday morning, coming back to the same landing at which our boat had docked on our way up. We took the day boat this time and had such a wonderful trip. . . . It is a wonderful river, full of such marvelous beauty as I did not know existed anywhere in the East.

Philip will return to Detroit a week from Monday, and will probably try to spend the weekend with you. How I wish I could come with him! But I suppose I may consider myself quite fortunate to have had two lovely visits with you already this year. Perhaps before snow flies, or at least before the winter is over, I shall be able to find some other good reason for coming again.

I expect to spend a day or so at the office clearing up some unfinished work, and then I shall feel no more responsibility toward the People's Council, for the time being, at least. I shall speak for them and help in whatever way I can. But the reactionary element has been so strong that I doubt whether much of constructive work can come from it now. Rebecca is still in doubt whether she will take up her work with them again. I think she will probably do so for the present, but I am certain that sooner or later we shall organize the young people's movement of which we have both dreamed so much.

For the present, however, I am determined to stick to my decision and not do any active work until I have had time to refurnish my mind and restore my body. I have chosen a course in history and one in psychology which I will take at [Columbia] University. Philip has a fellowship and will also work for his doctor's degree this winter. The months ahead look very wonderful to me. We shall settle somewhere in the university district, and will keep Miss Ward to do the housework so I can devote myself entirely to my work. I shall probably do a little writing, also, and we shall try to draw around us a coterie of interesting people, which will make the winter a most delightful and profitable one.[10] I shall take up some active work again within two or three months at the latest, but just now I am not worrying about what it shall be, or when I will do it.

Miss Ward has been so amusing. Rebecca told her before I came back that I expected to keep my own name. She was very much shocked and "made a statement." She insisted that SHE would call me Mrs. Florence, because that "was the right way." So when she welcomed us upon our return home, she greeted me with great dignity as Mrs. Florence. I laughingly told her that I would keep my own name and be Miss Secor just the same, even though I was married. But she didn't choose to hear, and has gone on very solemnly addressing me as Mrs. Florence. There is something so funny about it that both Philip and I go into spasms of suppressed laughter every time we hear her. After a consultation with Rebecca, we decided that we would either have to let the matter go or run the risk of losing Miss Ward, which was a prospect too black. So we admitted that on two scores our modern ideas had been beaten—when we registered at the hotel, and when we encountered Miss Ward. Fortunately, it isn't a matter of great import with me. Philip feels it more keenly than I do, I believe. What I insist upon is keeping my own individuality, and retaining my own name—smirched (though it be) with pacifism—will help to do it.

I expect next week to look for houses in New York, and if I find something desirable I will probably try to get moved while Philip is away. I am anxious now to get settled for the winter so that I can take up my work seriously.

I had a telegram of congratulations and love from Lew. I haven't heard anything from Ina. I wired to both Lew and Ina as soon as we knew definitely what day the wedding was going to take place.

And now about your own winter, Mother. If you do not feel that you can winter in Michigan, I think you had better spend the next few months in California. It would be quite essential I think for you to pay Ellsworth a visit on your way back, for they felt so hurt about your neglecting them when you came East. I think you ought to visit Ina also, but I would not favor your staying there this winter. It would be far too lonely, and besides, I am going to urge Ina to close up the house for the present, and take rooms in the city this winter. . . . I have laid aside some of the $500 which Philip gave me, to pay your expenses back West if you want to go. I am depending on the remainder to apply on our obligations and to cover running expenses until I am working again. In the meantime, I hope very much that Ina will find work for several reasons. I think she would be happier to be independent again, and interesting work would help to draw her out of herself, a thing which she so much needs. . . .

. . . I don't mind a notice being put in the B[attle] C[reek] papers. We have kept it out of the New York sheets, both because we hate the publicity and because I was afraid it might injure Philip's prospects if it were known that he had married one whose name has been so constantly associated with anti-war propaganda. . . . I suppose it might interest some of the old Battle Creek friends who will not learn of our marriage otherwise.

Boundless love to all,
Lella

P.S. I found the yellow nightie here when I got home. It is charming! I conclude one after another that each is the most wonderful.

To Lena and Llewelyn Case

127 Matilda Terrace
Long Branch, N.J.
Saturday, October 6 [1917]

Dear Lena and Lew and the Darling Kiddies,

And lo, after many months of soul-trying labor, there came unto her a period of rest and leisure. And in the midst thereof, she sat down and began to remember all those whom she had loved in past years. And behold, there appeared unto her a woman who was called Lena; and with her her husband whose name was Lew. And they were led by the hand by two little children who were called Mary and Esther. And the scribe looked upon the man and the woman, and upon the little children who led them by the hand, and said, "These have I greatly loved and long neglected. Behold, in the first hours of my new Happiness I will commune with them." And as it was written, it was done. . . . Selah!

. . . I feel much like a Rip Van Winkle who has just returned to earth after a long sleep, except that my sleep during the past two years has been disturbed by pretty lively dreams. I hardly know where to begin, but I suppose you are most anxious to hear about my wedding and my dear Man. So I'll pass over all of my activities—about which Mother may have kept you slightly posted—

except to say that the past two years have been a season of wonderful growth and development for me. I feel that I have lived ten years since I left Seattle. Week by week, more of interest has been crowded into my life than normally comes in six months. I have given up my active work in the peace field for the present, though this was not contemplated in our original plans, and I shall take up active work again sometime in the near future. . . .

And now to come to Philip. . . . I reckon it will be enough for me to say that he is quite the most adorable person in the world, which means that he is all and much more than I had expected any man to be. Also I hadn't dreamed how radiantly happy one could be as the wife of such a man as Philip. I had always supposed I would feel hesitant and fearful finally about getting married. But I have never done anything more joyously or more willingly.

Our lives have been so utterly different up to this point that we bring a rich store of experiences to each other. Philip's life has been spent mainly in schools. . . . He has a wonderful Mother—an artist—who has brought him up free from restraint or tyranny of any sort—in striking contrast to our own experiences. I'm beginning to learn, under his guidance, that life is made for play as well as work and that one must have plenty of relaxation if one is really to enjoy the fullest development. You know how unyielding a slave driver I have been for myself, and how hard it has always been for me to allow myself any time for pleasure.

The winter which lies ahead of me now promises greater delight than any I have ever known before. We shall live in New York in the university district. I shall do much reading besides my studying and shall also write a little. In addition, we hope to draw about us a coterie of interesting friends, some of whom we already know—Dr. Harry Dana, grandson of Longfellow, who was one of my admirers; Lola LaFollette, daughter of the senator; Mrs. Henry Villard; and others whose names have often appeared in connection with the work I have been doing. Also, there are always coming and going in New York delightful foreigners like Norman Angell of England, who is here now; Henri La Fontaine of Belgium, etc. I am looking forward with happiness to entertaining these people. It is what I have always yearned to do and never had the chance to do before.

I cannot think of anything more perfect than those brief days of our honeymoon. Every day was balmier than the one before, and the whole experience was one which will linger in our memory forever as a golden epoch. Philip had to get out a report, so we had to make our stay short. But our honeymoon has been continued since at Long Branch. Philip has worked four or five hours a day and we have played the rest of the time. Tomorrow he goes to Detroit for a week, and the week following he will spend in Washington. I shall be a widow early. But I'm starting my work at Columbia, writing a million letters, hunting houses, moving and doing a thousand other things, so I shall be kept busy. Please do write. I shall be a better correspondent now. Much love.

Lella

In October Philip and Lella left Long Branch for New York, and Philip began his Ph.D. studies at Columbia University.

To Loretta Secor

[October 1917]

Dear Mother,

We are in the throes of moving! Also I'm helping to organize a Hillquit mass meeting![11] That is why this must be a hasty note written on the train. Philip leaves New York for Detroit Wednesday night. He expects to run in at Battle Creek just long enough to give you a greeting. He will reach you Saturday night at eight or nine o'clock and will be able to stay until Sunday noon. Not long, to be sure, but long enough to give you a load o' love from us both.

After Thursday we shall live at 418 W. 118th Street, N.Y. We have finally chosen a furnished apartment—one of the first that I looked at—because I got so desperately tired I couldn't look any more. I've been having another [swollen] gland—on the neck—and have come to the definite conclusion that I can't stand as much as I used to. I'm going to make every effort this winter to get strong again.

. . . Please take good care of my *dear dear* Boy.

Much love to all,
Lella Faye

On December 15 Philip wrote Lella's mother: "Now that Lella is writing fairly regularly, I hope she is telling you all the news. However she is probably not *telling you how much better she is getting on under the injections and her rest from work. Her weight is now 122 lbs. (with clothes) which is 10 lbs. more than at Long Branch and we hope to raise it much more yet. Also she has* got *to eat regularly now and can always lie down and sleep when she feels like it. Altogether I have great hopes that she will quite recover from the terrible life she led as journalist and pacifist!"*

To Loretta Secor

LAUREL-IN-THE-PINES
LAKEWOOD, NEW JERSEY

January 3, 1918

Dear Mother,

We have just come in from a day of skating and I've dropped into this lovely hotel to dash off this note to you. Philip has gone up to our old rooming place to see if there is any mail. It has been bitterly cold ever since we came, but today it's just bearable outside—cold but sunny. We first stayed at the Palmer House, then moved to Cody Cottage where we stayed last spring when we came for a week-end. But it was so bitterly cold . . . that we couldn't endure it and so moved to the Waldorf Cottage, Lexington and Third Street, where we are delightfully cozy. Philip bought me a pair of

English sport shoes this morning and a pair of skates. A few weeks ago he got me a gay yellow sweater and tam-o'-shanter. So I'm wonderfully fixed for the first time in my life with a complete sporting outfit. It is so wonderful to have these things, and to be the wife of a man who is constantly thoughtful of my comfort. We are *such* congenial companions, and are so supremely happy. Sometimes I am dazed with the great joy that has come to me.

I am feeling better than I have for years . . . I have completed my treatment with Dr. Neumann and have reached 125 lbs.—the most I have ever weighed.

I have thought so much of you during this cold weather—I hope so much that it isn't as cold in B.C. as it has been here. In N.Y. there is terrible suffering. Some of the great office buildings and hotels have closed for lack of coal, and 75 schools. The people are rioting and in readiness for a revolution. We just got a letter from Joe saying the gas was frozen and that my maid Helen had not shown up for four days.[12] I suppose I shall find things in a pretty mess when I get back. Phil has just come so I must cut this short for now. He is so eager to have every hour of my time while we are having this outing, and I am only too glad to give it to him.

Lovingly,
Lella

Lella and Rebecca Shelly now began the work of launching a new movement, The Young Democracy, founded on their longstanding dream of an international organization of young liberals. Its aims, along with universal peace, would be freedom of thought and speech both in and out of universities, and "economic democracy" for all people. More immediately, it would strive to abolish universal military training and to protect the rights of conscientious objectors.

An executive committee was formed, offices were rented, and two paid officials were soon hired: secretary Ray Newton and publicity director Devere Allen. Philip Florence was named chairman of a committee on industrial democracy and Lella "international chairman."

To Loretta Secor

418 West 118th,
New York
[February 3, 1918]

Dear Mother,

. . . I fully intended to write yesterday, but I felt so miserable all day that I did not get up to stay until just in time for dinner. It is the first day that I have felt wretched all day, but I suppose one must expect that occasionally.[13]

I am bothered a great deal with gas, which is quite as likely to become troublesome in the middle of the day or at night as in the morning. It makes it hard for me to eat, and yet I seem to need a good deal of food. I mean that I find myself empty much sooner than usual. I don't know whether that's the fault of little Philipino or not. We expect to select a good doctor next week, who will be able to advise me from time to time.

I was so happy to get your letter, and to know that you were all so pleased about our baby. . . .

I think I have been postponing mentioning the contents of that package, because I do not know where to find words to express my appreciation. I have never seen anything so beautiful as that luncheon set, but it makes me shudder when I think of the hours and hours of work [it took]. The package arrived just as we were having dinner and quite upset our meal. . . . I shall never want to use them for fear that I should not be able to launder them successfully. . . . Please do thank all those who have helped make these beautiful things for me. . . .

Philip and I are making weekly tours into surrounding parts in search of a place to live this summer. Last Sunday we went to Long Beach [New York] and were caught in a frightful hurricane. We got the next train back and decided that we didn't want to live there at any rate. . . . The problem is so much greater here in New York than anywhere else in the world, for the rich have grabbed every available spot until there is nothing left for the rest of us. Yesterday we went to Lake Mahopac [New Jersey] up in the hills. . . . We found one charming bungalow a mile from the station, facing the lake. It is $400 for the season and we cannot pay more than $200. However, it is possible that Anne and Hiram may take half of it, which would cut the expenses all the way around. We really want very much to be alone this summer, but sometimes it seems just hopeless for everything is so high. I do not feel that we could afford to keep a maid if we were alone, and yet I do not want to be tied down with housework all summer, and Philip objects to this arrangement even more than I. It is going to be a wonderful chance for me to read and study and write, and I certainly want to embrace the opportunity. Lake Mahopac is an hour and three quarters from New York, and it may be that we cannot get anyone who will come out every day. It is quite the nicest spot we have found so far, but I suppose we will just have to keep on looking. . . .

Philip and I would like to have you come to us the first week in April. . . . Let me know right away whether these plans are agreeable to you. I think you should plan your summer carefully, so as to be in the coolest place in the hottest weather. You ought not to take the cross-continent trip in the heat of the summer. Try to map out your visits as nearly as possible, and let me know also how much money you have on hand, and how much you will need. . . . I want you to come early here, so as to have as much time as possible, for we have to get out of this house the first of June and heaven knows where we will go from here. . . . I think the next two months will be about the best time for you to see New York.

I am so glad that you are feeling better. I am sure a few bright days when you could get out would work wonders. . . .

Much love to all,

Lella

To Loretta Secor

[New York]
April 4, 1918

Dear Mother,

I'm so sorry not to have written you before but I have been quite desperately ill and am only able now to be propped up slightly in bed. My naughty young son in his process of building seems to have thrown off more poisons than his mother could take care of. Quite unexpectedly and without warning, I began to vomit violently and continued it all day with only the briefest intervals. The doctor was afraid my kidneys were causing the trouble and could do nothing to relieve me until he examined the urine. Within the hour we sent a specimen to his office, and by evening he reported that there was no serious complication there. By midnight I was in a pretty bad state, which he finally relieved with a generous hypodermic of morphine. He planned to take me to the hospital the following day, for he feared I would lose my baby either through poisoning or through the terrific straining. But I was much better the next morning, and today was able to retain a little slab of toast and some orange juice—the first mouthful I've taken in more than two days.

I have placed myself in the hands of Dr. Bishop. He is a young chap with wide experience and an excellent record—a specialist in obstetrics. I have every confidence in him, and it is a great relief to have decided upon a doctor to whom to turn whenever I'm perplexed. He is full of sympathy and understanding, and I shall follow his suggestions carefully. He is sure we will have no serious difficulties in future.

But enough about me. When are you coming? It is clear that we can't expect you Saturday as we first planned. But I think you had better come sometime next week. If you'd rather do your other visiting first, of course you are perfectly free to arrange your plans that way. But you must remember that every week you delay now is just a week cut off from your visit with me. Already it is getting uncomfortably hot in [New York], though showers yesterday and today have cooled the air considerably. It seemed to me that two months was a short visit at best. . . . Philip and I have taken a four-room summer cottage in Connecticut, and plan to board with the lady next door. I shall do the bit of work needed to keep the cottage tidy, but otherwise I shan't carry many responsibilities. It is clear that I shall not be able to depend on myself much during these coming months. The cottage is about 3 miles from the city of South Norwalk, which can be reached by trolley—about ten minutes' walk from the house. It is about 1½ hours from N.Y. by train, and the few times it will be necessary, I shall come in to consult my doctor. I can send him urine specimens by mail every week or so, and this is the most important thing I guess. He says that if I'm in good condition June 1st I'll likely get along without any untoward happenings during the summer.

. . . Please write or telegraph the time when you will leave B.C. so I shall know exactly when to expect you in N.Y. I expect to be up and around again within a few days. . . .

I'm afraid I'm too weary to write more. Philip and I join in love and in happy wishes for your birthday.

Lovingly,
Lella Faye

P.S. I'm sometimes afraid you won't be able to stand N.Y. We live in a "quiet" neighborhood but the shouts of peddlars, the screams of children and the rattle of carts and cars have nearly driven me wild. Today, Philip has closed the windows sometimes to try to shut out the racket.

Loretta Secor visited Lella and Philip in New York in the late spring of 1918. Lella, who felt miserable during the first months of her pregnancy, welcomed her mother's company. The two women began working on a layette for the expected baby, while Philip sat studying on the fire escape in the sun.

After her mother returned to Battle Creek, Lella and Philip moved to "Rose Cottage," Bell Island, South Norwalk, Connecticut, which they had rented for the summer.

To Loretta Secor

Rose Cottage
Bell Island
South Norwalk, Conn.
[June] 1918

Dear Mother,

Philip has just rushed off to the post office to mail a part of his proofs which we have been working on for two days.[14] There is still much to be done, so I'm snatching this little time while he is gone for a hurried letter to you.

It is a week ago today since we went to New York for Philip's doctorate. . . . I thought the exercises at Columbia were particularly dull and stupid. I was inspired by the crowds of fine young people, but the old bellicose profs with their bald heads and antiquated ideas interested me not at all. My Own Boy was lovely in his cap and gown. I can be justly proud of him for I know of no one who has a doctor's degree at his age.

The exercises consisted of Butler's[15] (the impossible president) address, which he closed with the "academic" exhortation, "Be brave for the enemy is at our gates!" followed by various department heads who related that so many had donned the uniform, etc. The climax came when one woman prof told *how many bandages* her students had wound. The whole thing became pitifully ridiculous. But there was good music which helped some!

The rector of Trinity Church, a little shrimp of a man whose Creator ought to be ashamed of him, prayed for the destruction of every foe, etc. I prayed neck and neck with him that we might have "peace without victory" and that the enemy might be forgiven. It's hard to tell, of course, which one of us God will listen to. I yearned for an ammonia gun or a pea shooter. I had no murder in my heart—the poor wretch was too insignificant for that—but I should like to have mussed him up considerably!

After all these unedifying ceremonies, we all marched out and I spent a precious half hour looking for My Boy among the crowds on the campus. When I found him, he promptly doffed cap and gown and took me to lunch. Afterward I went to the doctor's. He didn't make an examination, considering that it was still too early. He listened for my baby's heartbeats but couldn't hear any and I'm to go back in a month.

In the meantime I'm feeling very well and working hard, though I've been suffering a good deal with backache. Philip and I have both been less vigorous than usual, and I feared he might be going to have a bilious attack. The change of diet to one consisting very largely of meat—we have now protested and are getting more vegetables—has been bad for us both. I have gotten the effects in a bad abcess under the arm which has pulled me down a little. But it is getting on hopefully. This, and a broken tooth which happened today, constitute our list of calamities. . . .

We are going to Bridgeport Friday to see about a piano. In S[outh] Norwalk they want $54 for the season which is quite too much. We may buy just a cheap one in case we can find one. However, we're feeling rather poor just now, and shall go slow for a time.

I went to S. Norwalk the other day and we bought a hammock which is strung on the front porch (when it's *not* raining) and I also got green cloth for a smock. [I] have it cut out and sewed up, but as usual it's not finished.

We launched our boat the other day and had a delightful row, but it began to leak so we put back to port. We have caulked and painted it but the rain has kept us from setting out again. It is a lovely craft—lighter than we thought at first—and we shall have great times. This is such a wonderful place and we are *so* happy. It is the first time we have ever been alone.

There are scores of the most interesting land and water birds and thousands of wildflowers, all of which we shall study with the aid of our little books. This afternoon, we rested ourselves with a little walk which led us through lovely woodsy lanes and past a cinema colony, where they will soon be taking moving pictures. It will be interesting to watch them.

Beginning next Sunday, I'm going to try to get breakfast at home and possibly some of our lunches, in order to give us the fruit and vegetables we need. If I find the lunches too irksome, I'll give those up for we are getting fairly good food at the boarding house now, and the arrangement is really ideal.

I have a woman every other week to wash and iron, and I do the little housework that is needed in our four tiny rooms. Philip is delighted with the transformation I have effected in the living room which is really quite cozy now. I've put up a couple of shelves for books, daubed a bit of paint here and there, shifted the furniture, and behold, as cozy a place as you could wish. We shall live a great deal on the veranda when the weather settles. I miss the bathroom most of all. . . .

We are looking for Rebecca and Freddie as soon as the weather clears. She is at a N.Y. hotel as his guest and they have told us of their engagement, specifying, however, that it was confidential, so you must say nothing about it. I don't know when they expect to be married, but I suppose the sooner the quicker![16]

It is just eight o'clock and the sun is going down behind the tree-tops and turning the water into opalescent beauty. Only fancy having trees and grass and a lovely sheet of water at one's very door. I realized only today that we are living in historic New England. . . .

Lovingly,
Lella

To Loretta Secor

Bell Isle
Rose Cottage
July 13, 1918

Dear Mother,

You have quite the laziest daughter in the world. For two days now I have not wanted to do anything but sleep—ten hours at night, two or three by day. Something seems to have gone a bit wrong with my tummy, and I have taken to the sleep cure. I feel better today, and hope I shall be able to keep awake tomorrow.

I went to the city last week to see the doctor, only to find that he had left . . . on his vacation ten minutes before I arrived. So I shall have to go in again next Monday and will probably stay over until Tuesday with Anne, as Philip will be in Waterbury those days, and I have a good many errands to do. I am especially anxious to ask the doctor about my precious bites. We are not bothered with mosquitoes, so I think it must be gnats or chiggers, or something. They attack one area after another, until my legs from ankles to waist are a mass of swellings and inflammation. After a bit, the bites spread into each other until there is one huge spot, larger than my hand, almost purple in color and tender to the touch. They itch night and day until I have almost been driven crazy. A few spots appeared today on my breast, and I am getting rather worried. Do you think it could have anything to do with my baby?

Philipino is behaving himself very well indeed in the main. He is so lively that he hardly gives me a moment's rest, night or day. The other evening, he rapped on the wall of his house so loudly that Philip heard it across the room. It was amazing to us. Is that the usual procedure? And may we conclude that he is probably going to be a Billy Sunday or a Theodore Roosevelt?

Thank you so much for sending the *Reflectors*.[17] I read them with much amusement. I fear we would find it pretty difficult to live in Bellevue now with patriotism of the worst kind simply running away with the place. I can imagine what a howler Mrs. Rodgers is—one of the non-thinkers.

I had a letter from Ina yesterday. She says she feels better than she has felt in her whole life before, and is very happy in her work. . . . I am so relieved to feel that Ina has at last found herself again, and is getting on her feet. I have so long worried about her, but I rather feel now, judging from the tone of her letters, that we may rest contented, knowing that she is getting along nicely. She was going to make my baby basket with all the fittings for me, and was disappointed to know that I had already purchased one. But I think I shall suggest that she make something which will not take so much time, for I know how busy she is.

I am so anxious to see the little things you have been finishing. I have not washed any of the things yet, for I am still somewhat respectable to look at and thought I would wait until my tummy gave me away before hanging baby things on the line. I have not yet hemmed the diapers but I am waiting for Philip to take a holiday, for then we shall be reading together, and I can sew while he reads without wasting extra time.

I have been expecting to send you a little money ever since you went back, but our funds have been slow in coming from England and we felt we must keep enough on hand in case of emergency.[18] Philip joins me in sending this $5 check. I know it only partly repays you for all the work you have done on our baby clothes. . . .

The Y.D. [Young Democracy] is having its troubles, and I sometimes fear it will never grow much until I am able to throw myself into the work again. Devere hasn't quite the initiative and hustle needed to push a thing of that sort through. The net of suspicion tightens around Keyes every day, but it is difficult to get proof.[19] We finally decided to ask him to resign, but things are being held up now by a disagreement in the executive committee over some of the details. However, I hope things will soon be straightened out. We anticipate a rather nasty mess.

I hear the postman whistling now, so I must make haste, for I want to write a note to Keyes. He has never delivered the shorthand reports of the Y. D. Conference—a suspicious fact in itself.

We are having very cool weather—so cool that we cannot make it seem possible that we are nearing the middle of July. It rains almost every day, but this morning has dawned bright and sunny.

Much love to all,

Lovingly,
Lella.

To Loretta Secor

Bell Island
September, 1918

Dear Mother,

I don't know how many times I have started a letter to you since I sent that hurriedly scrawled note, but something has interfered each time to prevent its completion. Now I'm trying my machine which seems very much inclined to balk.

I am so sorry tnat you felt I was ungrateful for the dear things you have made for the baby, and also for your characteristic thoughtfulness in sending the cakes and corn. I thought you would understand that that hastily scribbled note on yellow paper was not meant as a reply to your letter or as an acknowledgment of the gifts, but rather as a makeshift to let you know how I was until I could get off a better letter.

I have been feeling pretty miserable during the past few weeks, and as my strength becomes more and more limited I have been trying more and more to get finished some of the essentials which must be done in advance of baby's coming. I have all the flannels washed and ironed, but I must now mark them all as you suggested. I have completed the arrangements at the hospital. I shall be at Dr. Lloyd's Sanitarium, Corner of 151st Street and St. Nicholas Place. I find that they do not wash the baby's things but that I must depend upon someone outside. I shall, therefore, not take any of the little white petticoats, or the lovely little best dress which you sent . . . and I shall keep careful account to see that everything is returned.

Philip and I spent Monday and Tuesday in N.Y. I had an examination by my doctor who seems to think that everything is quite normal, except that he marvels at my size when I still have six weeks to wait. He assures me that I'm not going to have twins. I think it's going to be a little girl, for it lies high up on the right side. I suffer a good deal of pain, especially in one spot where the pressure seems to be continuous and severe. Also I have great difficulty to digest my food, and I cannot sleep at night. But on the whole I am getting on famously, and I think I have no cause for worry at all. Needless to say, I shall be glad when it is over.

We shall leave here probably on October 14th, and, unless the baby comes too soon, I shall still have three weeks in New York to get the house settled. I also closed the deal for our house while in New York, and I am enthusiastic about the possibilities. We are to have the entire third floor at 104 West 13th street, and the lady is going to let me use so many pieces of furniture that we will have to buy very little. Also, we had a letter from our young friends in Mexico[20] yesterday, and they offered to sell us or let us use their furniture which is in storage. They have practically everything we shall need, so that the expense of fitting up the place is going to be very slight. It seems to me that we are unusually fortunate. Yesterday I bought nearly $10 worth of kitchen things—brooms, ironing board, etc. Everything is very high now.

I had such a dear letter from Philip's mother yesterday and another from Joseph this morning.[21] Mother Florence wants to buy the crib for us, so we shall be able to get a very nice one. but I do not think I will buy the crib or the buggy until after I get back from the hospital. I have the house furnishings mostly planned out, and as soon as the place is finished, I'll take pictures of all the rooms so you can see just how we are living. . . .

Friday morning

I seem doomed never to finish this letter, which was started day before yesterday. . . . I find my machine is frozen up so it won't work, and my pen is dry. Hence in desperation, the pencil.

It is so cold here that we have about decided to go to the city earlier than we expected. I am beginning to feel that the baby might come almost any time. . . .

This morning we are jammed into our little kitchen in order to have the oil stove lighted. Philip insists it has assumed the aspect of a real shack—partly packed trunks piled in one corner, dirty dishes massed on the table, letter writing, shaving, and whatnot going on simultaneously. I'm trying to get packed little by little but I have almost no strength. Yesterday Philip packed one box of books, and I almost finished one trunk. But you know how long the process takes. I had another wretched sleepless night last night. I have despaired of feeling very well until the baby comes, which at best will not be long now. . . .

I cannot tell you how lovely I think the dear little dress with all its patient handwork. I supposed that was to be the very best one and so I was surprised to know that you're making still another with embroidery on it. I do hope you will not confine yourself to sewing when you might be enjoying yourself otherwise. I wish you could see all my dear things together. I have them wrapped in separate little bundles, but I shall have to undo them again to put the letter on.[22] I also have to cut down those white nightgowns, for the necks are too high to permit of nursing the baby. I want to finish that today so as to get the suitcase packed and ready.

I guess you remember how fond I am of dried corn! I know Philip will like it too, for he is devoted to green corn,[23] which they do not have in England. Thank you so much for sending it. I'm not sure I know how to prepare it. Will you tell me? . . .

[End of letter missing.]

To Loretta Secor

[104 W. 13th St., N.Y., N.Y.]
November 1, 1918

Dear Mother,

It is 2:30 a.m. but I have made vain endeavors to sleep and have abandoned the project in favor of a letter to you. It is astonishingly hot and muggy and has been for days. I am afraid it is the sort of weather to encourage influenza germs.[24] My windows are up and I am lying without covers, almost, on November first.

It begins to look as though I were going to finish out my full time until Nov. 7. But at best I have only another week, and I am trying to crowd that full. Yesterday afternoon Anne's mother came to help me hem curtains, and she is coming tomorrow again. I am so grateful, for the task seems pretty big to me now. I have ten windows besides bathroom and toilet, and as I'm putting two colors in Philip's room, my room, and the dining room, it means lots of work. I'll try to send you some little samples.

Everything is now just on the verge of being done, but it will still take several days to put the house in order. I guess I told you that we have some of Charles and Eleanor's things, including a big pile of book shelves . . . of just ordinary lumber. Part of this we used for a book case which Philip put in. The rest I have had made into a day bed. The carpenter charged only $5 and I picked up some splendid springs for $4.50. The mattress will cost $12 but it will make a charming bed such as we could not have touched otherwise for less than $50. I tried to buy a second hand one but the woman wanted $60.

We picked up an old Morris chair with good leather cushions. I painted this, the bed, and all the other living room furniture black, with a few little touches of white. Miss Peters[25] let us take an old fashioned gas table lamp which is going to be quite attractive. I painted it black, and will put a black and white shade on it. I even painted that wooden vase black with a white rim around the top. I'll use my black and white curtains in the living room and get touches of color in the sofa cushions. When I feel a little less miserable, I'll try to give you a detailed picture of each room.

I suppose I am feeling as well as I can expect, but it is so trying not to be able to sleep at night.

Several days later

I had no idea this letter would run into the week-end, but I've been feeling too miserable to write. I guess I worked too hard, but I'm much better today. The carpenter made the bed too large so I took it all to pieces and rebuilt it, cutting it down eight inches and making it shorter and narrower. Now it just fits the space in the wall intended for it. Today Philip picked up a used black velvet rug for $15. All our house I think will not cost us $100. I hope to finish hemming the black and white curtains tonight. Then all are finished except kitchen and bath. I have still to make dresser covers, cushions etc. galore, and I also want to get Philip's desk fitted up before I go. There will be many odds and ends left over, but in the main, the house will be presentable. . . . Philip is much pleased with all the arrangements. . . .

Freddie has had influenza very severely and is just recovering. Rebecca has spent all her time with him so that I've seen her not at all. We have had a good many callers already though I'd like to have finished the house first.

I wish you could see the lovely roses and taste the candy my lover brought me Sunday. He also took me to the theater last week. He is just an incomparable husband.

Philip's Aunt Fan and Uncle Joe with their 19-year-old daughter Katharine have moved to N.Y. and live just around the corner.[26] It was a tremendous surprise to us. She came to see me yesterday while Phil was in Waterbury. These days, he only stays away one day and not at all over night. . . .

Now I must rush along, for it's long past our dinner hour.

Much love,
Lella

On November 7, 1918, the world received a premature news story that the Germans had signed an armistice. In New York there were scenes of wild rejoicing, and Lella—nine full months pregnant—went out with Philip to join the excited crowd gathering on their corner, at the foot of the Sixth Avenue elevated station. Toward noon they thought of phoning Anne Herendeen. After making the call Lella discovered that her enormous girth would not allow her to open the door of the telephone booth. She signaled wildly to Philip, who, with much pushing and pulling, managed to extricate her. Anne met them for lunch at the Hotel Brevoort on lower Fifth Avenue, where patrons were singing, dancing, and jumping on tables.

On November 9 Kaiser Wilhelm abdicated and the war ended, the true armistice being signed two days later. At 5:30 p.m. on November 9, Lella gave birth to a son. Noel Secor Florence weighed eight and one-quarter pounds and was, in Philip's words, "a beautifully formed little human" rather than the raw lump of flesh he had been told to expect.

The scene at Lloyd's Sanitarium was one of great confusion, for part of its staff had been ordered to the front and the orders had not yet been countermanded. Lella's own doctor, Captain Bishop, was in uniform. Philip was permitted to stay by his wife during her labor and delivery, and slept on the floor by her bed afterward.

"Noel Florence" to Loretta Secor

[In Philip's handwriting]

Monday
9 days old

Dear Grandmother,

Mother & Father tell me that it was you made my beautiful clothes. They are lovely. Thank you very very much. I'll try to be ever so good in them & not to grow out of them too quickly—but I'm awful big.

Yours with all Love
Signed: Noel
Witness Lella
Philip Nov 18th 1918[27]

"Noel Florence" to Lida Hamm and Laura Kelley

[In Lella's handwriting.]

Tuesday, November 19, 1918

Dear Aunt Lida and Aunt Laura,

Mother has been telling me all about you, and I've decided that you must be the very nicest aunties in the world for a little boy to have.

I'd like to tell you all about this new life I've started. I think it's going to be pretty interesting to be alive, especially since peace has come and little boys will have a chance to grow into useful men instead of machines of destruction.

My name is Noel. I hope you like it. Mother and Father chose it because it means "great rejoicing." I guess it's pretty appropriate, for I was cradled in happiness from the beginning, and I came at the very hour when Father and Mother were rejoicing with such glad hearts over the coming of peace.[28]

I like my parents quite well. I get good meals off Mother, and Father just does everything in the world to make us both happy. He stands over my bed and gazes at me rapturously as though he thought me pretty nice. For my part I adore him and try to tell him so by rolling my big blue eyes and making queer faces.

You should see how lovely I look in my fine clothes. Yesterday I heard Nursie say, "I'll just put a plain petticoat on him," but she couldn't find a *plain* petty in my whole wardrobe. This morning even the doctor man exclaimed about my lovely nightie. Wasn't it just dear of Grandmother to make me all these pretty things?

I'm a pretty big boy! Last night Nursie discovered there wasn't really room for me in my big basket and had to get a little iron bed. Now I have room to stretch my pink toes.

Mother is sitting up in bed today and tomorrow the doctor says she may get into a chair for a little while. Saturday she and Father are going to take me to my new home. But the doctor says Mother and I must have a nurse for a little while longer, so a dear lady is coming to help us out.

I think Aunt Lida's cap is quite becoming to Mother. I like her to wear that and the little yellow silk jacket Aunt Ina sent her.

I guess I haven't anything more to tell now, 'cause my experience is rather limited. Mother and Father join in love, and I send heaps to you both and to Grandmother. . . .

Lovingly,

Noel Secor Florence

To Loretta Secor

104 West 13th
N.Y.
November 26, 1918

Dear Mother,

This is Thanksgiving evening and I'm celebrating the most wonderful of all Thanksgiving days by sitting up in a chair. Also I ate dinner in the dining room today. Our nurse, Mrs. Clark, is a perfect jewel, and a wonderful cook. We had a delicious feast—just Philip, Nurse, and I—chicken, sweet potatoes, cranberries, plum pudding[29] and all the fixings. I suppose no one has ever had so much to be thankful for as we have. I spoke of you all at dinner, and wondered just what you were doing I didn't need any surmises about the sort of dinner you were having! How we would love to have joined you!

Every day I wish more and more that you could see our little Noel. He is just the wisest young rascal you ever saw. He is growing every day, and seems just as well and sturdy as can be. Last night he slept from 10 [p.m.] until 6 a.m. without waking.

I should like to report in similar vein about his mother, but I have to confess that my recovery is taxing my patience. I think I have not told you what terrible care I got at the hospital—the whole place was so dreadful that the doctor wanted to bring me home in an ambulance after a few days. But that scheme was too costly, and so I stuck it out for two weeks. But I'm feeling the results, rather, now. One stitch has not held, and the wound is very slow in healing.[30] Last Sunday I tried to sit up for a little while but Monday I was much worse so that the doctor had to be summoned. I've been in bed ever since, until today, but I hope to get on my feet now.

I had another setback Tuesday, when Rebecca who had just run in for a moment was suddenly seized with a frightful spasm so that both the nurse and I thought she was dying. Philip and the nurse got her on the floor and brought her to, and we sent for my doctor. The anxiety and excitement upset me, and of course the baby, but we are all straightened out again.[31] The nurse will be with me another week. She charges $28 a week, but Philip insists on keeping her two weeks, which I guess is very wise after all, for I shall hardly be able to take charge of Baby before then. Meanwhile I'm going to try to get a good maid, so I shall not be alone at all.

You've no idea what a wonderful husband Philip is! He is ridiculously happy about his little son.[32] He just thinks of everything. This lovely stationery is one of his gifts. Besides flowers and dainty cakes and candies, he has given me since my illness six or eight books, . . . an exquisite necklace, and a beautiful muff of gray fur. No girl has ever been so blessed as I!

. . . [Noel] goes out for a ride with his father almost every day, and takes to the fresh air like a trooper. . . .

Yes, I got the house pretty well in order—and it is warm and comfortable. There are many little things still to do, but they'll have to wait. No, we haven't an elevator, so it will be some time before I'll be able to get out. But I'm *so* happy to be home with my two dear boys that I don't mind at all.

Mother Florence . . . is making great preparations for our coming. We plan to go in April.[33]

Hope to have some pictures of the baby to send next time.

Much love—
Lella

When Lella had fully recovered her strength, she and Philip took Noel to Battle Creek for a visit with Lella's family.

To Loretta Secor

104 W. 13th,
N.Y.
February 28, 1919

Dear Mother and Sisters,

Just a few lines while my little son sleeps. He is gradually getting unspoiled again, but the first day at home, he was hardly out of our arms all day. I thought he was probably crying for his Grandmother and Aunties, and did my best to comfort him. He was such a good little traveler. He slept all night on the train until six in the morning, and he has not been nursed before six since I came home. . . .

Our train got into N.Y. early Tuesday morning . . . but our baggage did not come until the later train . . . so we had breakfast at the station. I put Noel to sleep on two chairs . . . and we took a table where we could watch him. It worked beautifully, and by the time we had finished breakfast, our baggage had come and we took a taxi home, arriving shortly after ten. I nursed the baby in the taxi as we paraded [down] Fifth Avenue. He's a great sport; he could eat on a raft.

I entered the house calling gaily for Maggie,[34] but only echoes and accumulated dust of two weeks replied. Inquiry revealed the fact that she had fled to Texas, almost before we were out of sight. Here endeth the chapter on Maggie.

I have managed pretty well alone, but the house and baby take every bit of my time, and tie me down too much. So now I'm answering ads, and we may advertise again Sunday.

Philip has been in Waterbury for two days, but I expect him early today. . . . He's bringing Dr. Ryan[35] back with him; there's an all day Y. D. [Young Democracy] Conference here tomorrow, and a splendid Women's Conference ending with a dinner which I want to attend. Things have piled up during my two weeks' absence till I hardly know where to begin. I didn't enjoy myself much in Detroit. Florence Shelly came in the evening and I had a long session with her in my room. . . .[36] Then I fell asleep just as Philip was getting up in the morning and he sneaked the baby out and let me sleep . . . so that breakfast was all over before I awoke. I wouldn't have had it happen for the world, but Philip says he doesn't care, I was so worn out for sleep. . . .

John Reed has also been acquitted.[37] It begins to look as though the reign of terror were passing. I'm sending a few papers. They'll be a little old but anyway they may give you some news.

Thank you all again for the lovely lovely time we had with you, and for all the beautiful gifts and the gay breakfast parties 'n everything.

Noel misses you so much and sends loads of love as do his Mother and Father.

Ever lovingly,
Lella

To Loretta Secor

March 14, 1919

Dear Mother and Sisters,

I am afraid I have neglected you frightfully again. I had a few moments yesterday, but the instant I started a letter I fell sound asleep and could not go on. I hope to soon get back to normal, for since I have not had any maid I have had to get up at six in the morning in order to get my work done, and I have lost so much sleep in the last month and worked so hard that I am about at the end of my endurance. I am so tired and sleepy at this moment that I shall probably be incoherent. . . .

Well, Katherine arrived yesterday! She is a bright, talkative, scrupulously clean, devoted Irish Catholic, and I feel that I was especially fortunate to get her. . . .

This is the first time I have really felt the servant problem in all its force. Before, when we advertised, we got fifteen applicants. This time, not one nibble did we get, and we were forced to resort to the dubious process of answering ads that appeared in the papers. Last Sunday, we communicated with sixteen, either in person or by letter, and the Sunday before with something like a dozen. Out of this number I hired four, and finally actually succeeded in corralling Katherine yesterday. In desperation, I hired two people for exactly the same hour last Saturday, trusting to luck and my ingenuity to straighten out the tangle in case they both appeared. As I expected, neither one came. Tuesday I went to Seventeenth Street immediately after breakfast, climbed four dreary, foul-smelling flights of stairs, rapped on the appointed door, and received no response. Then just because something had to be done, . . . I began rapping on every door I came to, covering each floor systematically. Finally, an old woman in white pantaloons covered by an abbreviated long black coat, emerged from one dark corner, followed me persistently as I backed away down the hall and, thrusting her witch-like face under my nose, extolled the merits of the woman I sought and assured me that she had only gone to mass and would return presently. So I took up my position at the foot of the stairs, resolved that no promising subject should pass except over my dead body.

Meanwhile, I ingratiated myself with two women who were running a delicatessen store on the first floor, which proved a good diplomatic move, for they cordially recommended me later to Katherine as a "nice lady." Presently Katherine arrived . . . and I pounced upon her, hiring her upon the spot. But she couldn't come until Thursday. Meanwhile, other would-be employers began to arrive, and tried to seduce my prize. How near they came, I suppose I shall never know. The fact remains that I have had Katherine now for two days, and that I must tread carefully for she has discovered how great is the demand. She has never done any cooking, but seems to be picking it up pretty well. Also she is very nice with Noel, which is a great point.

Meanwhile, I have had a letter from Maggie, regretting that she ever left me, and wishing that she was back again. I think I shall have it framed. . . .

Wednesday, Dr. Lee, Philip's "superior officer," invited us to luncheon, and as it was my first appearance in his group of associates I was anxious not to disappoint him. . . . We had such a pleasant time at the luncheon. The Lees have a magnificent home on 65th (I think), beautifully decorated in Italian style, and filled with wonderful works of art. Dr. Lee is the person who has so often used Philip's ideas and the results of his investigations without giving Philip any credit at all. Recently Philip and his colleague Dr. Ryan revolted, and now everything is to be changed. It seems like a complete victory for them, over which we are of course rejoicing. Also there seems to be quite a large demand for Philip's book.[38]

Baby is asleep, and I have just gotten up from a little nap myself. The issue of the baby's napkins [diapers] came up, and I dreaded to tell Katherine to wash them for fear she would revolt. So I put them on to boil myself and then went off for a nap. Just now I find she has rinsed them out and hung them up to dry, so I guess I won't find any great difficulty there.

Philip started agitation for a passport the other day and came home feeling quite discouraged.[39] It is going to be very difficult and I think I shall have to begin to work on some of my influential friends if we are to succeed. I think he is almost certain that we cannot get passports, but I am by no means hopeless and feel confident that once we start pulling wires we shall be able to succeed. And by the way, as a first step I have to have a birth certificate, or some document to show that I was really born and did not just grow. Was my birth registered, and if so, can you get a birth certificate? If not, will you take steps to have an affidavit sworn to before a notary, "either by parents, attending physicians, or someone having actual knowledge of birth." I will pay whatever fee is required. . . .[40]

Philip is in Waterbury—or rather, I hope he has started on his way home by this time. There is just a possibility that he will undertake to investigate a factory in Washington D.C., which will be fortunate for us, for undoubtedly it will take several trips to Washington before we are able to get passports, and the trip is rather costly as a weekly stunt.

Philip and I are going to the theater tomorrow night. It will seem so good to get out again after our long siege at home. . . . The baby is calling, so I must bring this to a close. . . .

Lovingly,
Lella

To Loretta Secor

[March 1919]

Dear Mother and Sisters,

My Son is a bad little Bolshevik—he protests loudly every time I turn my back, and is threatening to organize a Soviet of the Babies. I have picked him up a dozen times this afternoon, only to have his tears turn like magic to smiles. So I am convinced that he is plain bad. He has slept only a half hour since lunch, and now it is dark and I am just writing by touch so I suppose this letter will be full of blunders. I continue to have a strenuous time.

Firstly, Katherine gave notice yesterday that she would leave today. But this morning she concluded that she would stay. She didn't like to see me so upset she said. So that problem is settled for the time being, and I was able to take off my hat and coat this morning and abandon my thankless search in smelly tenements.

The Young Democracy is taking a good deal of my time and energy and I have little left for anything else. I have a stenographer come to the house now so that helps some. Our new secretary comes on the job April 1, and the first two weeks in April will be pretty strenuous. Starting a new organization is always an uphill job.

How I wish you could see little Noel. You would hardly know him he has grown so. I guess I'll have to give up to him, for he's crying so hard—I'll try holding him on my lap and letting him help me at the typewriter. I shall be able now to blame all mistakes on him, for he is quite fascinated by the movement of the keys and biffs them with his little fists whenever he gets a chance. . . .

A day or so ago when it was particularly lovely, and I had to be away, Philip took him up on the roof. You never saw such rosy loveliness after his whole day in the sunshine. . . .

The Next Morning at Noon

Noel has just gone to sleep and before I rush out to get things for lunch I want to finish and mail this letter. He has developed so much since you saw him. Every day, as he shows some new trick, I long to be near you where you could share this happiness with me. His bibs are coming into fine use now. I sewed ribbons on them all, for I found it much easier to tie them than to work them with buttons.

I have also finished my blue smock and it is quite smart. I turned the bottom up on the right side, making a sort of cuff, decorated the hem with short stitches in black yarn, and finished it off with dangles of blue and black buttons. I got little round button molds and painted them. I want to make one now of dark brown, very long, to wear over my brown velvet skirt and cover up the worn places. I also got black crepe de chine for a dress, but I guess I'll have to get a dressmaker to do it. . . . I want just a loose flowing sort of thing, with a scarf lined with brilliant green. Won't it be lovely? . . .

Philip and I have taken advantage of our good Katherine and have gone to several plays and concerts. . . .

. . . I am going to try to get a permanent stenographer who will act as personal secretary as well. Then, with my faithful Katherine (if she only stays), I think I shall be able to manage my work a little better. I am frightfully tired out, and getting just a bit nervous, so that I felt I must do something at once to lighten my work.

Rebecca's condition is very critical. I have written to Dr. Kellogg, asking him to invite her to the Sanitarium, but he is in Florida and I have not yet heard from him. A wire from Florence two days ago said her condition was extremely serious and something must be done at once. The doctor says she will probably not recover under two or three years. Florence has joined with us to try to break up her engagement.[41]

Did you get the *Call*s I sent? That arch-fiend Burleson has declared them unmailable, so I thought they might have been held up.[42] I will try to send them every week if you enjoy them. They give much news that is not printed elsewhere, and it is the only paper on whose truthfulness you can rely. . . .

I had a delightful tea party last week—the Muscios from Australia and half a dozen other delightful people. Anne's new magazine *Judy* is having a coming-out party tonight at the Holland House [Hotel]. She wanted us to go, but it does not begin until ten o'clock, and I am too tired to undertake it. Besides, I know so little about dancing. Last night we went to hear *Patience,* a Gilbert and Sullivan opera which was perfectly delightful. We feel that we must make the best use possible of our stay in New York, for next winter we will probably feel that we must live out somewhere for the baby's sake.

I shall have to bring this to a hasty close—my son is howling a protest at being left alone any longer. I am so grateful that he is mostly so good and dear, else I do not know what I should do. . . . His Father bought him a lovely musical instrument which you play with two mallets and which is capable of really delightful

THE YOUNG DEMOCRACY

BY WAY OF INTRODUCTION

"The world needs a more articulate expression of the power and the vision which the young can offer as their supreme and unique gift."

OFFICERS

DEVERE ALLEN
Executive Secretary
Publicity Director
Editor of "Young Democracy"

HAROLD C. KEYES
Organizing Secretary
Treasurer

EXECUTIVE COMMITTEE

DEVERE ALLEN
HENRY J. CADBURY
HENRY W. L. DANA
ROBERT W. DUNN
HAROLD EVANS
HAROLD C. KEYES
LELLA FAYE SECOR
DONALD WINSTON
DAVID H. ROBBINS
ANNE GARRETT WALTON

Announcement will be made in a later bulletin of the members of the Young Democracy Bureaus, as follows: Bureau on Labor; Bureau on Education; Bureau on Universal Military Training; Bureau on Conscientious Objectors; Bureau on World Federation; Bureau to Promote the International Young Democracy.

Introductory pamphlet of The Young Democracy.

"Young Democracy"

A Live Magazine for Young Liberals

The Young Democracy will soon begin the publication of a new monthly magazine, "*Young Democracy.*" It will be MILITANT and FEARLESS, you may be sure; but it will also be, we trust, SANE and CONSTRUCTIVE. It will have a staff of young liberals with experience in magazine work, and among them you will see names familiar to young liberals everywhere. "Academics," "Laborites," spokesmen of downtrodden races and classes, will all have their say.

Not a propaganda magazine in the sense that it will have room for only a single idea or opinion; but at the same time a magazine that will speak with the voice of youth consistently and boldly for the principles and purposes for which the YOUNG DEMOCRACY itself came into being.

To all regular members of the Young Democracy organization, the magazine will be sent free of charge, the membership dues of twenty-five cents per month covering the charge for the magazine as well as for any supplementary bulletins and leaflets that are issued.

To all others, the subscription price is ONE DOLLAR A YEAR.

FELLOW LIBERAL:

Are you going to have a share in our fight?

Are you going to stand by us?

WE ARE GOING TO STAND BY YOU!

Announcement of the magazine *The Young Democracy.*

melodies. I think Philip is a trifle disappointed at Noel's inability to execute "Swanee River."

Much love to all,
Lella.

To Loretta Secor

April 14, 1919

Dear Mother:

I am afraid it will remind you of E. P. F. when you receive a dictated letter.[43] I am so overpowered with work these days that I hardly know whither to turn. The Young Democracy is giving a coming out party Wednesday night, when we hope to really launch the work on a larger scale. As usual most of the work has fallen upon me and on top of everything Katherine decided again to leave. I did not try to persuade her this time, because I thought it was foolish to have such a situation recurring every week or so. Just on chance I advertised again in the *World* and this time I think it is going to be successful. A colored woman who is unusually refined has promised to come tomorrow morning, but it is impossible to get anyone competent at the sum we have always been used to paying, and we have been compelled at last to pay what everyone else is paying, an advance of ten dollars on our usual allotment for this purpose.

. . . I have finished your birthday gift. . . . I am sorry it had to be late but I have so few moments to give to anything of that sort. It is something for you to wear and something which I hope will go with either gray or purple dresses. I so much hope that you had a joyous birthday. Two days later Noel was five months old. How jolly it would have been could you have celebrated together.

Noel is growing more cunning every day. . . . He now weighs seventeen pounds and I think it will not be many days [before] he will want to creep. I intend to put him on the floor now, as soon as the weather is a little more settled. . . . Yesterday he had his first real outburst of temper when I attempted to take a paper bag away from him. When I gave it back to him he was all smiles in a second and then when I took it away there was another grand uproar. Philip and I both felt that our responsibilities were beginning.

I want to thank you again for the lovely box of things you sent. . . . Baby's little dress fits him beautifully. I am letting him wear it as much as possible for he will soon outgrow it and besides it is getting to be a task to keep him in white. If you have plenty of time and really want to make him some more bibs, I could use them.

I am having a dressmaker make my black crepe de chine frock. I wanted so much to do it myself, but it was clear that I should never get to it.

Our plans are still quite indefinite, but they are beginning to come somewhat to a head. Philip has had two offers; one from Lexington, Kentucky, and one from Northfield, Minnesota, but the thing which interested us most is a possible engagement with the New School of Social Science which has been started in New York.[44] If he accepts a position for next fall, we shall make every effort to get to England for the summer. . . .

Much love from us all
Lella

On Monday, June 30, 1919, Lella, Philip, and Noel sailed aboard the Aquitania *for England and a visit with Philip's mother.*

To Loretta Secor

R. M. S. *Aquitania*

Sunday, July 6, 1919

Dearest Mother and Sissers,

I had expected to write volumes every day to make up for all the things I had to omit saying during the past hectic weeks. Instead I find myself, on the sixth day of our voyage, beginning to feel just a bit fit for the first time. I have behaved disgracefully. We have had a wonderful sunny voyage on a sea as smooth as a lake, except for one day when a brisk north wind whipped up enough waves to compel us to close our port hole. In spite of this I have felt miserable all the way, part of the time unable to leave my cabin. My conduct has been a great disappointment, for we had planned on having such wonderful times together on this new honeymoon. I can't account for my illness except that I had about reached the limit of my endurance before we came on board and was in excellent condition to be upset. I have enjoyed but one good meal, which happily was in the evening of the Fourth when there was an extra fine spread. Ordinarily the food has not been overly appetizing, especially to a capricious appetite.

We are traveling second class, but aside from the food the other accommodations are fairly good—as good as could be expected of a ship which has been partly converted into a transport for carrying troops. The ship seems literally to be hacked to pieces and is far from the usual Cunard standard. It is amazing how soldiers seem to cease to be human beings. They are treated like cattle—all locks, knobs, hooks, every portable thing is removed. It looks as though authorities were fearful that they all contemplated suicide.

Noel is enjoying his voyage immensely and has behaved in his usual exemplary fashion. Philip also has behaved as usual—simply wonderfully. He has had the entire care of Noel on some days, and has learned to change him, bath him and dress him since we came on board. Noel has an admiring circle of friends who have also been helpful.

For the most part, the passengers are uninteresting and dull. This is quite likely to be the case if one is traveling second class, and one would find it pretty stupid if one were alone. Together, we do not care who is on board. We had to pay $135 each even for second class accommodations—about $30 more than used to be charged for 1st class. We had first engaged passage on the *Baltic* which sailed the first. Then a bare week before that date we learned that the sailing had been postponed until July 17th because of a strike. We rushed about to all the other steamship companies but there were no accommodations to be had so we relaxed a little, thinking we had more than two weeks, and fooled away two precious days. Then suddenly came a phone message from the Cunard, telling us that a cancellation had made passage possible for us. We seized upon it—and then started the grand rush, for the *Aquitania* sailed a day earlier than we had expected even at first.

The Y. D. Conference had taken so much time and energy that I had done precious little up to that time. Into those few days had to be crowded a vast amount of shopping, sewing, mending, packing, cleaning, sorting, storing away, and what not. When we got on board Monday noon we were both too weary to have any sensations at all. To cap the climax, on Saturday I got dreadfully angry with a tailor who had pressed all the pleats *out* of my green serge dress instead of pressing them in (I've so few things anyway) and then insisted that I pay him for spoiling the dress. It is the first time my temper has been really exercised since Noel was born, and apparently my milk was poisoned, for he woke in the night and cried for two or three hours. . . .

I cannot tell you how grateful I am to you for fixing his clothes. Needless to say most of the sewing I had planned to do for myself is undone, and I am going over with almost nothing to wear. We had but one afternoon for shopping and that produced only one smart dark blue coat dress for traveling, and a blue terra cotta lined cape. Otherwise I am quite naked, but I have ceased to worry about that. . . .

. . . [Noel] crawls all over, sits alone, and yesterday pulled himself to his feet. He stands alone by clinging to a chair, but I'm not encouraging him in that for he's still so young—eight months in three days now. . . . He has his first leather shoes—little soft-sole moccasins for which I had to pay $2! The price of everything continues to amaze one. . . .

We are still not in sight of land though we expected to get in yesterday. It is probable now that we will dock tonight in the night and land sometime tomorrow. I suppose Philip's Mother is waiting impatiently in Southampton. I could almost wish the voyage even longer for I feel that now I could begin to rest, for I don't believe I shall be sick again. I am sitting on deck now—Noel is asleep in his carriage beside me and my Dear Boy is getting a little sleep down in the cabin.

It was so splendid to get your letters. . . . There is no doubt I think that I will take you to Europe some day. After all—you got to New York you know. I feel frightfully selfish to be making my second trip. . . .

Did I tell you that Philip presented me with a beautiful little typewriter which folds up and can be carried anywhere? I'm so delighted with it. . . . I hope to do a good deal of work on it this summer, but I've about ceased to plan on work. Philip insists this is to be my great holiday and I'm to rest—and I guess I'm willing.

The Y. D. conference was a splendid success—but I don't know how much will be done this summer. I despair of getting a real live wire for secretary. I drew up a plan before I left for sending help to Germany and trying to heal the wounds as quickly as possible. But I don't know how much will be done.[45]

. . . It is evident the captain is optimistic about getting in. There's a fog and we may be nearer land than we think. A sea gull just flew by—we must be near.

Loads of love to all from us all—
Lella
Philip
Noel

P.S. Did I tell you some friends had taken our house in N.Y. for the summer? I'm so grateful for I could never have packed and moved everything. I put away all my best things in lavender and tar flakes so that I know everything is safe.

Notes

1. September 22, 1917.

2. After the Chicago fiasco, a smaller People's Council convention was held in New York.

3. This remark must have shocked her family, but Lella was coming under the influence of Philip's rationalist beliefs.

4. Norman Thomas, who in later years was to run for President six times on the Socialist ticket, founded the Fellowship of Reconciliation and was active in many peace groups including the the Emergency Peace Federation and the American Union Against Militarism.

5. On a note to Lena Case, Lella pinned slivers of crepe de chine and wrote, "Mother and the girls made me nighties of these. I also have four under jiggers. They are made just like children's rompers and delightful. The tiny scrap is my wedding dress, clipped from a

seam. I wore my bronze slippers with it. My coat is smoke, with a big fur collar. I have a black velvet hat."

6. Famous for its French restaurant, the Lafayette—now demolished—was at University Place and Ninth Street. The party was enlivened by the reading of "telegrams" from famous people, typed on Western Union forms by Anne Herendeen. One from "London" to Lella Secor read, "Preserve your economic independence. Remember—no annexations, no indemnities. Sylvia Pankhurst."

7. The Hudson River Line operated passenger boats between New York and Albany.

8. Evidently hot-water enemas.

9. The automobile was chauffeured; neither Philip nor Lella could drive.

10. Lella's idea of a coterie was perhaps inspired by Philip's description of London's intellectual Bloomsbury group of which he had been a fringe member.

11. Morris Hillquit, author and lawyer, was the 1917 Socialist candidate for mayor of New York, and had been a member of the "Committee of 100" of the American Neutral Conference Committee. Lella's involvements were becoming more and more left-wing at this time, under Rebecca's influence. In December, Rebecca was to make a speech in Carnegie Hall to a group called Friends of New Russia (see Appendix C).

12. Joseph Cohen was sharing the apartment on 118th Street; "Helen" had apparently replaced the redoubtable Miss Ward.

13. Lella was pregnant. She and Philip had not planned to have a child so soon, but were ignorant of reliable methods of birth control.

14. Philip's Ph.D. dissertation was being published under the title, *Use of Factory Statistics in the Investigation of Industrial Fatigue.*

15. Nicholas Murray Butler.

16. Rebecca's friends were not eager for her to marry Freddie Robinson, fearing she would lose her independence. Joseph Cohen wrote Lella, "Both Phil and you can still . . . insist on a settlement before marriage. I think it your duty as a best friend."

17. Probably a Bellevue, Washington, newspaper.

18. Philip had a small but regular income from shares left to him by his grandmother.

19. Harold C. Keyes, a member of the executive committee, was suspected of being an F.B.I. agent.

20. Charles Phillips, who was one of the student delegates on the Ford Peace Ship, and his wife Eleanor. They had moved to Mexico to escape the draft.

21. Joseph Cohen had enlisted in a special division of the Canadian Army and was stationed in England. He was to prove himself invaluable to the British government when the Balfour Declaration of 1917 pledged support for Palestine as a national home for the Jews.

22. An embroidered "F."

23. Fresh corn, or corn on the cob.

24. A prophetic statement, since the great influenza pandemic of 1918–19 was soon to break out.

25. The landlady.

26. Fanny Keane was Philip's father's sister. She and her husband, a wholesale grocer, had formerly lived in New Jersey.

27. The day after Noel was born, Loretta Secor had written, "Laura picked the most beautiful little white rose . . . so characteristic of a baby darling. Just a bud so tight and then it began to open up, and so perfectly pure and white . . . until you could see the little pure heart. And I thought if one could raise them the little ones as pure as this little rose it would pay for all the pain and worry. . . . You will see dear now, as never before, why I have missed you girls and how hard it has been to give you up. I hope you and Philip won't be too happy and don't worship baby too much for you know you must not lay up treasure on earth."

28. If the baby had been a girl, she would have been named Ethel (after an aunt of Philip's) Peace Florence.

29. This traditionally English dessert may have been added for Philip's benefit.

30. The doctor had used forceps to hasten Lella's delivery and stitches were necessary.

31. Rebecca was in an agitated state, having just found out about a liaison of Freddie's with an "older woman." The fainting episode in Lella's bedroom caused Lella's milk to go sour temporarily.

32. Philip wrote Loretta Secor, "I wonder whether you realize the joy this gift of Lella has brought me! I have been feeling so excited ever since he came—so beautifully made and perfect—that I hardly seem able to sit down quietly and write about him. . . . Sometimes I can hardly believe he has anything to do with me, he's so much of an improvement: so good and contented and strong."

33. Philip was planning to take his new wife and son to England in the spring for an extended visit.

34. The most recent maid.

35. Howard Ryan, a physician, was Philip's colleague at the Scovill factory.

36. Philip had business in Detroit and while they were there Lella took advantage of the opportunity to talk to Rebecca's sister. Rebecca was on the verge of collapse from the accumulated fatigue of years of peace work combined with the crisis in her relationship with Freddie. She had been forced to give up her involvement with The Young Democracy and her friends were quite concerned about her health.

37. John Reed, author and revolutionary, was prosecuted in the famous *Masses* trial along with the magazine's editor, Max Eastman, and others. Reed's specific misdemeanor had been to write a headline for an article on mental illness in the army: "Knit a Strait-Jacket for Your Soldier Boy." The government's charges of obstructing the war effort were later dropped.

38. His doctoral dissertation, now in print.

39. Although the war was over, private citizens still could not get passports easily.

40. The original record of Lella's birth perished in a courthouse fire. Some other document must have sufficed at the time of this letter, for it was not until a visit to Battle Creek in 1956 that she obtained a duplicate birth certificate.

41. Rebecca did not marry Freddie but in 1922 became the wife of Felix Rathmer, a German. This meant relinquishing her American citizenship (although she continued to live in the United States). Denied repatriation because she would not promise to bear arms for her country in time of war, she did not regain citizenship until 1944.

42. Albert S. Burleson, Postmaster-General, had denied second-class mailing permits to Socialist periodicals.

43. Typed by a stenographer at The Young Democracy.

44. Philip hoped to teach economics at an American university and had applied to the University of Kentucky and to Carleton College in Northfield, Minnesota. The New School for Social Research was being organized, and for a time the Bureau of Industrial Research, where Philip was to give a series of lectures that fall, expected to be attached to it.

45. This is Lella's last mention of The Young Democracy. Beset by infighting, intrigues, and lack of leadership, it eventually died of attrition.

V

Abroad and at Home

To Loretta Secor

Lord's Wood
[Marlow, England]
Summer 1919

Dearest Mother and all the Family,

It is over two weeks since we reached England, and I am pursued with remorse at not having written before. Fact is, I have been so frightfully exhausted that I have not been able to force myself to do a single thing. I have been so near a complete breakdown that I have had to exert every ounce of will power to keep myself together at all. Those last hectic weeks in New York were almost too much, and though I realized before we left that I was nearing the end of my rope, I didn't believe that I could continue indefinitely to be so exhausted. I am still so dazed that events seem to make precious little impression upon me, and I am unable to realize all the wonderful things that are happening to me.

I do not want to alarm you, and except to explain my frightful neglect of you I would not mention these tiresome facts. I am feeling a little more fit today, and I think when things are a little more organized I shall be able to get more rest and recover more quickly. At all events there is no need for worry at all, and I promise hereafter to keep you more closely posted. . . .

And now with these explanations out of the way, where shall I begin? Perhaps with the day we landed in England, for that is where I left off in my last letter.

Our ship landed in Southampton at breakfast time on a dull misty Monday morning. We had a long tedious wait before we could get our baggage collected and passed through the customs. The whole English system of handling baggage seems so very primitive—and it is even worse since the war. All order and system seems to have broken down. There was no food to be had for any price—not even a piece of chocolate, and as we did not reach London until mid-afternoon, after a very early breakfast, we were famished. By a series of lucky accidents, Mother Florence reached the London station soon after we arrived, and bore us off to dinner. Afterward we traveled from Waterloo station to Paddington by taxi, through many of the historic streets of London about which I have heard so often and which even yet I cannot believe I have seen. A queer little English train with a sort of toy engine and compartments running crosswise, each with a separate entrance on the platform, carried us away from the bustle of London into the quiet countryside with its green sloping hills, its neatly tailored gardens, and its quaint thatched cottages. It was seven o'clock when finally we arrived in Marlow[1] and started on the last lap of our journey to Lord's Wood, in two open chaises with antiquated horses who pulled us leisurely through the quaint old town with its charming old buildings and its fascinating public houses.

Lord's Wood we came upon quite suddenly as we left the Common on a sharp curve. It is so like the pictures and sketches that we received before leaving America that I felt as though I were reaching home. It is delightful beyond words—a broad three-story brick structure with charming French windows which are always open—and clambering all over, in luxurious greens, rare and lovely vines—magnolia, the first blossom of which opened its waxy leaves today, wisteria, jasmine, and roses. The driveway is flanked on either side with roses which were in full bloom the day we arrived, and reminded me so much of California with their delightful smells. A row of pines and a thick hedge just to the left of the rose bushes shut off the kitchen garden, which includes also a little hothouse and a profusion of climbing roses, lavender and old fashioned flowers. Holly and laurel trees divide the house from the lawn in front, and a yew hedge shuts in the whole but still permits a charming view of the wooded Common beyond. The house is removed from the main road and enjoys delightful seclusion. At the left as you face the house, and separated again from the main lawns by a hedge and wicket fence, is the sheep paddock where [the sheep] Rebecca and Rachel and the latter's charming little daughter Rhoda disport themselves when they are not adding their presence to the picturesque beauty of the Common. Back of the whole is the loveliest part of all, though we have used it very little because the weather has been so cool. This is the lovely forest of beech trees with their slender trunks standing so firmly in a carpet of brown leaves, which crunch and crackle under one's feet as one follows the fascinating paths to the edge of the wood and to a glimpse of a lovely valley below, which rises again in gently rounded hills. To the right of this, but not visible from the main lawns, is a spacious meadow which skirts the valley and stretches away up the hill. And now you have a hasty picture of the home where my Dear Boy has spent so many happy years, though I have not been able to tell you how peaceful and quiet, how beautiful and luxurious it really is. Nor have I mentioned the farm which is reached by a short walk across the Common, and which has two charming cottages, one of which is over three hundred years old. Besides, there is Mother's spacious studio . . . a delightful building just in the rear of Lord's Wood.[2]

But I have hardly explored the place at all as yet, for I have been too weary to walk, so I shall have much to tell you as the summer moves on—which I am afraid it will do altogether too quickly.

I am so wonderfully happy here. There has been but one regret, and that is that I am too tired and stupid to really appreciate anything. . . .

Days later

When we first came to England we tried not to let anyone know, for I felt as though I could not meet anyone I was so tired. But it was not long before Philip's friends began to learn that we were here, and already our days have been filled to overflowing. I have been so eager not to seem just a fagged stupid person to his friends that I have used all my energy in meeting them. . . . I now have a little nurse maid who is to be with us temporarily, and later I shall have an older woman who is more or less trained, and who may go back to America with us if everything goes well. That will relieve me a great deal, for Emily is too young and inexperienced to be trusted with Noel's bath and preparation of his food. . . . On top of everything else, Philip has had another very bad carbuncle which had to be dressed every hour for a time. . . . Also, I tried to help him off the bed and strained my back so I could hardly move for days. This woeful recital is again merely to explain my unavoidable delay in finishing this letter. . . .

How I wish you could see Noel. He has one tiny tooth just through, and is getting so smart. . . . I expect he will be walking in ever so short a time. I have weaned him completely and am already feeling stronger. . . .

I am beginning to really enjoy the beauties of Lord's Wood. The house is a wonderful structure, with extraordinary mural decorations inside done by Mother Florence. She is very talented and altogether delightful, though one would hardly expect it at first meeting. She is quite tiny, with dreamy blue eyes and sort of autumn colored hair which is constantly escaping from her little top knot and hanging in ringlets around her face and neck. She is rather scornful of clothes, so that on first meeting she looks like a rather shabby but very cunning little lady. It is not until one sees her at home, presiding over the dinner or gracing her drawing room, that one appreciates her real charm. She has quite a reputation as an artist, and a good many artists come here to see her work.[3] I wish you could meet her, for I know you would find her delightful. . . . We get on splendidly, though I have sometimes feared that the sudden increase in her household after so many years of quiet has made her rather tired and confused. For that reason I have been extra careful to keep Noel rather quiet and to relieve the nursemaid myself when she had other things to do. . . .[4]

Uncle Willie,[5] the sculptor from Italy, has been for a visit and later asked us to take a several days' canoe trip with him. But I didn't feel I could leave Noel until the older nurse came so the trip was abandoned for the present. Later Uncle Eddie[6] and his charming wife came, and they have invited us to their home. They are all wealthy and live in a good deal of style, so you can picture your little urchin hobnobbing with a gay and cultured set and being waited on by many servants. However, the servant problem is quite serious here, though in no way to compare with the situation in America. Mother F. has only two house servants, a gardener, two assistants, and a farmerette who has charge of the farm. Philip is regretting that the old "feudal" system of his grandmother's time is past, for he greatly wanted me to see an establishment with fourteen servants—his grandmother always kept that many. Anyway, we shall probably get a little taste of it in August, for we have been invited to spend a week with Lady Sargant and Sir Charles.[7] But for my part, I'd rather lie under a tree and be left alone.[8]

Next day

My determination to post this last night was overcome when Joseph [Cohen] suddenly arrived for lunch. It was the first time we had seen him. Philip has a lovely little boat on the Thames, and so we took Joseph up the river. It was the first time I had actually started out on a pleasure jaunt, my only expeditions up to this time having been to London once to get some clothes, for I was quite destitute, and once to see the Russian ballet which I had . . . always yearned to see. On the way up the river we visited a charming old church built in the fifteenth century. Then we passed through two locks and had tea on the river bank. It was lovely. Today Jerome K. Jerome,[9] the author, and his wife are coming to tea. . . . We shall go to Cambridge next week, and I'll write you all the details when we return.

. . . Please don't worry about me. I am afraid I have been rather too free in discussing my woes, but I'm really feeling much better and I am sure I shall be quite strong by the time we leave. Loads and loads of love from us all.

Your little girl,
Lella

To Loretta Secor

Lord's Wood
Summer 1919

Dearest Mother and All the Family,

. . . I am beginning to feel a little better, though I still have such a dazed feeling that I can hardly realize all that is going on. I at last yielded to Philip's entreaties and consulted a physician who has given me a tonic to start with and I feel greatly improved. Now that Philip's friends have begun to learn about our arrival, we are constantly having guests, and next week we must begin to accept some of the invitations we have had. Up to this point I have not felt like meeting anyone and I guess Mother Florence despaired of ever getting me anywhere. But now I have a competent little nurse who takes most of the care of Noel, and, relieved of all responsibility, I shall be able to get about much more easily.

. . . [Noel] is getting along so beautifully—twenty pounds now, two teeth, and enough mischief for twenty babies. . . . He has been a great care since we came, for he eats everything, or else climbs around so that we can never leave him alone a moment. He is standing beside me just now, laughing with glee as the keys go up, and trying his best to keep me from writing. I expect to get a baby pen in London this week, and then we can leave him alone more. He is getting quite too much attention and care for his own good. . . .

. . . The photograph is one of me which I had taken in Cambridge for the police. We are aliens here, and have to register with the police wherever we go.

I feel so sorry that we had to make our Cambridge visit when we did, for now I should be able to enjoy everything so much more. But it was a marvelous experience at all events for, tired and ill as I felt, I got a good many thrills out of the lovely old college town where my Dear Boy spend five such happy years before we met. . . . The river Cam winds its limpid course back of the colleges, which connect with their gardens on the opposite shore by charming bridges, one of which was built by Isaac Newton. There is so much of historical interest about Cambridge. . . . Some of the buildings date from the tenth and eleventh centuries and in their time have housed many of the celebrities of all the centuries which have followed. There is much more an old-world atmosphere there than in London. . . . Attached to Jesus College is Jesus Chapel, built in the tenth century. Jesus College was formerly a nunnery, and the chapel is the same used by the nuns for their worship eight hundred years ago. We were shown through by one of those historic guides, whom Philip employed because he thought I would so much enjoy the experience. He was so proud of every crack and crevice, and explained all the statues, carvings and interesting bits of architecture, dwelling with especially loving emphasis upon the names of the Old Testament saints shown on the colored windows.

We had rooms at Mrs. Danes', where Philip spent his fifth year in Cambridge, being then unable to remain longer in the quarters attached to his college. Mrs. Danes is a typical woman of the English—what shall I say—lower middle classes. The class line in England is more clearly cut than Mason and Dixon's, though the war has done much toward breaking down the barriers between classes. The lower classes have the most servile deference for a lady or gentleman. For instance, in Cambridge I was never asked for my ration cards in buying provisions (which Mrs. Danes cooked for us), though the rationing system still prevails everywhere. Mrs. Danes insisted it was because I was a lady, for only the day before she had been told to produce her ration card, "and that at a shop where she had spent lots of money too." [Her house] was such a primitive sort of little place, without bath or conveniences, but that seems to be the general rule in England. We were fortunate to get any accommodations at all, for the housing problem is even greater here than in America.

After the first day or so in Cambridge we never ate at home at all. "Mr. Philip is a very popular gentleman," said Mrs. Danes, and so it seemed, for we were entertained continuously by his friends, . . . including lunch with various dons[10] and notables, some of whom were blest with more fame than manners. One don, for instance, invited us to his college rooms for lunch—a great honor. He has a great name,[11] and I approached him in great awe. He is contained in an immense frame which sags at the shoulders, and the frame is in turn encased in a loose baggy grey suit which sagged wherever there was an opportunity. As we came in, he somehow gathered all his massive bulk together and lifted it off the lounge, where he was sprawling, to an upright position on the floor. Then he shook hands, ran a bony set of fingers through an incorrigible tuft of wiry hair, and finally, like a self-conscious school boy, stretched himself until his long arms almost reached the century old beams of the ceiling. Finally he collapsed in a heap on the lounge again. I had a great impulse to go over to him, pat him kindly on the head, and assure him that we were quite simple folks and he needn't mind us at all. But just then lunch was served. I was frightfully hungry, and fell to with a will, but almost before I had finished the second mouthful, my host was lapping up the last drops of soup which a moment before had filled his bowl. It looked like a race to the finish, and I buckled down, but each course was swept away before I had a chance to satisfy my hunger. I might not have been so far behind in the last lap, except that I was finally overcome by nausea, so that I had to sit very tight for fear of disgracing Philip.[12]

. . . We also took tea at the home of a famous professor, who never said a word, chiefly, I suppose, because I chanced for the first and only time since I've been in England to feel in a very garrulous mood, and babbled disgracefully. One sunny lovely afternoon, Philip took me up The Backs in a punt. But we had to abandon many of the things he [had] hoped to do, because I hadn't the strength to carry them out.

. . . Since we returned [to Lord's Wood], I have hardly been able to obey the doctors instructions—breakfast in bed, never up before ten, and an hour's rest in the afternoon—for things have been far too bustling. But Philip has insisted on this luxury several mornings, and has brought up my breakfast himself. He is such a dear wonderful boy. I know his equal could never be found and I have never been able to comprehend the mystery of his loving me. I feel so riotously rich with my darling husband, and my little treasure of a boy.

We have spent several days on the river. Philip has a jolly little boat and one can always get tea at the locks. One day Uncle Walter[13] and a young friend of Philip's joined us, and afterward we all had dinner here together. It was the first time Uncle Walter had been here in three years, so Philip proudly boasts that our coming has made Lord's Wood the family center again after the differences which inevitably arose over [a] divergence of opinion over the war. I like all of Philip's uncles, but no member of the family is as charming as Mother Florence, who grows more delightful still on further acquaintance.

Crystal Eastman and Walter Fuller spent last weekend with us.[14] It did seem strange to meet our New York friends so far away from home. We expect to go into London Friday when we shall probably stay with them. From Aug. 27 to Sept. 4, we shall be at Aunt Millie's,[15] so I shall have much to tell you when we return. . . .

. . . The weather has been frightfully hot for England, and there has been day after day of sunshine. . . . Last night there was a little rain, and today the air is cooler. Has it been scorching in Michigan? By the way, Mother, did I tell you that our tenants have written to say they expect to vacate our house in Nutley this fall?[16] That settles the last of a long string of uncertainties which hung over our heads this spring. So we shall move into the house as soon as I return from England. It is very difficult to get passage, and it looks as though I would have to remain here until November 1st, but if I take the nurse over with me, it will not be so bad.[17]

Philip is sitting beside me waiting impatiently, so I must make haste. He and Noel send heaps of love to you all, and so does your

Little Girl.

To Loretta Secor

General's Meadow
Walmer, Kent
Summer 1919

Dearest Mother,

There is just a little breathing spell before dinner, and hence the *beginning* of this letter which I hope may be finished before the week ends. This is Friday, and we arrived at General's Meadow

Wednesday afternoon. Lady Sargant, who is Aunt Millie, is a delightful hostess. Sir Charles (Uncle Charlie), whom I have been expecting to regard with great awe, is rather a genial, quiet man of advancing years who plays golf in his leisure time and presides at court as a learned judge at other seasons.[18] He seems slightly surprised at the brood of romping children he has hatched, and is also, I think, a little subdued by them, for they take all manner of liberties with him. They are Millicent—about eighteen, not attractive but rather serious and quite determined to enter the medical profession, though a few years ago her father would have scoffed at such presumption in a woman. Janet is a few years younger—lovable, romping and full of life. Eddie the youngest is about a dozen years. He enters Rugby next autumn and is altogether charming.

. . . General's Meadow is a great, lovely house of three stories which contains quite enough rooms to lose yourself comfortably in. During the war the family was moved into a smaller home and the whole place was converted into a hospital of one hundred beds. It was a tremendous undertaking and Aunt Millie distinguished herself by her efficient organization.

There are lovely terraced gardens at the back, and a charming lily pond. Stretching away at one side are green meadows which nourish a flock of fleecy sheep, and above the meadows rise the chalk cliffs which separate Aunt Millie's from the sea. France is just across the channel and we plainly saw the shore line today.

This is I suppose quite typically a rich English country place with guests coming and going constantly. Aunt Millie confided that she had but four servants now when she usually had six—but in spite of this hardship we are pursued with service from morning till night. At 7:30 a.m. we are awakened by a maid who comes in with tea which we take in bed. If one throws down a dress for the moment and leaves the room, one returns to find it carefully hung up. At this moment I hear the maid in Philip's room adjoining, laying out his dress suit for dinner.[19] Now she has arrived in my own sanctuary and is turning down the beds and laying out our nighties for the night. If one steps out of a pair of shoes they disappear and are returned later with a neat polish. Philip protested that it was too much when they carefully folded a union suit which he had deserted for just a few minutes.

We spend most of our time in dressing, and I am having some puzzle, to make my scanty wardrobe go round. (I have seven dresses.) You dress for breakfast, you dress for tennis, you dress for tea, you dress for dinner—and most welcome of all, you dress for bed.

I arrived in a frightful state—the result I guess of too strenuous a time, for which I seem as yet quite unfit. To go back a little—last Friday and Saturday we spent in London. All day Friday I met more of Philip's friends, which is a tiring job in itself.[20] Friday night we had dinner at Crystal's and Walter's with also Mr. and Mrs. Henderson[21]—friends of Philip. Then we spent the night with the latter—and all Saturday morning rushed from place to place. In the afternoon I returned to Lord's Wood in order to prepare for this visit, while Philip went on to Buxton to consult his old doctor about his carbuncles. Philip arrived at Lord's Wood Monday night, and Tuesday morning I left for London again—Jerome K. Jerome had introduced me to a League of Youth and they had arranged a tea etc. for Tuesday afternoon. When I got there, I found the worst old crowd of reactionaries you can imagine—purely a scheme to back Lloyd George. So of course I had to lock horns with them, and we had a battle royal all afternoon. That was rather exhausting.

Then I joined Pyke, the friend of Philip's who had the thrilling escape from the German prison camp, and Leacock, the Canary Island friend who is now in England, and we had dinner.[22] About ten o'clock I joined Joseph—had more food, and then turned in at his apartment, which he generously gave up by going to the garrett himself. I had hardly fallen asleep when I woke up frightfully ill. I vomited of course and spent a miserable night. All next day I was so ill I couldn't retain a morsel of food or drink.

Philip, nurse, baby and baggage joined me in London. We went to Uncle Willie's (the sculptor uncle who has recently opened a house in London) for lunch, but I was too ill to eat. Then we had a three hour train journey to Walmer, and I tumbled into bed as soon as we arrived—nor did I show my face until next day at noon. I am much improved now, and on the whole I'm feeling much better but I'm far from my normal strength as yet.

Philip and the girls are coming in from the tennis court so I must bring this to a close. . . .

Noel . . . has 4 teeth—two huge ones in the upper jaw. He's been rather upset with so many people around and so much confusion, but I'm hoping he'll show off better in the next few days. We expect to leave here Sept. 4. Phil returns [to America] Sept. 27, and the nurse and I Nov. 2.

Much love to all—
Lella

To Loretta Secor

Lord's Wood
September 26, 1919

Dearest Mother,

I have just had a telegram from Philip, who has been in London today, and as usual his departure is suddenly hastened—like all our comings and goings. A great railway strike is threatened, and so he must rush to Plymouth tomorrow in order to be in readiness to go on board his steamer at nine o'clock Sunday morning. It seems such a pity that his last two days in England should be spent so near, and yet so far from us, but the risk of missing his boat is too great to allow of sentimental considerations.

I'm hastening to write this note . . . so that he may mail it for me. I expect him now every moment, so this must not be long though it is important.

Firstly it is to tell you about Noel's baby sister, who has been sent for and who greeted her Mother with a joyful kick a few days ago.[23] That's about all there is to be said for her at the moment, though she will probably make herself heard more forcibly a little later. Her name is Philippa Secor Florence. I am feeling quite well again, and have laid aside a heap of work to do while Philip and I are separated. Six weeks seems a long time to be apart and I shall miss him furiously.

I expect to sail with Noel and Nurse on Oct. 26th though I

am still hoping that I shall be able to get passage on Oct. 12th. . . . We would like to have you come to Nutley for a visit. Better make plans for Christmas but more of this later.

Much love,
Lella.

Upon his return to New York, Philip arranged for their household effects to be moved to his "ancestral home" in Nutley, where he had been born on June 25, 1890. A four-bedroom house with several acres of land, a separate studio, and other outbuildings, the place was very run down after many years of tenants. Philip moved in, arranged to take his meals at a boarding house nearby, and tried to make the house habitable.

The Niew Amsterdam, *bringing Lella, Noel, and the nurse, docked on November 4. "Lella had a rotten passage," Philip wrote his mother, "the nurse being sick all the time and the second class crowded. . . . However, she arrived looking very sweet and cheerful in your lovely fur coat and Noel enjoyed himself as usual. Today Lella has thrown herself into fixing the house. . . ."*

She continued energetically feathering her nest throughout December. "Lella has been working away to the limit and has become an expert wall-painter. My specialty is stripping off old wallpaper and painting ceilings."

A young Scottish housekeeper had been hired from an ad for $6 a week, but Miss Gilbert, the English nurse, would not eat with her, and took her meals with Lella and Philip. "We rather hope that Miss Gilbert and Lella's mother will get on," Philip wrote to Mary Sargant-Florence, "and do their gossiping together, as they both like that more than we do. At present Miss Gilbert spends her evenings at the Cinema down Franklin Avenue. . . ."

Mother Secor arrived after New Year's, expecting to stay through "Philippa's" birth. The Scottish housekeeper had left, but Lella was feeling very well and was able to manage the work alone.

On February 15 David Anthony, a "perfect brown boy," was born.

To Laura Kelley and Lida Hamm

115 Vreeland Avenue
Nutley, N.J.
February 26, 1920

My dear Sisters,

. . . The work and anxiety and hazards of the past months are over. Little David Anthony (named for Susan B. whose hundredth birthday anniversary fell on his birthday; David is for Philip's great friend David Leacock of the Canary Islands) lies asleep in his basket; Noel is recovering from the first cold of his life; Philip is again quite himself after several days of threatened illness as the result of strain and anxiety;[24] Mother is greatly improved after feeling quite miserable for several days;[25] I am recovering in a perfectly marvelous way—and I have a gem of a housekeeper who came yesterday! Ergo—a household which for a whole week has bumped along on one wheel over rough roads, so to speak, is once more settling into a semi-state of order and tranquility.

. . . I've had the most amusing and most distressing experiences for weeks past in trying to get a housekeeper. Finally when baby came three weeks ahead of schedule, I had only a woman who came in for weekends and occasional mornings. Mother has probably told you about the perfidy of the English nurse we brought over, so you see we were in a frightful hole.[26] In desperation we got an old Irish woman for a week. She was apparently slightly off her head, being possessed of seven or more devils. By the end of the third day she had Mother so buncoed that she dare not enter the kitchen, and when Nurse Clark (our beloved nurse who was with me when Noel came) came upstairs flushed and trembling after an encounter with the demon of the kitchen, Philip had to dismiss her peremptorily. Then there was a painful interregnum when we had no one, and finally came tripping along a brilliant idea to me. So we advertised for a couple to whom we would give room and board in exchange for the household services of the wife. We drew a wonderful pair[27]—she's scrubbing and dusting the house into wonderful order, and he's mending a thousand loose ends. It's too good to be true, and we're just holding our breath.

How I wish you could see my two dear boys. I'm so proud of them! Noel . . . goes from one thing to another like greased lightning, and is so strong that he completely does his grandmother out in half an hour. . . . David Anthony is almost as vigorous. At the tender age of one week he holds up his head and looks about with grave interest in his surroundings. He has a heavy silken thatch of black hair and bears a strong resemblance to his Father, who finds it hard to forgive him for not being a girl. . . .

I've never had a chance to tell you how much we appreciated your lovely Christmas gifts, and how much we have enjoyed the sleigh.[28] Noel simply loves it, and settles back with such a happy smile whenever he is put in. We have had such quantities of snow that Philip has been able to make great use of it. . . .

. . . Both the babies send kisses to their dear Aunties.

Much love
Lella.

By April, Philip wrote to his mother, the household was running fairly smoothly. A woman had been found to take the children out in the afternoons, but instead of napping as he felt she should, Lella was "terribly keen to spend her leisure digging the garden!" Mr. Bartel had turned out to be too erratic to perform gardening duties but Lella was determined to plant vegetables herself and had ordered seed.

By May, explaining that Lella had no time for letter writing, Philip described her daily schedule: "She rises at 6 a.m., goes to bed at 10 p.m., has to nurse Anthony at 2 a.m.–leaving six hours sleep or thereabouts. The day is spent in shopping, cursing tradesmen over the telephone, organizing the household, and, whenever possible, gardening. . . ."

The many fruit trees on the property were discovered to be badly blighted and Lella went into an orgy of pruning and spraying, with Philip's admiring assistance. The result of this foray was an attack of poison ivy which closed Lella's right eye and kept Philip awake at night.

In late May, Lella's sisters Lida and Laura arrived for a week's visit, later taking Mother Secor back to Battle Creek. "Mother has been very poorly," Philip wrote, "and I think it will be a great relief to Lella to have one less responsibility.

"Lella and I are happier than ever and we found even a week *of guests most distracting, i.e. distracting us one from the other. Of course Lella's family are pretty conventional . . . and not interested in thought. Indeed, though Lella and I* began *by thinking that Mother's ardent Christianity would be a stumbling block, we ended by discovering that it was her . . .* materialism *that separated us. . . . In fact, though we don't say grace & she does, it is we who are the more spiritual!"*

Lella had hired a woman described by Philip as a "coal black mammy from Florida, an absolute prize" for $50 a month. But "a careful statistical review brought out the fact that Lella did not gain more than one hour per diem thereby, at most one hour and a half. And this two-servant system was going to allow her to go back to work in New York next winter! [This] has so discouraged us that we have determined to leave America in the autumn unless I definitely get a position that makes it worthwhile struggling along."

To Mary Sargant-Florence

115 Vreeland Avenue
Nutley, N.J.
June 5, 1920

Mother Dear,

Isn't it amazing how swiftly events move! So much has taken place during the past three months that the bits of letter which I tried to piece together shortly after Anthony came now seem like the most remote ancient history. At the moment we are engrossed by the happy event of yesterday,[29] so that garden, nurse, housekeeper, books, music—all the interests, and problems too—which troop through our days are eclipsed. . . . We drank their healths at dinner in some home-made grape wine which has turned into wonderful port, and which was left by my sisters on their departure—for medicinal purposes only. Philip proposed the toast and concluded, "May they be as happy as we are"—which we both agree would be a mighty achievement for anyone. Do tell us, will Alix keep her own name, or has that custom not invaded England at all?[30]

Mother begs me to congratulate you on your new son-in-law but doubts whether yours can be as fine as hers. She loves Philip dearly, and in her first letter after her return to Michigan confessed a greater affection for him than for her own son.

I wish we could tell you how happy we have been, living in your dear old place at Nutley—in spite of all the rush of events which have pursued us madly ever since we returned from England. First we were engrossed with decorating and settling the house and acquiring some furniture—has Philip told you of our adventures at second-hand sales?—then came Anthony, and Mother and my sisters, with a steady procession of housemaids, nurses, doctors, artisans and tradespeople. Just now we feel like theatrical stars who have been trailing our company through a long series of one-night stands, and have at last settled down for a season's run. For the first time the house is sufficiently organized so that I am able occasionally to spend a few uninterrupted minutes with Philip, and the books we love to read together and the music we play together[31] are gradually coming into their own again after such long interruption that both of us were beginning to be rather upset. We have just concluded a wonderful week at work in the garden (I have new "overhauls" as Mammy calls them), the net result of which is:

Vegetables Planted
Corn
Peas
Potatoes
Swiss Chard
Lettuce
Radishes
Cauliflower
Egg Plant
Watermelons
Squash
Cantaloupes
Beans, etc. etc.

Flowers Planted
All the loveliest kinds

Also, walks laid out, paths made, trenches dug, hollow places filled, etc,etc.

In addition, we have carefully manicured, barbered, powdered and painted all the trees, shrubs and vines, and there is every promise of a bountiful crop of pears, peaches, cherries, some apples, grapes and strawberries. Of the latter we have a fine bed made from scattered plants left by [ex-tenant] Mr. Fitting who seems to have cared very badly for everything.

Second Installment—1 month later
July 5

It seems clear that part of this letter will be remote history. It is stupid to read of planting seeds when only yesterday we had peas from our own vines for dinner. Just at the moment when I began to think of books and music with the house organized and the seeds tucked away in the earth, the unreasonable stuff began to grow and ever since we have been having a mad race to keep up with things. We went out after a lapse of a couple of days to find a young forest of weeds. But other things are growing too, and I hope to have enough vegetables to last partly through the winter.

The cherries were rather disappointing. The large sweet ones were wormy and devoured by birds as well. The other trees are delicious but the fruit is small. Peaches, pears and grapes promise well, but I am almost terrified at the prospect of a large crop which must be cared for.

Philip has told you of course about the departure of the Bartels.[32] *He* became quite unbearable, and it has been nothing if not a relief to have them gone. We still have Mammy. She came back yesterday from a three-day holiday in New York, which gave me a chance to see just what I would do if left alone with two babies, house and garden. Her daughter has a fine "department" in New York. Mammy eats only pork and hopes to convert us to this indigestible diet. Why, she worked for Jews once who never ate pork until she cooked it for them, and then they ate nothing else, and they were "crocheted" (Kosher) Jews too. She loves the children and is at her best when after Noel in hot pursuit while she calls, "Here Sugah, come Sugah!"

We nearly lost her once. Her son . . . wrote from Jacksonville, Florida, that he had a cough which Mammy said had resulted from an attack of the "influence," and she was determined to leave on the next boat to look after him. . . . [He] had asked in the letter to have the doctor (Philip) send him some pills for his cough, and it was clear that either some pills must be forthcoming at once or Mammy would be forthgoing. Dr. Alling who brought Anthony responded to my S.O.S. and sent pills which have cured the cough.

I feel quite certain that she will stay until the autumn and then another readjustment will be needed. Two sisters or friends who will provide each other with companionship seem to be indicated, for it is clear that our establishment is not large enough to harbor a nurse, and a housekeeper and a husband as well. But in defense of the wife-and-husband scheme, which was mine, I must avow that it worked splendidly while it lasted, and that it might work very well indeed if a neat, clean, subdued husband could be found among the working classes—which Philip says cannot be done.

Meanwhile, I am doing the housework myself, taking a slash at the garden whenever I can. We are going to try eating out at a boarding house tonight—Mammy likes to cook her own food. . . .

I have tried every combination of scheme possible to encompass the work myself, and I can do it, but at the expense of all cultural interests, and all my strength. The vigor which I accumulated shortly after Anthony came—and I have not felt so splendid in years—is gradually being worn down, and I approach evening too tired to be any sort of intellectual companion for my husband. . . .

I am afraid this last will rather alarm you. Indeed we are getting along splendidly even without a housekeeper at all, but I should not like to contemplate an indefinite period of isolation for the intellectual companionship which has meant so much to us both. And [which] we are looking forward with greatest joy to resuming in the autumn *WHEN YOU COME.*[33]

By then the fruit and vegetable harvest will be over and the heaviest of the outdoor work at an end, and we shall be in readiness to organize a delightful autumn and winter which revolves completely around you. . . . There is every likelihood that we shall remain in America now until spring at least, and there is no definite assurance that we can get to England even then. I expect to take up my work again this fall if it is possible after weaning Anthony, and Philip's work may prove so lucrative and so desirable that it will seem wise to continue here in this dear old place. Meanwhile the babies are growing up and missing their grandmother. . . .

. . . We are certain that a change of environment for you will prove most happy and profitable. Ergo, if a change seems definitely indicated, why not a change to America while we are settled in this comfortable house and can well entertain you? There seems every likelihood that the exchange will approach a more equitable adjustment before long, and in any event, traveling on the continent—unless you were engaged in some lucrative work, would be quite as expensive as a trip to America. An additional argument of course is the one you advanced yourself, viz. the economy to be derived from a combined domestic establishment.

As for your work—and that seems to be the only question of importance which remains to be settled—is it not altogether likely that you would find it advantageous to try to pick up the lines connecting with the very desirable reputation you were making for yourself here[34] and to open up new lines of contact with the art world in America—even such as it is? You must remember that an intellectual foreigner, especially one pursuing the arts, has a great advantage in America—much more prestige than can be claimed by native talent, and particularly when she is able to present distinct and original work such as your experiments with the color analogy. I have every belief that we will be able to introduce you to persons of interest and influence whom you would find agreeable and helpful. And the studio will be ready for you—to say nothing of the rooms which we are leaving for your advice, notably the nursery and the smaller bedrooms which need doing over. Could you find it in your heart to disappoint us? . . .

The end of this document must approach, and I have still so much to enter therein, that I think, as the wife of a statistician, I should set it down as follows.

YOUR BIRTHDAY
It will be close at hand when this reaches you, and you will know that we are thinking all day of you and loving you hard and sending a hundred happy wishes across the sea. . . .

NOEL
Tall, slender and agile, of remarkably fine build. . . . Yellow hair worn cropped all around, eyes as blue as the skies in Italy, and pink and white skin. Unusually dexterous—it is difficult to keep any clothes on him for he loves to run about naked, and impossible to keep shoes or stockings on his feet. Yesterday we found him on the third rung of the ladder leading into the cherry tree. A few minutes later he had taken the screen out of one of the bay windows and

was leaning far out to hail the people passing by. Then he discovered a can of paint which I supposed was out of his reach and decorated the top of his bureau with a fine futurist design. Deprived of that, he found his father's flute which he used for a walking stick. His powers of imitation seem astounding to us, and his mental processes are quick and keen. He is so sunny and merry and extremely lovable. His attachment to his father is touching.

ANTHONY
A charming little boy whose distinct personality was early observable. He is quite the sunniest baby imaginable, with a ready smile for those he loves, and a happy flow of gurgling contentment when he is alone. It is likely that he will talk more quickly than Noel has. His eyes are not brown *yet* but I am still hoping. . . . He has grown very good and sleeps all the night through. His skin is like a transparent rose leaf which has fallen on a bronze autumn leaf. His forehead broad and beautiful, but not quite so high as Noel's, a charming mouth and nose. His face is rather round and delicate, so that most people mistake him for a girl. Mammy cannot understand why de Lawd done change his mind after Anthony was started and made him a boy instead of a girl. His hair which started almost black is now a dark brown with glints of gold like Philip's. His eyebrows are brownsilk beautifully curved, and his lashes heavy and almost black. And he loves music as does Noel. He is extremely observant and looks about with great interest at every new object. (Note: A fond mother craves indulgence if she has seemed too extravagant.)

PHILIP
Who grows dearer every day and sheds a radiance of happiness over his little circle and beyond, so that everyone who meets him loves him too.

—and who calls me now to go to dinner and sends his love with mine to our dear Mother.

Lovingly
Lella

Lella apparently wrote no other letters this summer, but Philip made regular reports to Mary Sargant-Florence. "Lella & I celebrated [*my birthday*] *with a ride on secondhand bikes we have bought. We went all along the Old Canal to the top of those high cliffs towards Paterson. . . . It was so lovely having Lella away from household & garden cares for a bit."*

He continued to press his mother to visit them in September, promising, "We could live very cheaply, having enough provender planted to feed a dozen vegetarians." . . . "Full preparations are being made for your stay. . . . I read that New York is to have a particularly brilliant musical season this winter & [*we*] *mean to DO this thoroughly."*

By midsummer his tone had changed. Writing that the U.S. Public Health Service would continue to employ him during the winter, he added, "BUT I don't think we can either of us stand American housekeeping conditions much longer–not unless I get a whacking salary. . . . I have determined that life in America is too degrading for Lella unless her husband can earn at least $3,500 and can afford to pay $100 a month for a housekeeper and $75 a month for a nurse.[35] *. . . If no decent job is offered from America by October I shall look around for something in England." A terse report on the state of the household followed: "Weeds overpowering everything. Cherries rotting on the trees. Beans going to waste. NO HANDS. Cultural pursuits: NIL."*

And in August, "Mammy's feet collapsed in some mysterious way & she is having them 'fixed' in New York so now Lella has the entire care of both children again. We got a housekeeper . . . who cooks beautifully. She is not likely to last though, as she is likely to be engaged to the grocer next door. . . . This sort of thing of course is going to happen all autumn & winter & spring. . . . The weeds have beaten us. Some are actually 8 feet high. . . . Mosquitoes ghastly . . . we can't sit out."

Mary Sargant-Florence had heard enough. She sent her regrets and Philip replied, "Your letter just came . . . with further reasons (economic-domestic) for not coming to America. I must confess that it was *worrying me considerably how you would take the 'state' in which we have to live . . . really more like peasants than anything else. Lella has no time to do any shopping for clothes or anything for herself . . . , working hard on the kids and whenever possible in the garden and sewing the rest of the time.'' He had been ''frightfully busy earning a living and not able to help at all,'' noting that he had found the studio ''an absolute* sine qua non *and am doing a lot of work there.''*[36]

By September all was gloom. ''Your surmise as to my & Lella's silence is correct; we have reached the nadir of our domestic fortunes and for the last two weeks have had no one *to help. Mammy, to whom we had got quite attached, lost her son and had to go to Florida to bury him. . . . Meanwhile Lella works from 6 a.m. to 11 p.m.—the Seventeen-Hour-Day—while her husband writes pamphlets advocating the Eight-Hour-Day for factory operatives. Unfortunately, though not being particularly busy, I was not able to help much owing to a beastly back-ache. . . . Had you come this month you would certainly have found a mess. Lella is trying, on top of all, to bottle the quantities of pears & peaches that have ripened.''*

To Loretta Secor

115 Vreeland Avenue
Nutley, N.J.
September 1920

Dear Mother—

Just a line before I start on the second lap—i.e. prepare A's food for the day, feed the children No. 2. and start on housework. I've already bathed and fed them both once, and fed my Big Boy and myself. Had a letter from Mammy this morning. I'm afraid it will be several weeks before she gets back. . . . She expects to come back to me, and her daughter—who lives in N.Y. and her little girl age 4—will come out during the week to do my [house]work. So the arrangement is ideal if it materializes and if I can hold out till then. I work regularly from 6 a.m. to 10 p.m. but I'm standing it pretty well so far.

I'm putting up as much fruit as possible but some has gone to waste because I simply could not get to it. Please tell me as soon as you can how to make grape jelly and spiced grapes—also what else can I do with pears beside preserving them and pickling them? I've cooked them all down rather thick because they mostly have to be cut into small pieces [because of] worms. . . .

So dreadfully sorry to know how miserable you feel. I'd so like to bring the babies home before we go to Europe and maybe it will be possible someway.

Love to all—and loads for Mother
Lella

Lella and Philip planned to spend the spring and summer in England, renting the Nutley house. Philip wrote his mother proposing that they spend "at least two months at Lord's Wood if you will have us. About June first Lella and I will try for our long-postponed honeymoon . . . first traveling around England a little . . . , then possibly France and anywhere else on the Continent. . . . Of course this involves a highly competent nurse with the kids at Lord's Wood."

To Loretta Secor

115 Vreeland Avenue
Nutley, N.J.
[September 1920]

Dearest Mother,

I'm about to stagger up to bed and as I'm in no condition for any sort of converse, this isn't meant for a letter but just a bow and throw you all a kiss.

I'm still alone. I've had no word from Mammy in more than two weeks. So everything seems extremely uncertain. Besides the housework and the babies I've put up almost 75 qts. of fruit—and still [have] a good many pears and some peaches I hope to finish this week. I'm standing the work remarkably well. Some days I get so tired that it seems as though I could never last until night. But I do. I've dropped from 159 to 133 pounds—for which I'm profoundly thankful. A few more weeks and I shall be quite respectably slender.

Thanks so much for your promptness, and Laura's, in sending on those valuable recipes. I know it isn't easy to attend to a thing like that at once, and I appreciate it greatly. I made twelve pints of grape juice which is *delicious* with Vichy, and about 20 glasses of jam-jelly—a recipe Philip brought from Waterbury. I've tried the pear conserve—using dates and raisins instead of figs, which I couldn't get—not so good but still excellent on bread. I've made a good many peach and pear pickles and shall do most of the rest that way. It's extremely hard to get cans—my last were $1.80 a dozen. All sold out everywhere. Sugar now 14¢ here.

The babies are growing so fast. Anthony is even livelier than Noel was at his age. He cannot be kept anyplace. Today he plunged out of his pram but I bolted down the path just in time to catch him. It gave me such a fright. It adds a good deal to his care when he must be watched every moment—and he gets out of straps as fast as I put them on. . . .

Noel adds a new word every few days. . . . I've taught him to say wee-wee when he wants to urinate. Today he was looking at a magazine and came across a black native with a bowl in his hand about to catch some sap from a rubber tree. He pointed with great glee and said, "Wee-wee." Noel considers it great fun to have learned this important function and I found him at first trying to fill every sort of receptacle he came across. . . .

Philip is in Waterbury for 3 days. It is the first time he has gone away since that terrible storm two weeks ago. I was all alone—both babies were wakened by the storm and too frightened to sleep so I held them both until the storm abated after midnight.

The little dress and petty came yesterday. I'm so grateful, for Anthony hasn't another whole dress left. I'm trying to darn the others and keep them on until I have a chance to get to the shops. . . . I've tried in vain to see how you fixed the little dress. It is just like new, and so lovely. . . .

I do hope you are feeling better again. How I wish I could be near you so you could see the babies.

And now to bed.

Much love to all,
Lella

To Loretta Secor

115 Vreeland Avenue
Nutley, N.J.
October 1920

Mother Dear—

Every single day for weeks I thought I would be after mailing a letter before I slept. You would have volumes if all my thoughts of you were typed.

I am still alone, and getting rather tired. Mammy has been back from the South for two weeks, but she has not been able to come, and I don't know when she will be well enough. Also her grand-child, Ruth, has a bad cold so Esther [her daughter] cannot come either. So I am just hanging on, but Philip is determined that we shall not wait on them any longer, and is going to see them tomorrow to find out just what they mean to do. It is seven weeks now that I have been entirely alone. . . .

Yesterday I finished the last of the fruit—and I feel like a kite cut loose. I have put up over ninety quarts, besides about twelve little glasses of rich preserves, and twenty-five of grape-lade. Also ten pints of grape juice. IT HAS been a job.

When the last of the fruit has been bottled
  And the vines are withered and dry
And the labels have all been adjusted
  With many a groan and sigh,
Faye shall rest, and faith, she shall need it,
Lie down for a minute or two;

Till her children, the blessed darlings,
Shall call her to work anew.
With apologies to Kipling, ''L'Envoi''

How I wish you could see the babies. They grow so interesting from day to day. . . . Aunt Fan has asked us to bring the children to her house for [Noel's] birthday, and invite in some friends for tea. We are planning to do it, but it will be a rather a job if we have no nurse.

Philip has made a late tea, and also it is the children's bedtime. Also I have not washed my luncheon dishes, and also I have nothing ready for dinner. So I must rush off. But I determined to dash off these few lines at the expense of everything. . . .

The babies send you love and kisses and so do Philip and I.

Lovingly,
Lella

To Loretta Secor

115 Vreeland Avenue
Nutley, N.J.
November 13, 1920

Dearest Mother,

This letter has been in contemplation every hour, literally, for days and days. Sometimes when the day ends I am simply amazed to find things still undone which I started at eight o'clock in the morning. I hope soon now to be relieved of the very strenuous time I have been having. Things have come to a head with Mammy. After many promises and delays, ... I gave her one day in which to decide whether she could come back, since she was still in very poor health. A letter this morning said she was not able to come now . . . and so we have advertised for someone else. You can imagine how I dread taking chances on a new one, but perhaps luck will be with me.

Except that I am tied to the house like a prisoner and that my day does last pretty long so that I am overtired before it ends, I get along pretty well, especially now that the fruit is over. I feel badly about some vegetables that I simply have not had time to gather—we seem to have a plentiful crop of peanuts—but as the weather has been extremely mild perhaps there is still some chance. . . . It is hard to feel reconciled to the complete loss of these wonderful autumn days with their glorious coloring, which I have had to view mostly from my kitchen or nursery window. . . .

Where shall I begin to tell you about the children? . . . [Noel] is quite a big man now and appeared at his party in his first little pants—the charming suit Mother F. sent from England. . . . He is too smart for his Mother and keeps me guessing about what to do next. He has now learned to let down the side of his bed and climb in and out so that it is impossible to keep him anywhere. I hardly know how I should manage if it had not been for a happy idea of Philip's . . . to turn the Bartel room into a day nursery. . . . Often he plays alone [there] for several hours, sometimes with Anthony in the pen, and they amuse each other greatly.

The party was a great success. We . . . went by trolley to Newark and thence [to New York] by tube. We took the little folding go-cart, which was a great success as it holds them both. . . . Aunt Fan had prepared a dear little birthday cake with three candles—one for luck—and two children and their mothers came. . . . After the party, Aunt Fan made a little supper for us and we stayed almost until nine o'clock—a most extraordinary spree for me. . . .

So far we have had just one response to our ad—a girl of seventeen . . . perhaps the morrow will bring better results. . . . Philip and I want to celebrate our wedding anniversary which went by unnoticed except for some dear gifts which Philip bought—part for him to present to me and part for me to present to him. . . . We have decided to have a grand splash in New York, with a night at a hotel—theater and meals with friends. Won't that be jolly? But of course it depends on whether we get some competent person to stay with the children. . . .

I have just made a little beginning on my accumulated sewing, starting with about twenty pairs of socks for Philip. Also, I took those little knitted stockings of the babies', which had such narrow feet, cut the feet off and sewed the legs onto those lovely little woollen socks which I brought from England. They look cunning . . . I shall have to make Tony some plain little short dresses in colored goods, for he begins to want to crawl about. . . . He looks more and more like Philip, which of course delights me beyond measure, and there is no longer any doubt that his eyes are brown. . . .

Noel . . . still loves books and papers, and jabbers away pretending to read. Both the children love music as I discovered one morning when they were both so cross that I couldn't do any work and it was still an hour to their nap time. So I played to them throughout the hour. Anthony hummed most of the time and Noel never offered to get down from his chair. I thought it quite remarkable. We seldom have time for music any more, and never while they are awake.

. . . I think of you constantly, and pray that you may be feeling better. . . .

Much love from us both and from the babies too.

Lella

Philip wrote to Mary Sargant-Florence on November 16, 1920: "Stop Press News. Lella has engaged two [housekeepers,] Dora and Lily respectively, to come next week. She hopes to get work in New York so that we can afford this luxury and is setting off tomorrow to hunt through New York magazine offices for a 'job.' It's very exciting."

To Loretta Secor

115 Vreeland Avenue
Nutley, N.J.
November 30, 1920

Dearest Mother,

Anthony is asleep and it is not quite time to give Noel his dinner. Hence begins a letter.

Dora and Lily came and saw and went. Don't imagine that I am referring to two fair young blonds, as you might suppose. They are as black as a burnt pudding, and of Dora there is more than 200 pounds. At least there was when last I saw her, which was yesterday after dinner. Then she asked leave to go home to Newark to see a recalcitrant son . . . and later telephoned for Lily to join her to advise her on some weighty subject. So Lily departed also, and behold the night passeth and the day dawneth and the sun sitteth high in his heavens yet there comes no report either of good or evil from them, not from either one, and the mistress sitteth in the nursery and waiteth with anxious heart.

For behold, scarce a week hath passed over the earth since they did arrive, both Dora and Lily, promising faithfully to prepare food and drink and to watch tenderly Noel and Anthony, the sons of Philip. And now they have disappeared from the face of the earth and none knoweth whence they have fled or at what time they will return.

One thing I do know, however, and that is that they have left all their clothes and must come back sometime. Dora is an excellent cook, and Lily is patiently trying to learn how to take care of the children, though it is a sore task to force a little information through her well padded skull. I am sincerely hoping that they will come back, for I have been able to gather up so many loose ends during the few days they have been here. I have plastered a hole in Philip's ceiling and painted it, painted the windows, had the curtains washed and rehung, finished the day nursery . . . , cleaned the studio with Philip's help, waded through a stack of mending and sewing, classified magazines, music, etc. which have been waiting for action these many months, and done a heap of odd jobs. . . . As soon as I can get things straightened around here, providing of course that the ladies come back and prove efficient, I shall try to get a job. I want to renew my connections in the magazine field before we go abroad so I can take advantage of the splendid opportunity I will have to do some work over there.

. . . I am so glad you had such a happy Thanksgiving day. I thought of you so much and yearned to be with you as we sat down to our solitary Thanksgiving turkey. I picked up a bargain in a little bird. We ate in state with a grand mince pie and towering cake made by Dora. I have had no one else as competent as she is. Lily is not so intelligent, but she is patient and willing and perhaps she will learn—if she ever comes back. . . .

The Next Morning before breakfast.

The duo have just put in an appearance. Poor Dora is having some sort of trouble about a wayward son, and I feel the greatest sympathy for her. I am too glad to have them back to be very cross with them. . . .

[Dora's son was a cook on a ship. In a letter to Philip at Waterbury Lella related Dora's story: "This is the morning after and they have just returned. You see, it was this way. Dora's son got into an altercation with a man in the hold. Just how it happened she doesn't know. Maybe they was shaking dice. Anyway, Son has a good round with Friend Enemy and then plants a meat cleaver in his skull. Now comes the ship to port laden with wild threats of vengeance. The man with the cleavered skull will have Son arrested and clapped in jail. Enter Mother Love, daintily personified by Dora. She opens a League for the Settlement of the Disputes of Injured Colored Persons, and arbitrates. She argues the case soulfully all day long, first on the wharves in New York, thence to Jersey City; and finally, at an adjourned session in Newark in the evening, the matter is settled thusly: Dora pays for the stitched skull at the rate of about $4 per stitch, and presents its owner with $25 worth of

soothing balm. But it is clearly understood by the party of the first part and the party who is in two parts that said adjustment shall not be construed as in any manner whatsoever prejudicing a reopening of the case if and when a dark corner, a handy meat ax, and a moment of abstraction seem to indicate an auspicious moment for settling the score once and for all to the satisfaction of all parties surviving.

"Dora is sorry and it ain't going to happen again."]

. . . I look back upon my summer's work with amazement. I do not see how I managed to do everything, and sleep so little. I am simply starved for a little intellectual employment, and Philip avers it will be the triumph of his life to see me with my feet up, reading a novel. Also I think he stipulates a box of chocolates, which is taboo—too fat—I haven't touched a piece in three months.

. . . I often think of you and wish I could take you out in your chair.[37] Do you get any use of it now? I should think it might be nice for you to move about from room to room in. Mother thinks she's smart doesn't she, with a lady's maid to bath her and comb her hair?!!!! . . . How I should love to have seen you in your gay new lounging robe and foxy slippers. I really think you could afford to wear silk stockings *every* day. I am sending a check for $10 to Laura to help pay for the baths, manicuring, shampooing, marcel waving, eyebrow penciling etc. etc. . . .

Dora has breakfast ready, and I'm not dressed. So off I must dash. Much love from us both and many kisses from the babies. Philip thought for a second that he might have to attend a conference in Chicago, and though I miss him fearfully I was more than happy, for that would mean that I could lend him to you for just a bit. But he is afraid he will not be able to go. He grows dearer every day, and I love him some'n terrible. I don't believe another could be found like him in twenty kingdoms.

Much love,
Lella

To Loretta Secor

HOTEL MCALPIN
BROADWAY AT 34TH ST.
NEW YORK CITY

December 1920

Dearest Mother—

Well I *do* feel swagger tonight. Philip is giving me a two-day celebration in honor of our wedding anniversary two months past—and it was well worth waiting for.

Fancy your child, Mother, about to retire in a magnificent room in the McAlpin Hotel, with curtains which slide open when you pull a tassel and glide shut when you pull another (we mean to investigate the inward workings tomorrow) and lights that go plop if you just wink at them!

We've had a day that's too gloriously perfect to be genuine. Lunch with friends this noon—a lovely concert—then a walk in Central Park when the sun was coloring all the fleecy clouds in roseate splashes—supper on Broadway—a few minutes for shopping—then Galsworthy's new play *The Skin Game*.

Even the jam of people, who were poured out of the theaters like so many peas from a basket, was distinctly thrilling.

I have had hard work to keep my mind off the babies even though I know they are quite all right—Philip phoned once to make sure.

Tomorrow we mean just to lie in bed till we feel inclined to get up, but I'm sure I shall hear my little Noel call "Mamma, Mamma" or "DaDa, DaDa" at 6 o'clock in the morning.

We shall lunch at noon with Freda and Evans,[38] then the great treat of the trip—Shaw's *Heartbreak House,* which Philip read to me while Anthony was still keeping me in bed. After that we shall be entertained at tea at the Civic Club by one of Philip's friends—then "Home, James."

I am trying to cling to these two wonderful days, but I know they will just run away like quicksilver. But every day is a wonderful day when I have my Boy. And more than that I have my two little Bambinos thrown in. Was ever Woman so rich? . . .

About their Christmas—We shall make it exceedingly simple with a gay little tree. Tony could use a little brush and comb—real man's stuff you know, not the infant kind—or little shoes or little dresses. He is also prepared to push a tiny wagon, or toy on wheels, back and forth as he sits in his pen. . . . But he still puts things in his mouth—so it mustn't run color.

Noel might have handkerchiefs, linen books with bright pictures, a rag doll or some stockings. . . . But *please please* get only simple and inexpensive things. . . .

Philip wants to sleep. Goodnight—and much love—

Lella.

Lella and Philip returned from their weekend in New York, Philip wrote, "to find three inches of dust on the nursery floor and about one inch on the children's faces. On remonstration [Dora and Lily] *offered their resignation which was accepted!"*

To Loretta Secor

115 Vreeland Avenue
Nutley, N.J.
[late] December 1920

Dearest Mother and Sisters,

This is an eventful day—that is to say it is the morning of the day on which my Boy will return from three days at a convention in Atlantic City, it is the morning after my new 'elp has arrived, and it is the morning when I have a chance to sit down and write that long delayed letter to you.

Firstly, Christmas. I do hope you had a merry day. . . . My

thoughts were with you all day and I yearned to join in your merrymaking. Our own day was exceedingly quiet. I sent the little colored girl, Ruth, home in the morning, because Philip couldn't abide an outsider at our Christmas table, and because I didn't have the heart to put the little thing alone in the kitchen for her Christmas dinner. Philip helped with the children all day, and I prepared our Christmas dinner—chicken and cranberries and a few of the fixings—which we ate in quiet state with our two children, both of whom behaved very badly. We had trimmed the tree the night before—it was set up in the drawing room in front of the mirror—and put on the gifts, including the lovely package for the children from Lida which arrived that day. The other package came Christmas morning and Philip would not allow me to open it until the tree "came off" at four o'clock.[39]

After dinner we packed the babies in the pram and had a walk through the park. At the park entrance Noel begins to say "Pease" and point to the ground, for he knows that here he is allowed to get out and walk. All through the park—it is a good long walk—he runs along with his Father, and it is a toss up which one enjoys it more. Then came the tree. It was gay with its lighted candles and bright fixings left over from last year. The children were both quietly passive at first, but grew enthusiastic as the gifts began to be discovered.

As for Philip and me, we sat limp and speechless on the floor when we saw the lavish display of gifts which those Battle Creek packages disclosed. Up to that moment, it hadn't really seemed like Christmas at all. I didn't even see a shop throughout the whole holiday season, and all the usual festiveness seemed remote indeed. I was overcome with chagrin to see how much you had done, with all your other cares, when I had done nothing at all. Dora and Lily left the day after we got back from our two-day celebration in New York, and there was another interregnum of a week before I got two colored girls. The cook, however, was taken sick on the day she agreed to come, and the young nurse girl came alone. She was entirely inexperienced, and I could not leave the children alone with her[40]—hence the Christmas shopping days came and went while I was still tied to my babies. But perhaps they will reward their Aunties and Grandma by growing up to be great men. Who knows?

Anyway they are adorable children and I just wish you could see them. But I wander.

To get back to the gifts. Of course I can say "thank you" a thousand times on paper, but it will not express a tenth of the loving appreciation we all feel. And if I were to say that you did far too much for us, it would not restrain your loving impulses the slightest degree another time.

My beautiful silk undie and silk stockings are such luxuries! I needed them both badly, for I seldom have a chance to do any shopping and when I do, a thousand things for the children and the house must be attended to. I shall save them to wear when I go traveling. . . .

Lida dear, when I said Tony could use a brush and comb, I didn't expect you to fit them [both] out for life with such beautiful things that I can't bear to let them use them until they are old enough to appreciate them. . . .

They adore the Teddy Bears. What a splendid idea! Noel's has been named Bebob. . . . He started as Bobbie, but Noel himself starts it backwards—so Bebob it is. Noel is a picture running about with Bebob in one arm and Loony in the other. Loony is the green and red clown whose face is soiled with many kisses bestowed affectionately by Noel. . . . Noel cannot eat or sleep, or have his face washed, or his nose blowed, or wee-wee, or perform any other function pleasant or unpleasant which is not shared by Loony. . . . Anthony . . . will love his Teddy more when his affection is not measured by his ability to eat the object in question.

Mother Florence sent me a magnificent silk lounging robe [of] which she made every stitch herself—without a machine. I am deeply touched and greatly complimented by this evidence of her affection, for I know how laborious sewing is for her and how little time she has to give to it away from her art work which engrosses her entire day. It was also partly Philip's gift as he had to pay $7.50 in duty. In addition he gave me adorable slippers to go with it, and some little household necessities. I got him a pair of skates and a fountain pen, so you see what a modest Christmas we had.

I had to rack my brain to arrange Christmas gifts to go the rounds without buying any perfectly useless things in the Nutley shops. I am ashamed that my ingenuity ran out and compelled me at last to send such minor and impersonal gifts to you as money checks. . . . To Ina I sent enough linen to make her tablecloth and a dozen napkins. For [the children] Esther and Mary I framed some of those lovely reproductions of the great masters, and wrote a little sketch of the artists' lives. Also I got a little wooden set of household utensils for Mary, and sent Esther a ribbon I had in the house—Roman stripes. . . . To Philip's various young relatives, we dispatched books selected from our shelves. How was that for a shopless Christmas?

I think I shall like my new 'elp. They are a mother and daughter, very much the type of our own family, to wit: gentle and kind and guaranteed to stand without hitching and perfectly good slaves if you pat them kindly on the head! The mother . . . is very much Aunt Dell's type, except a little more meaty. The daughter is a sort of half-witted female Uriah Heep, who goes about rubbing her hands and reiterating in a rasping voice that she hopes they'll please me, and they'll do their best. She snuffs—I shall be driven soon to offer her a handkerchief and also a nail file—and has eyes like a hammock upsidedown. I should be in despair if the children were entirely at her mercy, but the mother is a bright active little woman and is apparently going to do most everything herself while Florence rubs her hands.

They are both outcasts from factories as was also Ruth. And there are many more again turning to domestic work and glad to get a job at reasonable wages. We tremble no more. We laugh!

In the few weeks—almost three—that Dora and Lily were here, I managed to do quite a few odd jobs—bits of painting and repairing, a great stack of mending, and greatest achievement of all, a really pretty smock from that blue velvet I brought from England. I cut it and made it entirely without a pattern except the old one that I had to look at. It has the points around the bottom and a gold cord girdle. The latter was the cord I had on a dressing gown when I went to the Sanitarium. It has tarnished with age until it is lovely, and I finished the ends with two little bead ornaments I had on a hat. I wore this with my new plaid skirt to New York, and took along a little almost-Alice-blue velour dress that I bought months ago at $10. I fixed it up a bit with some scraps of brown fur and it is really quite dressy.

I wish you could see Noel and Anthony together! They amuse each other immensely. Noel shows Anthony how to do things and also imitates him very cleverly. . . . [Anthony] is a very bright little boy. I had absolutely no trouble in training him to sit on the chair. Twice was sufficient, and now he is as regular as taxes. . . .

Dearest love to you all,
Lella

Lella continued to contact editors in the hope of finding magazine work but, as Philip told his mother, "Lella . . . has been rather disappointed in her supposed friends and is having difficulty in getting a 'job.'" Philip was equally unsuccessful at finding a teaching position in an American university and reported, "The chances of a definite trek to England have in fact been greatly increased," adding that he had written to his former professor, C. R. Fay, about the possibility of securing a lectureship in economics at Cambridge.

To Loretta Secor

[Nutley, N.J.]
January 24, 1921

Dear Ones All,

. . . Philip has been having a week's holiday, and that really keeps me busier than anything else. For I try constantly to be on tap when he wants me to play with him, and in the interim I have to dash about to do my other work. We have had a wonderful week. Several days we spent on the ice, and I am actually learning to skate. One day we went up the canal for almost three miles, most of which I skated alone! I was fearfully stiff the next day, but I determined not to spoil Philip's holiday so I went hiking with him just the same, and it seems to have done me good. You know what a silly boy he is—he can't have any fun on a holiday unless I share it with him, and of course I love to share. One afternoon we took the children out in their sleigh. Philip carted the sleigh to the lake in the wheelbarrow, and I headed the procession with the two youngsters in the little gray pram. They simply loved it.

. . . We still have Mrs. Howard and Florence. They are stupid and incompetent, and the heavy burden of the work falls on Mrs. Howard who works so ineffectively that it takes her from morning till night. She is beginning to complain just a little so I don't know how long they will last. I have to help to prepare any company dinner and frequently do things for the children, which is absurd with two people hired for the purpose. I don't think I should be able to stand it if it were going to be an indefinite arrangement, but as it will not be many weeks before we shall be packing our trunks, I hope the arrangement will last out until the end.

Since Christmas I have been valiantly trying to finish the nursery, but it is still in a fearful mess. I have had to do a good bit of plastering, and the paper came off pretty hard. However, I expect to have it finished when Philip comes back from Waterbury, and also I hope the little room which you had when you were here. I have so often wished that last winter had been like this one—so mild and beautiful that we could have been out of doors most of the time instead of shut up like prisoners as we were. Philip and I have taken several walks, and I am getting able to do four or five miles without feeling especially tired. I have never felt so well and vigorous in my life as I do now, and I do hope I shall be able to keep it up until we go to England, for I was so miserable before, and made such a bad impression I am afraid.

We do not know exactly when we shall go. We had expected to get off by the first of April but I think it will be much nearer the first of June, especially if I get a good job which I now have in prospect. It is on *Everybody's* magazine—which pays excellent salaries. . . . I have another offer from *Collier's* for next month, but if I wait too long I shall not get started before I have to stop. However if I do get a good job, we shall probably remain in America longer, for it's going to be a great big task to get all our clothes ready, get the house ready to rent, and do all the details connected with getting off. We are planning our tour now, and I am fearfully excited. Switzerland, France, Italy—Venice which I have always yearned to see—and perhaps Austria and Germany. Fancy that now, Mother! Can you imagine your little Lella Faye having such a wonderful chance as this? And more than this, having it in company with such an incomparable person as Philip. It seems really too fantastic to be real. I don't suppose anyone was ever as happy as I am.

I had such a lovely letter from Ina the other day. She seemed more like her old self than in any letter I have had for ages. She has put the place up for sale, and I hope she sells it so as to be foot free. With only herself, she ought to be able to travel and broaden her experiences. I would love to have her come and stay with us for a while, for I know she will love the sort of life we lead. But I don't suppose she could be induced to come. It will be a wrench to part with the place, for I did so want to take Philip out there before we let it go. But it would be foolish sentimentality to tie Ina there against such a remote date.

Anthony will soon be a year old. Does it seem possible that a year has passed since that fearful wintry night? He is a beautiful child, and will walk and talk early I think. . . . I am shamed to say that Noel had a little upset with his stomach last week—the first in his life, due perhaps to having meat three days in succession. I spent several days entirely with him, for he felt just mean enough to want me to hold him continually. . . . So you see my days have been pretty full in spite of two helpers. Sometimes I have felt greatly discouraged, for I don't seem able to get much more sewing and extra tasks done than when I was attending to all my work myself. I am also in the throes of dentist work, and as soon as that is over, I must have that little cyst removed from my cheek. It has grown quite large. And so the days speed!

How are you feeling today I wonder? That is the question I ask myself every morning. How I wish we were near enough for a telephone call! I wonder if you have had such a winter as we have? . . .

I forgot to include in my activities of the past weeks a vast amount of typing which I did for Philip, helping him to get out an article.

Lovingly,
Lella

To Loretta Secor

115 Vreeland Avenue
Nutley, N.J.
[January 27,] 1921

Dearest Mother,

Anyway, I have got the ceiling in the nursery done. It is a lovely soft gray, and now I've splashed half the walls with a brilliant French blue. I still have the walls to finish, all the woodwork to paint, and the floor. But it will all have to wait this sunny morning while I dash off a letter to Motherkin. . . .

For three nights, a rat gnawing in the wood work at the head of my bed has kept me awake, and although I threw all the shoes in the closet in his direction last night, it seemed to have no effect.

It was only a day or so ago that [the rat's] presence was discovered. Mrs. Howard said the potatoes were about gone, and as I had put in a big sack full—enough I thought to do us all winter—I was surprised. When I went down cellar to fix the furnace, I saw a potato partly gnawed. I called Mrs. Howard who is very brave, and we pulled aside boxes, and there was a great cache of potatoes—half a bushel I should say. We found an immense nest in a hollow of the wall, and poked out at least another two quarts of potatoes. I don't know how many more have been carried in too far to be available. We tore up the nest, and now the miserable wretch is determined upon revenge. We have started a vendetta, and I mean to use poison today. But if he escapes me, you mustn't be surprised to read great headlines in the newspapers how a whole family was gnawed to bits by a fierce and furious rat! . . .

. . . I have just given [Noel] a magazine to amuse him, which had the usual beautiful lady on the cover. Philip has taught him to call all beautiful ladies Mama, and he would have been greatly bucked if he could have seen Noel point to the cover at once and say Munah Munah—which he now calls me. . . .

It doesn't look now as though I were going to get my job at *Everybody's*. . . . But anyway, I shall consider whatever comes as for the best. Perhaps I should find the task of house, children and job, coupled with the extra work of preparing for an ocean voyage, a bit strenuous. But I need the mon. Philip was greatly amused the other morning at breakfast when I reeled off some jingles about Miss Maloney, the editor—which he added to as we went along—I remember this much:

O Miss Maloney
You big baloney
Don't be so phoney
I need the money
To go to Coney
And feed my Tony
On milk and honey
You are so stoney
I'd like the loan-y
Of just one bone-y etc etc etc etc etc etc.

Philip is coming back from Waterbury tonight, and I shall be so glad. The whole place seems upset when he is gone. He has been away three days and it seems three months.

. . . Much love from your Nutleans—two big ones and two little ones.

Lovingly,
Lella

To Loretta Secor

February 1921

My 'elp is still 'ere.

Dearest Mother,

I've been expecting to write hourly, but as I wanted to send some money, and [as] we were overtaken by our biennial crisis[41] (blame the exchange) I have waited. . . .

. . . It's just possible we shall go to Fayetteville, Arkansas—of all places—next autumn. In that case we shall certainly stop to see you on our way. There is open at the Arkansas State University the position of head of the Economics Department which would promote Philip at once to a full professorship, and offer him such a good salary that it would probably justify removing to such a remote corner.[42]

I've got the nursery about finished, all but the molding in fact. It does look charming. The walls are blue, the ceiling and woodwork French gray, and the floor mahogany. I've painted every inch of the room—also the clothes rack, Noel's high chair and the weewee chair—all gray. I expect to begin on your room tomorrow.

I'm just rushing this off so that it can catch the six o'clock mail. . . .

Such love from us all—but most from your Philip and your Baby.

From "Noel" to Loretta Secor

[In Lella's handwriting.]

115 Vreeland Avenue
Nutley, N.J.
February 1921

Dearest Gran,

I was just having dinner when my lovely Valentine came and Mother stood it up on my table so I could see it all the time. I tried to give the lovely little girl some of my dinner and spilt a little on her dress. But she didn't seem to mind.

Just as we were beginning to look around surreptitiously for crocuses, what do you think happened? Snow! Bushels and bushels of it so that it looks just like it did last year when you were here. I was so excited when I saw it out the window that I rushed to Munah crying "Snow Snow," although I had never remembered being told what it was but once, and that was a good many weeks ago. Yesterday Munah and Dada took Brudah and me out in our lovely sleigh. Munah does the pushing count of Dada's bad back, and she pushed and tugged till she most wore out and consequence—today she feels miserable. Brudah and I both have colds—it's the second one I ever had and Brudah's first. Also Munah and Dada. So we're all feeling a bit out of tune.

Munah and Dada took me to the barber the other day. I didn't like the creature, and I howled till my tones echoed as far as Passaic. Munah finally brought me home and finished the job herself, and here is a little of what came off.

Such love from your little Grandson,

Noel

Lella's days held at least a measure of frivolity which she didn't mention to her mother, but Philip described fully to his: "What do you think is the latest adventure? Dancing Lessons! *An excellently taught class has been started a few doors away & Lella and I are in the midst of the Fox Trot, Something Amble, Hesitation Waltz and all the rest. We're even planning for May Week at Cambridge."*

To Loretta Secor

[Nutley, N.J.]
February [12–]21, 1921

Dearest Mother,

Philip and I dashed to the station this morning to find that Lincoln's Birthday was considered a holiday, and the usual train was off. Consequently we have 20 min. to wait and Philip will be half an hour late for his lecture. I'm going with him so as to take notes on his lecture in order to write an article for him. He is greatly in demand by scientific magazines and has precious little time himself. So I'm going to have a hand at it.

I'm working incessantly trying to get the house finished. . . .

And here this letter stopped to be resumed a week later when I'm again waiting for a train. I have just returned on the ferry from New York—such a marvelous sunny day—and must wait in this dingy Erie Station for half an hour. I went to New York in pursuit of an erratic editor of the *Delineator* who has been dangling a job before my eyes for weeks. In spite of the fact that I had an appointment with her, she had to put me off until Monday—So sorry you know!!! I think I shouldn't pursue her any longer except that the job is particularly choice and carries a nice fat salary. Even so I am rather indifferent about the whole thing for I fancy we shall not get to Europe this summer if I get a job which is too good to leave. So I am determined just to see the thing through to the finish, and accept whatever results.

I have the walls and woodwork finished in your room and half the floor, which I shall try to do now that I am to get home so early. The walls are a curious shade of red-brown, but quite charming. I'm rushing to finish it so as to have it ready for Philip's friend Brian Lawrence. . . . We do not know what moment he will arrive.

You ask why I did the rooms instead of sewing—which, by the way, I have not touched for over two weeks. It is because the rooms had to be redone if we expect to rent the house. I tore the paper off the little room last summer . . . and Noel took it upon himself to tear a great strip off the nursery wall, so that nothing remained for me but to finish his work. I did not intend to do the nursery—but now it is done anyway, and really lovely.

Anthony and I had a joint birthday celebration Sunday morning. We got him a doll and a little sulky to push it in, and a toy dog on wheels. . . . He is such a darling, and is devoted to his mother. . . .

My 'elp asked for a raise this morning which naturally I refused. So I don't know how stable my house is.

Thanks so much for the lovely birthday cards and the dear pink hanky which I'm using this very minute. Philip took me to the opera to hear Mary Garden. . . . My 'elp had a huge birthday cake made at the bakery with 33 candles on it.[43] I did so appreciate it but—it was such a foolish extravagance.

Thank you so much Laura for writing to the dressmaker. I hate to burden you with one extra task when I know how full your days are. I'll select a pattern [for the coats] sometime next week. I think it will be lovely to have the fur cuffs & collar[s] if Mother has enough. Also if there is enough material & fur left I'd like to make little caps to match. Perhaps I'd better make those myself so as to get them to fit. I think they will be too dear for anything. . . .

My station's next so I [must] stop. I think of you most every hour, and pray that you may be much much better.

Such love from us all—

Lovingly
Lella.

This was Lella's last letter to her mother, for Loretta Secor died on March 1. "As you know," Philip wrote his mother, "it was expected, though of course the exact date could not be prophesied. Lella wanted to be there at the end, but once death occurred she did not see much point in the long journey to Battle Creek that was involved, and I was away at Waterbury at the time. So we did not attend the funeral. However, as all Mother's friends live [near-by], *. . . our absence did not make much difference and the ceremony was well-attended. Lella, though very much upset, was sensible of the horrors of a middle-class funeral. We shall, of course, pay our share of the expenses."*

To Laura Kelley and Lida Hamm

[Nutley, N.J.]
March 1921

Dear Sisters,

I waited so anxiously for your letters after I knew that Mother was gone, and I never expected to wait so long in replying. It is so hard for me to realize that Mother is really gone—that those busy hands will never toil for us again, or make beautiful stitches, or write those long letters. She is constantly in my thought, and often in the midst of the very strenuous activities which have filled my days in the past few weeks, I have found myself weeping without really knowing why at first—just a sense of irretrievable loss. Day after day as I perform a hundred thousand services for my babies I think how many times she did those things for me and for the rest of her children, always without any help at all. I don't think it is possible really to appreciate a Mother until one has been that oneself, until one has washed faces and changed diapers and kissed bruises and fed and clothed and guarded helpless little ones.

Then, when I remember that besides all this she earned the bread we ate, I am filled with admiration for her extraordinary ability. I used to be afraid that memories of the unhappy times which we sometimes had would finally predominate. But this isn't so at all. She was so much that was good and clever and tender and fine that all her foibles seem swallowed up and forgotten. I would so love to have seen her once more—and yet I know that my parting with her was far easier than yours, who watched her sufferings and saw the inevitable darkness creeping in upon her.

At first the thought of her lying alone in the night out in the cold earth was intolerable to me. Over and over I asked myself—I wonder if she is comfortable, I wonder if she is happy, I wonder if her spirit wanders free and is perhaps here with me now. Then with the advent of these magnificent summer days when the brown earth is so warm and stirring with life, I have felt more reconciled to her lying there. She is not suffering, and she is not toiling, and there must be rest and peace for her. There is comfort too in remembering that she lived a full rich life despite its hardships, and that she was not cut off before she tasted the goodness of life.

I confess that the thought of death leaves me in great confusion. I am no longer able to accept many of the theories and beliefs on which we were reared. I do not know whether we shall meet again after death, or whether, leaving life, we enter again that mysterious oblivion from which we sprang. Perhaps we shall see her again some time, perhaps my spirit will mix with hers in some un-understandable manner. But however that may be, I am glad that she lived, grateful that she gave me life, and I cherish with tenderness all the happy recollections I have of her.

If I could have shared your care of her at the end, I would have been happier. There seemed nothing I could do at this distance, especially as I knew that you were giving her everything she could desire. But I want to meet my share of the expenses, so I wish you would tell me just what they would be. I know you have said in general what the nurse, doctor, funeral, etc. cost, but I want to know who has met the expenses—that is, have you two girls done it alone, or have the others contributed anything? If you have paid everything yourselves, then I shall want to pay a third. If not, perhaps my share will be slightly less. I know that I did not quite keep up my promised payments on the nurse's salary—that is, $10 per week—and I want to make that up in addition to my share of the other expenses. Please let me know—and also whether you have had difficulty in raising the money and need it at once. In that case, I shall get some money over from England without delay, regardless of exchange. If not, I shall send it a bit later when we shall be a trifle more flush than at the moment. Had the insurance been kept up? Is it possible for you to tell me how much Philip and I sent to apply on the nurse's salary? I expect I can find it but I shall have to look up old check stubs, and perhaps you have the figure in mind. Please do not neglect this financial detail, because I feel that you both bore more than your share of anxiety and care, and I do not want you to have the lion's share of the expenses as well.

I know how greatly you must miss Mother, and how silent the house must seem after these months of watching and waiting. I can understand too, how relieved you must feel to know that Mother is spared further suffering. What really was assigned as the cause of death? Could you send me any clippings? I do so appreciate the details contained in your two letters.

Indeed I shall make every effort to keep in touch with you even though Mother is no longer there, especially as it seems likely now that we shall remain in Europe for some years. I refrained from mentioning our plans in my last letter for fear of upsetting Mother. Philip has received enthusiastic letters from his old associates in Cambridge, urging him to return and take up his work there, and our present plan is to do so. Meanwhile, however, Philip is proceeding with negotiations already started with several American universities, and there is always the possibility that some offer over here may prove to be so good that we shall remain here instead of going abroad. But the probability is that we shall go to England for several reasons—Philip's mother is there, and we can get servants easily and for a third what we pay here. I am really getting exhausted trying to cope with the situation in America. They are all so incompetent, and I never feel that I have the slightest control over my house. I still have my mother-and-daughter arrangement, but it is not entirely satisfactory, for they are only about one-third present—"Nobody home." I shall try to keep them until June, however, as the thought of another change terrifies me. We have also decided to sell all our furniture, and rent the house unfurnished. It is much easier to get good permanent tenants for an unfurnished place, and besides we shall probably be able to realize quite a smart sum out of the stuff as people in Nutley buy anything at a private sale. We should have to accumulate furniture for our English place anyway, and it seems rather absurd to have money tied up in so many bits of furniture.

While I think of it, I want to mention Mother's things. I would like to have just a few mementos of her, but I don't want to ask for anything which you or the others might want. I shall love to have her five o'clock tea [set], for that is something which will always last, and I shall have a picture of her as she used to pour her tea here in our little dining room. Could you manage later—there is no hurry—to pack it and send it? I think you had better have the plum colored dress, Laura, for it might fit you without too much alteration—also the underthings. I would rather like to have the marabou cape and muff I gave her—I don't know whether she finally ever got the muff made. If I could have a few of her hankies I would treasure them. I can wear her gloves—I don't know whether she had another daughter who has large hands like I have. I might also have my rings which I gave her to wear when she was here—the amethyst and the emerald with pearls. She gave them both to me. Otherwise, for my part, I should want you two to make whatever disposition of her things you think best. I would find the trunk and traveling bags extremely useful, but I don't know whether you want to part with them. . . .

I do so want to see you both. Can't you manage to take a run up here again before we go? I do so want you to see the children, and a change now is certainly what you both-need. Please don't consider this question lightly! ! ! ! ! ! I would be prepared to do so much more for you this time than last year when I was so tied by a tiny baby. They are both growing like mushrooms. . . .

Brian Lawrence, Philip's old friend, arrived two weeks ago, and I have simply been bobbing ever since. Now he has postponed his sailing so that he will be here until April 10th, and I am trying to settle down into a less hectic routine. . . . He is a delightful person, and we love having him here. Last night he took me to hear Galli-Curci[44] while Philip stayed with the children—day off for 'elp. We were both rather disappointed in her. It has been so long since I have had any company or much social activity that I feel rather dazed. . . .

Lunch is ready—such love to you both from all of US.

Loretta Secor's death allowed Lella to focus her attention with a clear conscience on leaving America and taking up a new life in England, where Philip had been appointed junior lecturer in economics at Cambridge University. According to Philip, she was "fearfully excited" about the move.

To Laura Kelley and Lida Hamm

115 Vreeland Avenue
Nutley, N.J.
April 1921

Dear Girls,

I was so glad to hear from you again. Indeed I mean to keep in touch with you even though it is only with postals. Which reminds me that I found a card in my boy's pocket which I wrote to you weeks ago!

I have settled down to hard sledding after a month and more of gaiety during Brian's stay here. I took him on the rubberneck on the bus, up the tower and over to the Statue of Liberty all in one day.[45] I am so sorry we didn't take you over to the Statue. It is really quite worth while. You can climb right up her tummy if your legs hold out—which ours didn't. The stairs go round and round in a tiny spiral which make one dizzy before one starts.

Noel is sitting beside me, patting me with his little hand, and putting his dear head against my arm. He is so affectionate—and so is Tony. I do wish you could see them again before we go. They are such darlings—and so full of mischief. The other morning Noel got out of bed at about 5:30, climbed up on the table in the nursery, got a box of Graham crackers, and then proceeded to treat himself and Tony until they couldn't hold another crumb. I slept until 7:30 and then rushed in wondering what in the world had kept them quiet so long when I am usually routed out at 6 o'clock. They both looked like stuffed toads with their eyes fairly bulging. . . .

Well, we have sold a strip at the back of our place to the man next door for a peach orchard, and we think we have also sold the house. It is really so old that we consider ourselves lucky to get rid of it. . . . If our prospect takes it, the joke will rather be on us, for she intends to PAPER the house at once. Farewell to all my painstaking decorations! If we had thought of selling a little earlier I certainly would not have tried to do much to the walls. Now we shall try to sell the two lots next door and save for ourselves only the studio and a strip of ground around it with a right of way to the road. So you see I shall soon have some money to send you. We have been running as usual on one wheel so as to avoid losing on the exchange, and it has been a fairly close squeeze with the extra expense of a guest. . . .

Never mind about the ring Mother sent Esther. It does not greatly matter. You did not mention the trunk. Can you let me know about this at once so I can make plans? If Mother's isn't available then I must look out for one here. As I have but five weeks in which to do everything, I am beginning to feel a bit panicky. We shall probably not sail before mid-June or July, but we shall have to clear out here the first of June if we sell. So I shall let my 'elp go and just take the children to a hotel or boarding house at the sea somewhere until Philip can finish up his work and get away. I am rather looking forward to taking care of them myself if I can only get my sewing done up in advance. . . .

I think you had better keep the dress, Laura, as it will fit you more nearly than anyone else. Of course you can send it to Lena if you rather—it doesn't really make any difference to me. But it would be foolish to cut it over for me—I am quite decently slender again. I've lost 20 pounds. IF you plan to send the trunk, could you do it pronto, so I can gradually get it packed? I packed our little trunk and sent it over by Brian, which is a great help for we shall have so much luggage.

I am so sorry Laura that you are having such a miserable time about your job. I know exactly how ill it makes one feel to know that intrigues are going on behind one's back. I had that experience in my organization work. But don't let it worry you. [B]attle [C]reek is just one tiny dot on the map, and with your experience you could land any number of jobs . . . Do keep me posted, for I am so keen about your work.[46]

And now for the dentist!)(#=4$@*#! !''!''!''!'' (polite profanity).

Much love to you both.
Lella.

Philip Florence and Lella Secor to Lida Hamm and Laura Kelley

WHITE STAR LINE
S. S. *Cedric*

Mid-Ocean
September 8 [1921]

Dear Lida and Laura,

It seems extraordinary to have a little time for writing to one's sisters after the hectic work of the last three months. I finished the third of my government reports and mailed it at 7:45 p.m. on Friday; next day at 12 noon the boat left the dock. Meanwhile Lella was hectically repacking at Nutley, even sleeping in the leaky and mosquitoful studio.[47] If it hadn't been for our wonderful little colored lady who watched the kids in New York, we should never have got off at all. Pity we didn't find her earlier!

Our final exit from America was typical of our whole life there—one long hectic struggle. It's extraordinary the way Lella has survived it. She looks lovelier than ever and you would think she had done nothing but sport around all her life—which I gather she has NOT. Anyway I mean to give her a better time in the next few years—even a mere professor like myself can live pretty well in England, without going into business.

. . . Mother has got us a house in Cambridge—four floors (ten rooms) beautifully furnished with baby grand—for five pounds a week, which is now equivalent to less than eighty dollars a month. You couldn't get *two* rooms in New York for that! . . .

There are practically no passengers [on board] and all the stewards are nice kind Englishmen from Lancashire, most sympathetic with the "kids."

The first four days we had lovely bright weather (a great relief after the terrific heat when we left New York) so we all got used to the ocean gradually and none of us are sick. The "kids" manage to tire us both out pretty well, though, and we seize every chance to

PROGRAMME OF CONCERT

GIVEN ON BOARD THE

R.M.S. "CEDRIC,"

Commander G. R. METCALFE, (Lieut-Commr. R.N.R.)

On FRIDAY, SEPTEMBER 9th, 1921,

COMMENCING AT 8-15 P.M.

PROCEEDS IN AID OF SEAMEN'S CHARITIES
(LIVERPOOL AND NEW YORK)

Chairman Dr. P. S. FLORENCE.

PROGRAMME.

Selection		s.s. "Cedric" Orchestra
Song	"Perfect Day"	Mrs. K. BOYES
Recitation	"Gunga Din"	Mr. H. WARDER
Song	"Valley of Laughter"	Mrs. W. EVANS
Song	"Good Bye-ee"	Mr. R. THOROLD
Song	"In my Garden"	Miss E. CROSSLEY
Song	Selected	Mr. WILL EVANS

Chairman's Remarks.

Pianoforte Solo	Selected	Mrs. L. FINLAISON
Song	"The Tumble Down Shack in Athlone"	Mr. J. McDONALD
Song	"Down Here"	Miss E. CROSSLEY
Song	"When the War is over, Laddie"	Mr. J. HENNESEY
Duet	"Carry me back to Old Virginny"	Mr. and Mrs. W. EVANS
Song	Selected	Mrs. CAMPBELL
Song	Selected	Mr. M. WEYMES

Accompanist - Mrs. L. FINLAISON

MY COUNTRY 'TIS OF THEE.
GOD SAVE THE KING.

Shipboard concert organized by Philip Florence.

get a nap. The food is very good and you ought to see Lella eat! I enclose a menu checking what your dainty baby sister partook of. . . .

(Lella shoulders the pen here.)

Friday a.m. the 10th

We are now within 24 hours of Liverpool, riding in a joyously rough sea with brilliant sunshine. One could hardly hope for a more perfect voyage than we've had with only a little cloud and rain. The babies have been wonderfully good and none of us has been ill in the least. There are very few passengers, which always means better service, and in our case meant a beautiful stateroom on an upper deck far nicer than the one we had engaged. We've had our porthole open every night, and you can't imagine the joy of lying beside it and looking out into the starlit sky with the great white flecked sea beneath.

Philip has made a great impression by just sitting still and looking wise. An old lady talked to me about him and said he looked very brilliant. I replied with enthusiasm that he was even more brilliant than he looked and added that he had made a brilliant record. She was a little deaf and thought I said he'd made a world's record. So now he is looked upon as a world's champion of something or other and deeply revered. . . .

You can address us at Lord's Wood, Marlow, Bucks, until we send you our Cambridge address, which may be a few weeks as we shall be fearfully busy getting settled. Anyway, you will know we've landed safely when you get this.

Such love from us all.

Notes

1. A small town on the river Thames northwest of London.
2. Mary Sargant-Florence was an artist of some repute, especially noted for her frescoes, and at age sixty-two continued to maintain a rigorous work schedule. In addition to her painting, she was writing a book on color theory.

3. Mary Sargant-Florence originally settled in Marlow because of its reputation as an artists' colony.

4. Although Mary Sargant-Florence was delighted to have a daughter-in-law with such advanced views politically, the two women never saw eye to eye on clothes, child care, or general comfort. Mary considered Lella a butterfly in dress, a domestic drudge in her willingness to push a baby's pram, and a sybarite in her love of warm rooms and cosy furniture. Lella thought her mother-in-law both Spartan and impractical, found her insistence on fresh air and early rising a trial, and her sense of humor entirely lacking.

5. Francis William Sargant, the youngest of Mary's four brothers. Of the four Sargant sisters, Mary was the eldest, and the only one still living.

6. Edmund Sargant, the eldest brother, a civil servant.

7. Mary's brother, Sir Charles Sargant, a very successful barrister who was knighted and became a Lord of the Court of Appeal.

8. This temporary unsociability was brought on by Lella's ill health. In fact, her first experience of a life enhanced by servants was to make a lasting impression on her.

9. Humorist and playwright. The Jeromes lived nearby and were close friends of Mary Sargant-Florence.

10. In England a don is a head, fellow, or tutor of a college.

11. Prof. C. R. Fay, an economic historian, who had greatly influenced Philip's undergraduate career.

12. Lella was pregnant again although ignorant of the fact. She appears to have shared her mother's belief that a woman could not conceive while still nursing a baby, and Noel had only recently been weaned.

13. Walter Sargant, the fourth of Mary's brothers, headmaster of Oakham School, Rutland.

14. Lella's friendship with Crystal Eastman dated from the American Neutral Conference Committee. A journalist, pacifist, and attorney, she had a strong political influence on her brother Max Eastman. Crystal was staying in London with her English husband, Walter Fuller.

15. Sir Charles's wife, Amelia—Lady Sargant.

16. Mary Sargant-Florence was the real owner of the house in Nutley, New Jersey, where she had lived from 1889–92 and where Philip and his sister, Alix, were born. Upon returning to England she had left the house in the hands of an agent, who had rented it to a series of tenants for $25 a month.

17. Philip would be required to return early to begin his lectures with the Bureau of Industrial Research.

18. Uncle Charlie had remained a bachelor until age forty-four when he married Millie, his nurse during a serious illness. He was now sixty-three.

19. Dressing for dinner was still *de rigueur* at General's Meadow, although the war had forced many upper-class households to relax their standards.

20. The friends were mostly intellectuals with whom Lella—lacking formal education, pregnant, and ill—felt herself at a disadvantage.

21. Economist Hubert Henderson and his wife, Faith; Philip had known them both at Cambridge.

22. Geoffrey Pyke and David Leacock were both friends from Cambridge undergraudate days.

23. "Sent for" certainly did not mean "planned." Lella was frantic at the thought of another baby so soon after the first. This perhaps explains her advocacy of the birth control movement which became one of her passionate concerns a few years later.

24. And disappointment at the baby's being a boy; Philip had never considered this possibility, and admits to having had to "take to his bed."

25. Now seventy-six and a semi-invalid, Loretta Secor was often more of a care than a help to Lella.

26. The nurse, who had promised to care for both children in exchange for her passage to America, deserted the household before Anthony was born.

27. Mr. and Mrs. Bartel.

28. Lella's "baby sleigh," which Loretta Secor had brought from Battle Creek.

29. Philip's sister, Alix, had just been married to James Strachey, who later translated Sigmund Freud's works into English. Alix herself was to study with Freud and become a practicing psychoanalyst.

30. Alix preferred to be known as Alix Strachey, although the custom of using one's maiden name was certainly practiced in England.

31. Philip played the flute and Lella often accompanied him at the piano.

32. Philip wrote his mother, "Mr. Bartel . . . got on our nerves and Mrs. Bartel seemed to leave more and more of the cooking to Lella, so when they broached leaving us we made no effort to detain them."

33. Philip had been pressing his mother to visit them in Nutley and here Lella adds her own invitation.

34. During the years 1889–92 when Mary Sargant-Florence lived in Nutley.

35. In England, where competent servants could still be found for relatively low wages, these two could be hired for ten pounds, or about one-fifth what it would cost in the United States.

36. Philip was writing a technical manual for employers on statistical control of labor losses.

37. Loretta Secor was now confined to a wheelchair.

38. Freda Kirchwey, daughter of George Kirchwey, was to become editor of *The Nation;* her husband, Evans Clark, was an instructor at Princeton.

39. According to British tradition, Christmas dinner was eaten at midday with the tree and gift-opening ceremony to follow.

40. Lella dismissed her shortly after Christmas.

41. When funds were running low and anticipated money from England had not yet arrived.

42. Lella was unexcited about moving back to the Midwest; Philip, on the other hand, was eager to explore the American academic scene.

43. Lella has dropped a year from her age.

44. Amelita Galli-Curci, soprano.

45. The "rubberneck" was a sightseeing tour; the tower probably was the Woolworth Building, then New York's tallest.

46. Laura worked for the Battle Creek police department.

47. The house was already occupied by its new owner.

VI

England: A New Life

In September of 1921 Philip began his work in Cambridge, where his lectures were popular because he talked to the students about real factories instead of mere economic theory.

Lella found the new life much to her taste. Servants were quickly found and she began to pick up the threads of her old career. She joined the Women's International League, spoke on women's rights, and became a member of the Cambridge Labour Party, using the name Lella Secor. (When Philip sat on the platform with her, he was introduced as "Mr. Secor.") She helped organize meetings, canvassed before elections, and drove her car in parades for local candidates.

Learning to drive had been one of Lella's first objectives when she reached England, particularly since Philip eschewed this responsibility. Her skill behind the wheel of their Model T Ford allowed her a mobility and scope of operation most unusual for women of that period.

In 1925 Lella helped found the Cambridge Birth Control Clinic, only the second such facility in England. As secretary she interviewed each woman patient and kept records of each case. Later she was to write a book called Birth Control on Trial,[1] *based on her pioneering work in Cambridge.*

In the beginning, Lella had been deeply shocked at the inequality of the sexes which prevailed at Cambridge. On one occasion she attended a lecture by a famous, though woman-hating, professor and found all female students segregated at the side of the hall. As she told it, "In a burst of indignation I walked boldly to the best seats in the centre and had a bench all to myself because no undergraduate had the courage . . . to sit next to a woman."[2]

Lella was determined to fight this sort of male prejudice on her own terrain, and invited young people of both sexes to her home at 55 Chesterton Road. Her soirées were looked on askance by the dons, who preferred a life of unruffled monasticism, but many undergraduates and young lecturers found the Florence home a haven of warmth and hospitality.

Ivor Montagu, in his autobiography The Youngest Son,[3] *remembers:*

> *One pioneer hostess stood out against the barren tradition. This was Lella Sargant Florence, born Lella Secor, a freckled American redhead who had been . . . a spirited battler against the violence with which the U.S. authorities assailed pacifist protest towards the close of the 1918 war and, vindictively, afterward. She had sailed on Henry Ford's ill-fated peace ship. Her husband, a thickset and amiable young British economics don, looked stolid as a rock; but he had hidden depths. . . . Dear Lella! she found Cambridge a backwater that could not possibly be permitted to go on benighted. She set up a salon that attracted young people of both sexes by her political glamour and held them by her effervescence and charm. Here she set out to introduce them to one another. The old-fashioned Establishment regarded her as some sort of transatlantic modernistic bawd come to disturb their peace of centuries. Really she was just a respectable broadminded matchmaker, crusading to bring their fossil society up to date at least with Jane Austen's Bath. . . . This couple . . . did us all a very great deal of good.*

To Laura Kelley and Lida Hamm

5 Scroope Terrace
Cambridge, England
December 18, 1921

Dear Sisters,

I never meant to neglect you so long—these three months have been so full. We have such a store of delightful places and things to show you when you come. . . . I shall never be able to catch up with events and tell you all we have seen and done since we came. It is simply glorious here, and we are so satisfied to remain that we have bought a house overlooking the river where we shall move in next autumn.

Getting the family settled in at Cambridge, getting used to English life, meeting scores of delightful people, attending lectures, entertaining . . . all these things have filled my days to overflowing. And now I am rushing to get myself and the babies ready for the holidays, which we will spend at Aunt Millie's. . . . After Christmas, Mother and the nurse will come back to Cambridge with the babies and Philip and I plan to have part of that long postponed honeymoon—a week in Paris . . . and two weeks in the mountains of Austria. . . .

The children are an ever increasing joy. . . . Noel has grown so sweet and charming, and now says everything in his own fashion. Tony is talking almost as much—probably because he has had Noel to teach him. Tony is quite handsome with his big brown eyes and very light [brown] hair. Noel is as flaxen as ever. . . .

There are a million things I long to say to you, but I must content myself now with this hastily scribbled note. Philip (dearer than ever if you can stretch your imagination that far) sends love to you both. . . . Please do write occasionally, I so long to hear from you. . . .

Lovingly,
Lella

To Laura Kelley and Lida Hamm

55 Chesterton Rd.
Cambridge
January 31, 1923

Dear Sisters,

You will see that advancing years do not improve me at all in the matter of letters, which I always put off to that day of leisure which never comes.

We did so enjoy the Christmas bundle which arrived when we were still in such a mess of paints, plaster and planks that we found it hard to realize the proximity of Christmas. In fact I painted almost all night just before Christmas so as to get ready for Mother F. who came to spend the holidays with us. We seized the confusion of getting settled in our new house as an excuse for not going to Lady Sargant's, which none of us really enjoys. So we had a happy quiet Christmas at home with a big tree for the boys and many more toys I'm afraid than was good for them. The package from home which reached us a few days before Christmas proved too great a temptation for me and I opened it, and just peeked at my lovely gown. It so happened also that the children were at that moment feeling miserable with vaccination, so I felt justified in cheering them up with their jolly little dolls which they love. Philip like a proper gentleman refused to open his until Christmas.

We thought of you often on Christmas day and of Mother who has been absent now on two Christmases. What did you do I wonder—and Ina—and Lena. We seem now all to be separated at such great distances. . . .

. . . Please tell me something more about Ina. Last August I sent her a power of attorney and wrote a long letter to say that I didn't think the place[4] worth any quarrel or misunderstanding and that I would leave the whole business in her hands. Since that moment I have never heard from her, not even a card to the children at Christmas. I long to see her again and yet I sometimes wonder whether I should be able at all to understand her. . . .

I had Noel's tonsils and adenoids removed a week ago today.

He is quite recovered, though it was rather a trying job while it lasted.

How I wish you could see them both. Tony will soon be three and Noel is already beginning to learn to read. They are jolly youngsters full of vim and mischief. My little nurse has been with me now more than a year. She is splendid with children and they love her. Her sister Grace does the housework so that now that we are almost settled I shall have more time for outside work. I am making a few speeches now in Cambridge and London for the Labour Party and the Woman's International League, and I'm helping with a new young people's Labour Club which seems most promising. I take both the maids with me [to meetings] which is an unheard of thing in England. They are lovely girls.[5]

Except for a few trips to London we have remained steadily in Cambridge since autumn. There is such a tremendous lot of activity during term that one has time for nothing else. Philip is getting on very well at Cambridge and we hope to stay put here for a number of years. But it would not surprise me much if a good offer from America should take us back to our native shores at almost any time.[6] I should hate to leave England mostly. It is so lovely living here.

Have I told you about our house? We have a charming outlook over the river and away across the common, which is a sort of green park. The house is high and narrow—four flights of stairs from the kitchen to Grace's room on the top floor. Below her is the nursery floor—day nursery done in orange and blue with a jolly [balcony] overlooking the river, night nursery in buff and purple-blue and Nurse's room. Below that is a large drawing room which faces the river also. We've done it in old blue and pale yellow and it's quite jolly. Next [to] it is our bedroom and bathroom and, on the floor below, Philip's study and my study. Lastly comes the dining room and kitchen and a pretty little garden at the back. There are still odd bits of painting to be done, but mostly the place is finished. And now, when are you coming to see us?

We have had central heating (hot water system) put in, but it has been so beautifully mild this winter that we've hardly needed it. Today we have all the windows open and spring flowers are blooming in the garden.

I do hope your job is more settled, Laura. I've just joined the Penal Reform League in England, and last week heard Miss Frye—a descendent of the pioneer prison reformer Elizabeth Frye, speak in Cambridge. . . .

Much love to you both from us all.
Lella

To Laura Kelley and Lida Hamm

June 19, 1923
We shall be back
at 55 Chesterton Rd.
when this reaches you.

Dear Sisters,

At last the hectic summer term is over and we have retreated to the sea for a fortnight's holiday before taking up in earnest work on that long delayed book which we hope to bring out in August.[7] We have a dear little thatched cottage which is part of a large farm, a stone's throw from the beach. To be specific we are at Waxham, a tiny old village in Norfolk which, inch by inch, is being eaten up by the sea. We came up Friday (this is Tuesday) in our Ford which I drove from Cambridge—about 90 miles. We had a record load. Philip, his mother, the two children and their nurse, to say nothing of trunks, bags, spades, pails, and a stock of rainy day toys which, alas, we sadly need. We have had the most dreadful spring—cold and rainy. We are sitting today before a roaring fire in the grate, without which we shiver. And it has been a struggle to find blankets enough to keep us warm at night. I long for some baking hot American days, but when we even approach such a one the English go about with their tongues hanging out!

In spite of rain and cloud we are contriving to amuse ourselves. The children love the beach, and we dash out whenever it's not pouring. The sea is kept out by enormous sand dunes which have been planted with strong wirey grasses to keep the sand from shifting, and these little hills and valleys of sand make an admirable hide and seek ground. It is far too cold to bathe or even to wade though Noel, who shows a sudden spirit of adventure, wades about icy pools and swears it is warm.

They are such jolly youngsters. I do wish you could see them. Noel is very tall and slender and fair, while Tony is round and chubby and brown. They are inseparable playmates and on the whole get along very well together. . . .

When we return from the sea, we expect to remain in Cambridge until September when, if the weather is not too beastly, we shall take the boys to Grandma's for a time while we attend the British Association meeting at Liverpool, and make a little tour of Wales. We are all well and thriving, except for Philip's back which gives him trouble still. . . . I am doing a good deal of work in the British Labour Party, and have been asked to become organizing secretary for Cambridge. This, with my house, and helping Philip with his book and keeping up rather a giddy social life which is part of the term's work,[8] gives me precious little spare time. The house is practically finished now except for those persistent details which never do get finished, but anyway it is a vast relief not to have paint pots around any more. . . .

How are you all? I do so much wish I could hear from you more frequently, but I know of course that I am the worst offender—except in the case of Ina. It is just a year now since I have heard from her, though I have written a number of times, sent her little gifts etc. I have been hoping so eagerly to hear from you Lida, since your visit to Seattle. How did you find Ina? . . . Has she sold the place? Or has she simply lost it for debts? I feel that she has treated me abominably. . . . I have given up worrying about Ina. It does no good and she does not desire it. But I would like to know what has become of the place and all our belongings—piano etc. Can you throw any light?[9] . . .

We've got chicken for dinner! It's a real treat in England for they seem too expensive to be indulged in often. One is simply ravenous in this air by meal time—and we eat four times a day at that![10]

Philip and I send love to all. Do write soon and give us lots of gossip!

Much love
Lella.

Notes

1. Lella Secor Florence, *Birth Control on Trial,* London, George Allen & Unwin, Ltd., 1930.

2. Lella Secor Florence, typescript of a speech called "Is Britain a Man's World?"

3. Ivor Montagu, *The Youngest Son*, London, Lawrence and Wishart, 1970:186.

4. The house in Bellevue, Washington, which Ina was trying to sell.

5. Grace and Lillian Ward were intelligent young women, but in England they would have been confined forever to the servant class. This horrified Lella, who had herself come from a working-class background, and she later helped them obtain assisted passage to Canada, where one married a doctor, one a well-to-do farmer.

6. Although England was to remain home, Philip managed to arrange visiting professorships at several universities in the United States.

7. P. Sargant Florence, *Economics of Fatigue and Unrest,* London, George Allen & Unwin, Ltd., 1924.

8. Only in Lella's eyes. Cambridge society was strictly a man's world and wives were expected to stay at home while their husbands dined together "in hall" or otherwise enjoyed each other's company.

9. Ina did sell the old house and moved to Berkeley, California. Lella never saw her again.

10. Lella had adopted the English custom of afternoon tea.

Afterword

AFTER THE FIRST few years in Cambridge, Lella became increasingly impatient at its restraints upon her outgoing nature. Finally she rebelled and during the spring term of 1927 took a flat in Paris, where Noel and Tony attended an *école des enfants* and became bilingual. Philip joined them every other weekend, journeying by train, boat, and second train between Cambridge and Paris.

When she returned to Cambridge, Lella again became deeply involved in the work of the Cambridge Birth Control Clinic and began gathering material for *Birth Control on Trial,*[1] a personal follow-up of the clinic's first 300 cases, based on many months of visiting former patients in the Cambridge area. A review in the *Medical Press* stated: "Mrs. Florence's book. . .is written in a spirit of scientific inquiry rather than of dogmatic didacticism. It is not that Mrs. Florence is not as ardent a contraceptionist as the best of them, but she is possessed of a critical spirit uncommon among propagandists."

In the autumn of 1929, Philip was appointed to a chair in economics at the University of Birmingham, in the largest city of the industrial Midlands. Lella and Philip bought a large early-Victorian house called "Highfield," with nearly four acres of landscaped garden and a small lake. Although such an estate was much too big for them, Lella realized that by turning parts of the house into rental apartments, Highfield could be made self-supporting.

It was soon apparent that Highfield and Lella were meant for each other. After finding tenants—mostly faculty members—for the newly created flats, she resumed her Cambridge practice of entertaining students and young faculty at frequent informal parties. Birmingham was a "red brick"—provincial—university and many of the students were daily commuters who had never been entertained at a professor's home before. Nevertheless, Philip's kindly manner and Lella's vivacity and charm put them at ease, and an invitation to Highfield became a coveted item among undergraduates. Picturing her as she was then, a young admirer called her "this wonderful, articulate, witty, talented, generous, classless, American liberated female."

During the 1930's Highfield became a focal point for thought and action, providing what one visitor called "the first germane intellectual climate at a provincial university." The guest list included members of the intellectual aristocracy mingled with local business leaders, artists, actors, and politicians. Lella's hospitality embraced such houseguests as philosopher G. E. Moore, anthropologist Margaret Mead, biologist Julian Huxley, Bauhaus architect Walter Gropius, the Bishop of Birmingham, labor leader Ernest Bevin, American Ambassador John G. Winant, and poet Louis MacNeice, who had rented Highfield's converted coachman's quarters.

The tenants of the flats were an interesting community in themselves and provided the nucleus for Lella's famous impromptu parties, when guests danced to the phonograph, had picnics on the lawn, or skated on the frozen lake. On Sundays—cook's day off—Lella prepared simple suppers for huge numbers of drop-in guests. A friend who remembers those days says, "Highfield *was* Lella . . . it was her Americanism, a sort of live-wire quality." Another adds, "Highfield was the only really *civilized* rendezvous in Birmingham in the thirties. It was amazing how distinctive it was and how hospitable."

Full as her evenings were with socializing, Lella's days were given over to hard work for the causes in which she had always believed: world disarmament, left-wing politics, women's rights, birth control. Many successful projects were born or nurtured at Highfield, with Lella's incredible energy spurring other workers on.

In 1931 she was the driving force in a Birmingham Disarmament Campaign, which attempted to gather 137,000 anti-war signatures to be sent to the League of Nations in Geneva before the 1932 world disarmament conference. A co-worker described their efforts: "We hired a shop and decorated the window with borrowed mannekins to depict a family before and after an air raid. The arrangement was crude but the idea wasn't. The number of people that poured into that shop and the number of leaflets and the propaganda! And we had people outside, everywhere, collecting signatures to go to Geneva.''

The following year the dining room at Highfield was turned into a studio where artists, organized by Lella, painted enormous anti-war posters which on Sundays were paraded through the streets of Birmingham. In 1933 a play called *DISARM!,* with a tremendous cast recruited, in part, from trade unions and factory dramatic societies, was rehearsed at Highfield for performance at the Birmingham Town Hall.

Lella's ready wit and unorthodox point of view made her a popular speaker, and she was often asked to address civic groups in the Birmingham area on such subjects as ''What's Wrong with Women?'' ''England, a Man's Country,'' and the differences between Britons and Americans. Lella's obvious sympathy and interest led many women to approach her after lectures for advice, and many of them were steered to the Birmingham Family Planning Association clinic for information on birth control, in line with Lella's growing conviction that a high birth rate was responsible for many of women's—and the world's—problems.

In 1935 Lella contributed a chapter to *We Did Not Fight: 1914–18 Experiences of War-Resisters,* along with Sir Norman Angell, Adrian Stephen and others.[2] Of her chapter, ''The Ford Peace Ship and After,'' *The New Statesman and Nation* said, ''Mrs. Sargant Florence, who began without political conviction and who revolted against useless slaughter and found herself drawn into a political struggle for peace . . . writes one of the most interesting essays in this book.''

Politics consumed most of Lella's attention at this time. Highfield and the university were in the King's Norton ward, and although Birmingham proper was strongly conservative, that branch of the local Labour Party was—according to a former candidate for Parliament—''an absolute hive of political industry and excitement.'' Lella herself was invited to be the King's Norton candidate for the Birmingham City Council but, as an American citizen, was unable to run and had to content herself with speaking—usually on pacifism—to local ward meetings.

The period of Hitler's rise to power was a difficult one for pacifists. Many of Lella's friends believed that Hitler must be stopped at all costs and England protected against invasion. Although Lella still believed war to be morally wrong and world disarmament the only real chance for peace, she appears to have accepted World War II's inevitability. Comparing World War II with the earlier conflict, she wrote:

> The war situation then was vastly different from today's. The German Government [then] was, in fact, no better and no worse than many other European governments. It was not proposed to impose upon the whole world a completely new and abhorrent way of life as Hitler aims now to achieve. It is this profound difference which has led many 1917 pacifists to feel that, stupid and insane as war is, the immediate alternative of a world under Nazi tyranny is too unthinkable to contemplate.[3]

Lella soon channeled her activism into plans for helping displaced Basque children and for enabling German students, forced out of their universities by Hitler, to study in England

The outbreak of war brought new difficulties. In 1940 Lella and Philip visited Egypt, escaped to America when they were unable to return to England through a hostile Italy, and spent most of the following year in Washington, D.C. As American citizens, they were refused permission to travel to wartime England, and only arranged passage home after much difficulty. Lella described their adventure in her book *My Goodness! My Passport.*[4]

When the United States entered the war, Lella went to work at the American Embassy in London, trying to promote, through talks and exhibits, a greater understanding by Britons of America. These efforts culminated in two volumes in a series comparing life in England and the United States.[5] During the war she lived in a flat in London, and returned to Birmingham every Friday on a train often hours late because of the blitz. On Saturdays and Sundays she labored from dawn to dusk in the Highfield vegetable garden, catching a late train to return to London and her job.

Lella was enraged by the inequalities perpetuated by the war crisis. In *My Goodness! My Passport,* she protested:

> I honestly believe that some men would rather lose the war than grant women equal wages with themselves. It's just too much to ask women to make the same sacrifices as men, shoulder the same responsibilities, do identically the same work, and get considerably less pay for it. I don't blame women for not flocking in their thousands to take up work on these conditions. I'm damned if I would do it myself.
>
> But the inequality goes farther than wages. The Ministry of Labour has issued a leaflet called "Welcome the War Worker." It is addressed to landladies who are to billet the workers. I quote two succeeding paragraphs:
>
> "If you have any time to do any darning or mending for him, he will be grateful. Such attention to his comfort will be appreciated.
>
> "If your lodger is a woman, she will like to have hot water sometimes to do some of her washing. . . ."
>
> It doesn't occur to the Ministry to suggest a little darning on behalf of the girl worker who stands at the bench exactly the same hours, doing the same work, for less pay. Let her do her washing when she gets home![6]

After the war her continuing belief in the rights and dignity of women led Lella to channel all her energies into the Birmingham Family Planning Clinic. For ten years she was its powerful and controversial chairman, a job she called "the most satisfying I've ever done in my life." Always a pioneer, she was one of the first to insist that the Clinic provide not only reliable methods of contraception but also assistance with fertility problems and marital and sexual difficulties.

In 1956 she published her book *Progress Report on Birth Control,* based on painstaking research into the case histories of lapsed patients of the Birmingham Clinic.[7] *Progress Report* frankly discussed the Clinic's failures as well as its successes, hoping to encourage new research. One reviewer called it "a very human document."

Lella was outspoken in her impatience with existing methods of birth control and was excited by the news that an American, Dr.

Gregory Pincus, had developed an oral contraceptive. In 1960 a friend arranged for her to meet Dr. Pincus. In what was to be her final and most flamboyant *coup,* Lella went into action without the approval of the more cautious Central Committee of the Family Planning Association in London. She arranged for "the Pill" to be tested on a large scale in Birmingham, advertising for married women to volunteer as guinea pigs. The response was staggering and Birmingham was well into clinical trials before London knew what was happening. As the Birmingham Family Planning Association Newsletter later put it: "To work with Lella Florence in the heyday of her leadership was an exhilarating experience. Everything and everyone was subordinate to her desire to give the best birth control service that was possible."

Due to her activism and her outspokenness, Lella always made good copy and was frequently interviewed by local newspapers on a variety of subjects. Never hesitant about expressing her opinions, particularly *vis a vis* the status of women in England, she was quoted in one interview as saying:

> Women are near revolt—the time has come to liberate our slave wives. . . . What a lot of fuss and bother it would save if the opponents of proper recognition for women would give in gracefully and accept the inevitable! For the old-fashioned idea that woman's place is only in the home, and that women are inferior in intellect and ability was so amply disproved throughout the war years as to place the final issue beyond dispute. . . . The sooner we get round to a 50-50 co-partnership arrangement in marriage, the greater the chance will be for a happy home life.[8]

As early as 1936 she said, "Instead of asking to which sex a person belongs, it would surely be more practical and sensible to consider his or her abilities and qualifications for the particular job that needs doing. . . . If boys and girls were sanely and sensibly educated on co-educational lines and every girl encouraged to find a career quite apart from marriage, then her marriage would simply be a happy event in a busy life. . . . It seems to me so wrong to set out with the idea that marriage is the aim and end of all."[9]

In 1944 she declared that "there would never be a satisfactory organisation of industry with equal right and equal pay till women took up a full share in trade union organisation."[10] And in 1952, "We must educate men to realise that women are their equals and have equal rights."[11]

Lella also spoke out, from time to time, on such subjects as courtship ("We would beg families to make some use of [their] parlours besides corpses and aspidistras");[12] dress ("Perhaps if British women felt themselves less insignificant, they would take pains to dress more fashionably");[13] and food (Nearly all your food is yellow. There [is] always something on the menu encased in a yellow substance. But the British people [eat] it without a murmur.")[14]

In January 1966, Lella Secor Florence died of pneumonia following a stroke. She did not, as she had wished, die "with her boots on." But one woman spoke for many when she said, "Mrs. Florence's influence will still be upon all who knew her, and many who will benefit from her creative wisdom will never know who was the real instigator of their relief."

Notes

1. Lella Secor Florence, *Birth Control on Trial,* London, George Allen & Unwin Ltd., 1930.
2. Julian Bell, ed., *We Did Not Fight: 1914-18 Experiences of War-Resisters,* London, Cobden-Sanderson, 1935.
3. Lella Secor Florence, *My Goodness! My Passport,* London, George Allen & Unwin Ltd., 1942: 109.
4. Ibid.
5. Lella Secor Florence, *Only an Ocean Between* (vol. 1 America and Britain), 1943; and *Our Private Lives* (vol. 3 America and Britain), 1944; London, George G. Harrap & Co., Ltd.
6. Florence, *My Goodness! My Passport:* 215
7. Lella Secor Florence, *Progress Report on Birth Control,* London, William Heinemann Medical Books, Ltd., 1956.
8. "Our Slave Wives," Birmingham *Sunday Mercury,* May 26, 1946.
9. "A Midland Woman's Diary: An American Woman Looks at England," Birmingham *Evening Dispatch,* March 8, 1936.
10. "Equal Pay," Birmingham *Gazette,* December 4, 1944.
11. "Woman's Week: Can You Legislate for Housekeeping Money?" Birmingham *Gazette,* April 24, 1952.
12. "Sex and the Citizen," *Picture Post,* October 20, 1951. Lella felt British working-class families should allow their young people use of the front parlor for courting, as was the custom in America.

13. Lella Secor Florence, typescript of speech entitled ''Is Britain a Man's World?''

14. Lella Secor Florence, speech at conference of industrial catering managers, *The Caterer and Hotel Keeper,* April 8, 1950: 46.

Appendix A

Press Release by Lella Secor to Washington State Newspapers

On Board *Oscar II*
December 13, 1915

Henry Ford's peace ship, *Oscar II,* is due to arrive at Kirkwall, Scotland, today, and if no complications arise, it is expected that she will be released sometime tomorrow, and proceed on her way to Christiania. The vessel entered the war zone early yesterday afternoon, and at about four-thirty o'clock the sudden stopping of the engines announced with rather an electric thrill that the anticipated intervention by English warships had occurred.

All meetings in progress were summarily adjourned, and the entire ship's company found vantage places on the decks to watch the slow approach of the big black cruiser, vaguely discernible in the pale moonlight of early evening. The war vessel anchored a short distance away, and a small boat put out for the *Oscar II,* bearing a prize crew consisting of a lieutenant, an ensign and four marines, who boarded the ship, and will accompany her as far as Kirkwall. At Kirkwall the ship's papers, and the passports of the passengers will undergo examination.

The ship carries a stowaway, "Jake," from New York, whose fate is not yet determined, since he is not equipped with a passport. Jake was a Western Union messenger boy who had a hankering for learning and travel. Realizing the utter futility of hoping to be invited to join the Ford peace ship, he decided to go anyway. He faked a message to one of the guests on board, and promptly stowed himself away in the dark recesses of a bathroom. He was clever enough not to make his appearance until the pilot boat was well beyond recall. Then he made a clean breast of his adventure, and has proven himself a most useful ally as errand boy throughout the voyage.

The story of the peace ship, and all the events which led to the culmination of ideals in a definite undertaking, reads like an *Arabian Nights* tale. The struggle of a small group of people who believed that the present is the most acceptable time to strike for a permanent peace throughout the world; the disheartening efforts to secure financial support in Detroit, Chicago, and New York; the generous support of Detroit newspapers whose editors caught a glimpse of the dream it was hoped to realize; the sympathetic hearing given by Henry Ford and his final unreserved support of the definite peace movement; constitute a historical story of unprecedented interest.

The sailing of the *Oscar II* on December fourth created boundless enthusiasm in New York. Hundreds of people thronged the docks an hour or so before sailing time, and the crowds increased until it was almost impossible for passengers to get aboard the boat. One after another the prominent people on board were called to the rail while the throng cheered and shouted in their enthusiasm. Among the prominent people who were presented were William Jennings Bryan; Thomas Edison; Dr. Jenkin Lloyd Jones of Chicago; Madame Inez Milholland Boissevain, the noted suffragist; Mr. Ford, multi-millionaire manufacturer and host of the occasion; Dr. Charles F. Aked of San Francisco; Judge and Mrs. Ben Lindsey of Denver; Mrs. May Wright Sewall, honorary president of the International [Council] of Women, and others.

In spite of decided differences of opinion which developed on board ship as to ways and means of accomplishing the desired end, and in spite of the many arguments in which detached groups of peace enthusiasts indulged, a spirit of democratic congeniality has prevailed throughout the voyage.

[But] a storm blew up on the fifth evening out, which lashed the peaceful deliberations of the peace body into temporary fury.

A committee headed by Dr. Jenkin Lloyd Jones and supported

by Dr. Aked, Mrs. Joseph Fels of Philadelphia, Mrs. Lola M. Lloyd of Illinois, and [Rev.] Arthur Weatherly of Lincoln, Nebr., presented a platform of principles, with the idea of crystallizing the sentiment of the party in some definite form, in order that there might be a basis for the negotiations into which it is planned to enter at The Hague. The platform contained three planks, the first two having to deal with the desire to establish peace, and the loyalty of the ship's company to Mr. Ford's efforts; the third consisted of an unequivocal declaration against any increase by the United States of her naval or military forces, and it was this section over which dissension arose.

S. S. McClure jumped to his feet and declared that he would be unable to give his support to the platform, for while he was an ardent advocate of peace, he supported President Wilson in his preparedness program, until such time as international disarmament could be accomplished.

The meeting was adjourned at once without further discussion but arguments for and against the platform continued for several hours. Many of the guests signed the platform at once. Others did not favor any disapproval of the policies of the United States, and still others made accusations that the document had been "railroaded" through.

Oil was poured upon the troubled waters two days later when Mr. Ford issued a personal letter to each of his guests, which explained the situation so clearly that there remain only about a dozen who have not felt that they could endorse the platform. Mr. Ford explained that the paragraph to which objection had been made was merely a reiteration of his idea, expressed clearly in his letter of invitation, in which he had said that the international conference of nations which he had hoped the expedition would be able to bring about would be "further dedicated to the prevention of future wars through abolition of competetive armaments."

"What could be more absurd and inconsistent," says the letter, "than for us to ask Europe to stop adding to her own military burdens, while supporting either actively or passively a proposed increase of them in our own country?"

The letter closed with the statement:

"I wish to make it perfectly clear that, though some do not agree with all our principles, all can be useful, and all invited guests will still be my welcome guests to the end of the trip."

The entire party will proceed to The Hague, having the unanimous desire to aid in establishing peace in Europe.

Many interesting events have marked the progress of the voyage. With so many celebrities on board, eloquence and brilliancy have marched in attack and counterattack on wit and humor. Dr. Jones of Chicago and Dr. Aked of San Francisco conducted two memorable services the first Sunday on board. During the days which have followed, from two to six meetings, addresses and discussions have been held daily, and many mooted points in the great problem of permanent international peace have been thrashed out. Early in the week, Mme. Rosika Schwimmer, one of the leading spirits in the expedition, presented an eloquent exposition of the purpose of the voyage. Judge Lindsey has been heard on several occasions, as has Mme. Aino Maimberg of Finland, a noted lecturer and publicist. There has been no more popular and logical speaker than Mrs. May Wright Sewall, [who] clearly expressed the sentiment of the women of the world who have risen to declare that they will no longer bear sons to be sacrificed on the field of battle.

Miss Grace Wales of Wisconsin, a young Canadian who strangely enough conceived the idea of continuous mediation for the settlement of all disputes at almost the same time when the thought began to make a tremendous appeal to other women in a different part of the country, presented her ideas.

One of the most logical and convincing addresses of the voyage was made by Louis Lochner, secretary of the peace expedition, who set forth the reasonable possibilities of international disarmament. Other speakers have been Judson King, well known in Seattle, S. S. McClure, . . . John Barry, journalist and author, Mrs. Joseph Fels, Mrs. Inez Milholland Boissevain, . . . Gov. L. B. Hanna of North Dakota, and others.

Appendix B

Jamestown [*N.Y.*] **Evening Journal,** *Tuesday, December 25, 1916*

MISS SECOR WAS DISAPPOINTED

CAME TO JAMESTOWN TO SPEAK, BUT WAS ONLY INTERVIEWED

LATE FOR ENGAGEMENT

Good Audience Gathered To Hear Her In Peace Address At Eagles' Auditorium But Storm Delays To Train Service Prevented Her From Reaching Jamestown Until Late Sunday Afternoon—Miss Secor Tells Journal Representative of Her Experiences and Plans.

The town clock has just tolled nine this Christmas morning, and I'm at the office after having shouted "Merry Christmas," and "Bon Voyage," after Miss Lella Faye Secor of Seattle and New York, aboard the 8:45 train for Buffalo. Miss Secor, one of the organizers of the American Neutral Conference Committee formed about six months ago with the express purpose of exerting every possible means of hastening a just and lasting peace, was to have addressed the meeting in Eagle Temple Sunday afternoon. The heavy snowfall of last Friday is the reason she failed to carry out the program. At the time Chairman James S. McCallum was explaining to a fair sized audience in the Temple that late trains were responsible for the non-appearance of the speaker, Miss Secor was pacing the Lake Shore station at Westfield with every hope of keeping her appointment dashed.

Delegated official hostesses by the Jamestown Aerie, Miss Elizabeth Bealer and I met the 4:15 traction car on which Miss Secor was expected, and accosted every woman who alighted. Elderly ladies with gray hair and mufflers, some of them undoubtedly venerable grandmothers, constituted my prey, because I had read Miss Secor's list of achievements and felt positive she must have reached maturity, plus. Miss Bealer's most interesting experience was when she asked a smartly attired young woman with a shiney hat if she was Miss Secor. Looking somewhat startled and as if she wasn't just sure who she was, the lady gazed round at a robust young fellow and Miss Bealer fell back abashed at sight of spick and span suitcases and traveling bags and the very noticeable evidences of a recently performed ceremony. Of course, she was not Miss Secor.

At 6 o'clock in the evening we were summoned to the hotel and imagine our pleased surprise when we discovered Miss Secor to be a young woman with red, not white locks. "I wish there were a few gray ones mixed in," Miss Secor smiled, "because they lend such dignity. People persist in making youth a liability and not an asset. It remains for the young people of this nation to do better than our forebears have in the establishment of peace and its exaltation to a glory equal to that in which war has always been clothed, or I really feel we shall have lived in vain. And when we manage to make peace as dramatic, spectacular and colorful as we have war, then we will have the young people with us."

Over plates of Welsh rarebit and cups of fragrant coffee, Miss Secor recited some of her varied experiences. It was mighty difficult to determine whether her sparkling eyes matched the blue of her modish velvet "Tam-o-Shanter" above them or her traveling dress of sea green below. She was intensely interested in this big peace movement which hopes to arouse a huge public sentiment to back President Wilson and his peace overtures to the belligerent nations of Europe. All animation and with stray curly tresses escaping from the Tam (or perhaps they had been arranged with malice aforethought) it seemed nothing short of a miracle that this girl and one other, Miss Rebecca Shelly, could have inaugurated a peace movement with which many of the country's most famous and most learned men have since become identified.

"A year ago tonight," Miss Secor reminisced, "we were having a Christmas banquet in the Winter Garden of the Grand Royal Hotel right opposite Sweden's royal palace." (The "we" refers to Henry Ford's peace party of which Miss Secor was a member, first as journalist and later as an active participant in all its activities.) "At the close of dinner, the splendid orchestra played Sousa's *Stars and Stripes Forever* as a special tribute to we Americans."

Miss Secor is particularly attached to the Swedish people, and she told of how she addressed great mass meetings in Sweden, speaking through interpreters, line by line. Also of how she spent two hours learning, like a parrot, to say a paragraph in Swedish, and how it was enjoyed and appreciated by the audience. One time in Denmark only 24 hours notice was given of the appearance of the peace party, and at the end of that time Miss Secor looked down from a pulpit-like arrangement and spoke to an audience of some 2,500 persons assembled in the stadium.

There were just quantities of interesting things about that Ford trip but space considerations forbid their repetition. However, I will say that Miss Secor, newspaper woman as she was, frankly admitted that there was more of fiction than fact reached the American press on the doings of that party. She declared it was wonderful and that Henry Ford himself was one of the most charming, simple and wholesome men she had ever chanced to meet.

Miss Secor and others are arranging a tremendous New Year's Eve demonstration to be staged in Washington Square, New York, in which ten or twenty thousand persons are expected to take part. A community chorus of 1,500 voices will sing, and messages from cities in all parts of the United States will be flashed on screens. Jamestown, by the way, was especially invited to send some sort of greeting. The responsive service for citizens contains such expressions as "Ring out old wars; ring in world peace," and "Not from governments, but from the will of the people of all nations can come a lasting peace.'' The following New Year's message will be wired to President Wilson:

''Citizens here assembled send New Year greetings. The year is dawning brighter throughout the world because you have dared to speak to the warring governments in the name of peace. The repressed people of the war-ridden nations in the trenches and in countless homes are thanking you this day. We are with you heart and hand in your stand for peace. We pledge ourselves to support your further effort toward international good will and liberty for all nations.''

If Miss Secor's calendar permits, she will appear in Jamestown Thursday, Jan. 11, under the auspices of the Business Women's Club, and the entire public will be invited to hear her.

Appendix C

The [*N.Y.*] World, *Sunday, December 23, 1917*

SINCE FORD'S PEACE PARTY MANY THINGS HAVE CHANGED

It Cost $420,000, but Its Financial Backer Is Now a Militarist—Detroit Automobile Manufacturer Doing All He Can to Help the Government—Others Have Had Strange Experiences.

BY JOSEPH J. O'NEILL

Just at this time, two winters ago, there was much talk throughout the world of ''out of the trenches by Christmas, boys, never to return again!''

The famous peace expedition financed by Henry Ford had just reached Scandinavia and its members were turning upon the half-curious, half-amused Norwegians the rapid fire guns and heavy mortars of their oratory.

That Christmas passed, and the next, with more trenches—and more boys in them—than ever. And now here is another Yuletide, with the lines still further flung, and our boys in olive-drab holding a sector against the common foe.

The peace expedition, as such, flivvered out, though it cost $420,000 and was, on the part of its backer at least, well-intentioned and sincere. On the part of others—well, there may now be some doubt.

A few of us survivors of the great junket met in a New York hotel the other day and raised a "skaal" (as the Scandinavians term a toast) to its memory. It was a fervid toast too, as recollections awoke of the joy rides de luxe in specially chartered steamers and trains and motors and sleighs, with the liberal little genius of Detroit footing all the bills. "Oh, bo-oy!" as the survivors unanimously exclaimed.

Then the talk turned to "what a difference just a few months make"—what a difference there was between now and then, in the various members of the peace party, particularly in Henry Ford himself.

In December, 1915, Mr. Ford was undoubtedly the most laughed at man in America. There was scarcely a newspaper which did not turn loose its most humorous writers to deal with his peace scheme. There was not a small-time comedian on the stage who did not win chuckles from his audiences by allusions to the steamer Oscar II which carried the weirdly assorted Pilgrims. The motor manufacturer himself was regarded as the gentlest dove of all pacifism—which was going some.

In December, [1917], if there is a scrappier patriot or more energetic war worker in the United States than this same Henry Ford, he must be concealed somewhere out of public notice. This is how he stands:

He has $10,000,000 in Liberty bonds, purchased from his own private funds.

His company has $10,000,000 in Liberty bonds, taken in the second loan, not to mention what it took in the first.

He is turning out thousands per day cylinders for the new Liberty motors which are to drive our airplanes on the fighting front.

He is turning out thousands of small but capacious motor trucks to carry soldiers or supplies.

He is a member of the staff of the Emergency Fleet Corporation, and is putting into effect in the shipbuilding line what he has learned in his own business about "multiple production."

And he says he is in this fight, with his personality and his fortune, until both his strength and his money are gone (and he's pretty strong and wiry and has half a billion or more dollars).

In the last interview he gave me for The World some time ago he said he believed the most efficacious method of getting peace was to lick the other fellow, because when the other fellow couldn't fight any more there was bound to be peace. Which seems a simple enough bit of philosophy and incontrovertible.

So much for the chieftain of the peace forces—the gentle dove has been transformed into an eagle.

Next to Mr. Ford, the most-mentioned person on the expedition was Mme. Rosika Schwimmer, the Hungarian woman, whose claims that she had great influence among the neutral nations of Europe were largely instrumental in gaining the Detroit man's financial backing for the peace plan.

Mme. Schwimmer Has Disappeared.

Where Mme. Schwimmer now is is a mystery. After being detached from the Ford payroll when he scrap-heaped the peace conference which he allowed her to operate in Stockholm for a time, the Madame returned to America and sought out Mr. Ford in Detroit. But he refused to see her or have anything to do with her, and she sort of dropped out of public life.

A few weeks ago, however, before we got into war with Austria-Hungary, Mme. Schwimmer was frequently to be seen about the Waldorf-Astoria, and it was no secret to those close to the British and American Secret Services that both investigating agencies were keeping eyes upon her. She is now, of course—wherever she may be—an alien enemy.

There were many who felt at the time the peace expedition was under way, that it had a pro-German tinge because of Mme. Schwimmer's position as the associate head of it. The English newspapers did not hesitate to say so. Who knows?

Another personage who figured prominently in the doings of the expedition was Louis P. Lochner, a former Young Men's Christian Association worker, who was rated as "Ford's peace secretary" and who was attached to the Ford payroll with a very pleasant salary and a comfortable expense account.

Lochner's last exploit was his leadership of the laughable pilgrimage in the summer just past of the "People's Council of America for Democracy and Terms of Peace." The experiences of the Ford trip may have been funny; but the adventures of this outfit were funnier yet. They tried in Washington, just before we entered the war, to see the President and beg him to keep out. But they never got near him.

Then Lochner and his crew planned to have a huge convention somewhere in the Middle West on Sept. 1 to seek peace. "The country is wild for peace!" Lochner telegraphed back to New York after a jaunt westward.

In the last week of August a few score members of the "P.C.O.A.F.D.A.T.O.P." chartered a train—"The Rabbit Special" it was dubbed—and started for Hudson, Wis., where they were going to hold their convention, by the irony of chance, in a disused prize fight arena. But the Hudson citizens promptly proclaimed the whole business a pro-German move and warned the peace seekers to keep away.

Next they tried to have their meeting in Minneapolis, but Gov. Burnquist said "nothing doing." Finally they got down to Chicago, jeered and hooted [at] all along the line, and managed to engage a hall through the influence of the pro-German Mayor, "Big Bill" Thompson. Their meeting was scarcely under way when the Chicago police, defying "Big Bill," broke it up. The hapless pilgrims returned individually to their homes, probably feeling that the Nation was not so wild for peace as Lochner had intimated. Since that time Herr Louis and his crew have not figured prominently in the news.

Miss Shelly Still Here.

Still another member of both the Ford expedition and "The Rabbit Special" pilgrimage was Rebecca Shelly, a young woman who acted as sort of secretary and bodyguard to Mme. Schwimmer on the foreign jaunt and who became Treasurer of the People's Council. She is still in New York, and a fortnight ago made a speech at a meeting of "Friends of the Russian Revolution," many of whom call themselves the "New York Bolsheviki" (and look the part).

Miss Shelly intimated she was ready for arrest in case any of the Secret Service men present found her talk seditious; but she carefully refrained from making any direct attack upon America or its institutions.

There were fifty young students who went along with the Ford expedition, it may be remembered, twenty-five boys and twenty-five girls. One of these was Charles Francis Phillips of Columbia University.

Charles Francis became known to his fellow travellers as "the Talking Kid." He was willing to make a speech at any time about anything. The Press Club formed aboard the Oscar II as a joke formally invited him to deliver an address one night. But when he announced as his subject "Proof of the Absence of a Deity in the Universe" he and his lecture were promptly canned.

Phillips was arrested in this city last May with another boy student and a Barnard girl, Miss Eleanor Wilson Parker, for circulating literature urging protests against the Selective Draft Bill. He was held in $10,000 bail, later was convicted and was fined $500 and one day's imprisonment, the Judge who inflicted the sentence giving him clemency because he was "only a foolish boy." He was arrested again for refusing to register on June 5, and was sentenced to five days' imprisonment for that, but he finally did register and was set free. Later he married Miss Parker, his fellow-culprit.

But Phillips was an exception. Most of the students, forgetting the words of peace-wisdom which Lochner, Mme. Schwimmer, Miss Shelly, Phillips and the like used to pour into their ears, are now in the service of their country. Some volunteered as soon as we entered the war. One or two are "over there." Others gladly entered the National Army.

Vanderventer Crisp, who was the attorney for the peace expedition, is now a first lieutenant, stationed in the Northwest in charge of purchasing wood for the manufacture of airplanes. Several of the "Snakes in our Garden of Eden" (as Mme. Schwimmer called the newspaper correspondents with the party) have commissions in the army or navy, and are in active service.

Gaston Plantiff, Ford's financial manager of the Great Junket, recently—and romantically—married Miss Ellen Kaae, a young Danish girl he met in Copenhagen.

It was a queer outfit, to begin with—this company which set sail to have "The boys out of the trenches by Christmas" of 1915. Incidentally, that expression was Lochner's, not Ford's. But queerer are the things that have happened since that time. And the best of those things is the transformation of Henry Ford's resources to the militaristic, instead of the pacifistic, side of the national ledger.

For Further Reading

ADDAMS, JANE. *Peace and Bread in Time of War.* New York: Macmillan, 1922.

ADDAMS, JANE, Emily Greene Balch, and Alice Hamilton. *Women at The Hague: The International Congress of Women and Its Results.* 1915. Reprint, New York: Garland, 1971.

BELL, JULIAN, ed. *We Did Not Fight: 1914–18 Experiences of War-Resisters.* 1935. Reprinted in BLANCHE WIESEN COOK, ed., *Reminiscences of War Resisters in World War I.* New York: Garland, 1972.

BOURNE, RANDOLPH. *War and the Intellectuals.* New York: Harper Torchbooks, 1964.

BUSSEY, GERTRUDE, and MARGARET TIMS. *Women's International League for Peace and Freedom 1915–1965.* London: George Allen & Unwin, 1965.

CHATFIELD, CHARLES. *For Peace and Justice: Pacifism in America, 1914–41.* Knoxville: University of Tennessee Press, 1971.

CHATFIELD, CHARLES, ed. *Peace Movements in America.* New York: Schocken, 1973.

COONEY, ROBERT, and HELEN MICHALOWSKI, eds. *The Power of the People: Active Nonviolence in the United States.* Culver City, Calif.: Peace Press, 1977.

CURTI, MERLE EUGENE. *Peace or War: The American Struggle, 1636–1936.* New York: W. W. Norton, 1936.

DEGEN, MARIE LOUISE. *The History of the Woman's Peace Party.* 1939. Bound with: LELLA SECOR FLORENCE "The Ford Peace Ship and After." 1935. Reprint, New York: Burt Franklin, 1974.

KRAFT, BARBARA S. *The Peace Ship: Henry Ford's Pacifist Adventure in the First World War.* New York: Macmillan, 1978.

LINK, ARTHUR S. *Woodrow Wilson and the Progressive Era.* New York: Harper & Bros., 1954.

MARCHAND, C. ROLAND. *The American Peace Movement and Social Reform, 1898–1918.* Princeton, N.J.: Princeton University Press, 1972.

NEVINS, ALLAN, and FRANK ERNEST HILL. *Ford: Expansion and Challenge 1915–1933.* New York: Charles Scribner's Sons, 1957.

RANDALL, MERCEDES M. *Improper Bostonian: Emily Greene Balch.* New York: Twayne, 1964.

Index